RETHINKING EUROPEAN UNION FOREIGN POLICY

MANCHESTER
1824

Manchester University Press

SERIES EDITORS *Thomas Christiansen* and *Emil Kirchner*

Ben Tonra and Thomas Christiansen
EDITORS

RETHINKING EUROPEAN UNION FOREIGN POLICY

MANCHESTER UNIVERSITY PRESS
Manchester and New York

distributed exclusively in the USA by Palgrave

Published by Manchester University Press
Oxford Road, Manchester M13 9NR, UK
and Room 400, 175 Fifth Avenue, New York, NY 10010, USA
www.manchesteruniversitypress.co.uk

Distributed exclusively in the USA by
Palgrave, 175 Fifth Avenue, New York,
NY 10010, USA

Distributed exclusively in Canada by
UBC Press, University of British Columbia, 2029 West Mall,
Vancouver, BC, Canada V6T 1Z2

British Library Cataloguing-in-Publication Data
A catalogue record for this book is available from the British Library

Library of Congress Cataloging-in-Publication Data applied for

ISBN 0 7190 6001 X *hardback*
    0 7190 6002 8 *paperback*

First published 2004

13 12 11 10 09 08 07 06   10 9 8 7 6 5 4 3 2

Typeset in Minion with Lithos
by Northern Phototypesetting Co Ltd, Bolton
Printed in Great Britain
by CPI, Bath

CONTENTS

PREFACE

The initial idea for this book arose from the discussions at a conference held at the University of Wales, Aberystwyth. This conference brought together scholars of European integration, international relations and foreign policy analysis in order to exchange views on the ways in which the European Union's evolving role in global politics could be conceptualised. The ensuing debates and discussions demonstrated not only that across disciplines and approaches different conceptualisations of the EU's foreign policy existed, but also that a dialogue across these boundaries proved useful in furthering our understanding of the nature of this particular beast. We decided that the next logical step would be a book project that brought these different perspectives together and contributed the particular insights from the study of EU foreign policy to the wider debate about different approaches to European integration.

We have been fortunate that our enthusiasm in launching this venture was shared not only by the contributors to the volume, but also by others without whom this book would not have been published. The Department of International Relations facilitated the initial conference by awarding us a grant, and Steve Smith, then Head of the Department, was instrumental in helping us to get this project off the ground. Many colleagues in the Department contributed to the conference and helped to make it a success, but we would like to acknowledge in particular the organisational work done by Elaine Lowe. We are grateful for the support and encouragement which we received from Emil Kirchner, Series Co-Editor of *Europe in Change*, and Tony Mason, Commissioning Editor at Manchester University Press, from the moment the idea for the book was born until its publication. Efficient editorial assistance was provided by Susanne Kempe at the Department of International Relations in Aberystwyth.

Above all we would like to thank the contributors to this volume who endured the usual suffering of chapter authors – first impossible deadlines, then unreasonable requests for revisions and finally a seemingly endless wait for the actual publication – without any complaints. We are grateful for their cooperation throughout this process, and we hope they – and the reader – share out satisfaction with the finished 'product'.

Ben Tonra, Dublin
Thomas Christiansen, Maastricht

Notes on contributors

Lisbeth Aggestam is a PhD candidate in the Department of Political Science at the University of Stockholm.

Sibylle Bauer is a Researcher on the Export Control and Non-proliferation Project at the Stockholm International Peace Research Institute (SIPRI). She obtained her PhD from ULB, Brussels.

Thomas Christiansen is Senior Lecturer at the European Institute of Public Administration, Maastricht.

Adrian Hyde-Price is Professor of Politics and International Relations in the Department of Politics at the University of Leicester.

Knud Erik Jørgensen is Professor of International Relations in the Department of Political Science at the University of Aarhus.

Henrik Larsen is Associate Professor in the Institute for Political Science at the University of Copenhagen.

Jakob Øhrgaard is an official in the European Commission, Luxembourg.

Eric Remacle is Professor of International Relations and European Studies at the Institute for European Studies, Université libre de Bruxelles, Brussels.

Helene Sjursen is Senior Researcher at the ARENA Programme at the University of Oslo.

Karen Smith is Senior Lecturer in the Department of International Relations at the London School of Economics.

Ben Tonra is Jean Monnet Professor of European Foreign, Security and Defence Policy and Academic Director of the Dublin European Institute at University College Dublin.

Brian White is Professor of International Relations in the Department of Politics and International Studies at the University of Warwick.

List of Abbreviations

ASEAN	Association of Southeast Asian Nations
CDA	critical discourse analysis
CEEC	Central and Eastern European countries
CFSP	Common Foreign and Security Policy
COARM	Council Working Group on Conventional Armaments
COREPER	Committee of Permanent Representatives
COREU	Group of European Correspondents
EC	European Communities
ECJ	European Court of Justice
EDC	European Defence Community
EFP	European foreign policy
EFTA	European Free Trade Association
EMU	European Monetary Union
EP	European Parliament
EPC	European political cooperation
ESDP	European Security and Defence Policy
EU	European Union
FCO	Foreign and Commonwealth Office of the United Kingdom
FPA	foreign policy analysis
IGC	intergovernmental conference
IR	international relations
NATO	North Atlantic Treaty Organisation
OSCE	Organisation for Security and Cooperation in Europe
PSO	peace support operation
RAM	rational actor model
SEA	Single European Act
TEU	Treaty of the European Union (Maastricht Treaty)
TOA	Treaty of Amsterdam
UN	United Nations
USA	United States of America
WEU	Western European Union
WTO	World Trade Organisation

Ben Tonra and
Thomas Christiansen

1

The study of EU foreign policy: between international relations and European studies

The European Union's foreign policy is an ongoing puzzle. The membership of the enlarging European Union has set itself ever more ambitious goals in the field of foreign policy-making, yet at the same time each member state continues to guard its ability to conduct an independent foreign policy. As far as the EU's ambitions are concerned, foreign policy cooperation led to coordination, and coordination in turn gave way to the aspiration of developing a common foreign policy. Concern over foreign policy was the precursor to endeavours to cooperate in matters of security and eventually defence policy. And the desire to maintain the national veto over decision-making within the 'second pillar' of the Common Foreign and Security Policy (CFSP) gave way to the acceptance that, at least in some agreed areas, detailed policies – joint actions and common positions – would be determined by qualified majority vote.

Yet, despite these advances the reluctance of member states to submit their diplomacy to the strait-jacket of EU decision-making has remained. Individual states have maintained distinct national foreign policies, whether this is about specific regional interests, specific global issues or special relationships with other powers. This has been reflected in the institutional arrangements based on the principle of unanimity. Indeed, the very pillar structure of the EU treaties – separating the 'Community pillar' from the special regime that governs CFSP and parts of Justice and Home Affairs – is a hallmark of an arrangement in which member states have sought to minimise the role of supranational institutions and preserve national autonomy.

And yet, despite the sensitivity of member states in the area of foreign policy, and their caution to move beyond intergovernmental decision-making mechanisms in this field, foreign policy has been one of the areas in which European integration has made the most dynamic advances. This includes institutional innovations such as the establishment of the post of High Representative for the CFSP and the creation of an EU Military Staff, both based within the

Secretariat of the Council of Ministers, as well as the development of new approaches to humanitarian assistance combining the work of economic, civic and security policies.

What we have witnessed since the mid-1990s is a rapid expansion in the policy-scope and institutional capacity of EU foreign policy-making. However, it has been a development that has been about more than just the choices of member states to further integrate in this area. Structural changes in the international system – the end of the Cold War, the rise of new security concerns, the emergence of a unipolar world – as well as factors external to the EU – the violent dissolution of the former Yugoslavia, the security implications of EU enlargement, the implications of economic and political instability on the southern and eastern borders of the Union (the aftermath of 9/11) – have combined to compel the EU to make greater strides at speaking with a single voice. Arguably, the single greatest push for reforming EU foreign policy-making has come from the experience of its performance in dealing with the wars that accompanied the break-up of the former Yugoslavia. Unity of purpose, on the one hand, and institutional and material capabilities, on the other hand, have been the key issues that the EU has had to confront in the development of an effective foreign policy, and the desire to address deficiencies with respect to both of these dimensions has engendered the institutional changes that have occurred over the past decade.

In addition, there has been the link between foreign policy, on the one side, and the Union's trade, enlargement, economic assistance and humanitarian aid policies, on the other side, which have been increasingly difficult to ignore. With the latter being made within the first pillar, and involving substantial input from the European Commission, the wish to employ these policies towards the wider foreign policy goals of the Union has also contributed to a greater push for the 'communitarisation' of CFSP.

The prospect of these first and second pillar policies being drawn together towards the outward projection of the Union's interests is one of the factors giving rise to the prospect of a European Union foreign policy. EU foreign policy, in this perspective, is more than just CFSP. It involved the totality of the EU's external relations, combining political, economic, humanitarian and, more recently, also military instruments at the disposal of the Union.

It is the study of this broader concept, going beyond the traditional, exclusive focus on CFSP, which is the purpose of this volume. In particular, the present volume addresses three challenges that arise from the development of foreign policy in the EU over the past decade: first, it suggests ways of reconceptualising the external relations of European Union as *foreign policy* and therefore to apply concepts to the study of this area that draw on the insights of approaches from the wider field of foreign policy analysis. Second, it discusses the positioning of the study of EU foreign policy in relation to the discipline of international relations, in recognition of the transformation that the European construction has undergone in the recent past. And third, it links developments in the debate about integration theory, in particular the constructivist challenge to the established rationalist and intergovernmentalist approaches, to the study of the Union's foreign relations. Taken together, this volume suggest new ways in which European Union foreign policy can be studied in the context of the significant theoretical advancements and empirical developments that occurred during the 1990s.

The study of CFSP

Many texts on the international capacity of the EU focus upon the development of decision-making and policy within CFSP, Peterson and Sjursen (1998), Regelsberger, de Schoutheete, and Wessels (1997), Nuttall (1992) and Holland (1991 and 1997) being among the leading examples. Such studies are important because they provide an analytical insight to the way in which business is conducted within CFSP and how the process has developed – at least in terms of how policy-making and decision-making have evolved. They frequently highlight the gap between what the member states formally aspire to in the realm of European political cooperation (EPC)/CFSP and what decision-making capacity they actually give to EPC/CFSP as a policy process. What is often missing from such accounts, however, is a reflection upon how EPC or its successor CFSP thus related to the process of European integration more broadly and what such cooperation says about the relationships between EC/EU member states and their evolution as international actors.

Another larger segment of the literature relates to thematic/regional case studies or those looking more broadly at the Union in the world (Allen and Pijpers 1984; Ifestos 1987; Buchan 1993; Nørgaard, Pedersen, and Petersen 1993; Holland 1995; Piening 1997; Smith 1998; Bretherton and Vogler, 1999). The critical value of this category of study is that it provides the empirical meat of substantive analysis. What the Union does (or does not do) is crucial to any serious understanding of the Union as an actor. Its failures, more often than its successes, provide the analyst with an important 'reality check' in any assessment of the EU's capacity in the international environment. Such studies, however, may miss crucial aspects of foreign policy change. By focusing upon policy outputs there is a danger that the evolution of policy-making and, crucially, the impact or significance of that evolution upon the member states is undervalued or dismissed.

Fewer studies have sought to make explicit theoretical claims upon CFSP and to situate it in broader debates within either European studies or international relations. Certainly the realist school is dominant – whether or not this is explicit (Ifestos 1987; Pijpers 1991)). Even where theoretical ambitions are more modest, an interest-based/rationalist approach predominates in the mainstream texts on the subject (Hill 1996a; Eliassen 1998). In terms of integration theory, there have been recent attempts to return to older ground with the application of neo-functionalism to EPC/CFSP (Øhrgaard 1997) while the only other significant theoretical challenge has come from a neo-Marxist or world systems perspective (George 1991; Smith 1995). These accounts privilege the socio-economic interests of the Union and its member states over the political but they have the added advantage of – appropriately – seeing CFSP as part of the broader foreign policy process – a component of the Union's foreign policy. Other writers who have chosen to make theoretical claims from analyses of either CFSP or its predecessor EPC have employed domestic politics models (Bulmer 1983; Holland 1987).

In sum, the field of study in EPC/CFSP has been dominated by empirical accounts of decision-making, policy-making and regional or issue-based case studies. Only infrequently are such accounts grounded in an explicit theoretical framework and even then such analyses are, more often than not, dominated by realist/rationalist accounts of state behaviour (Bretherton and Vogler 1999 is an important exception from a social constructivist perspective).

Just as much of this literature lacks an explicit theoretical focus, so the broader literature on European integration theory lacks a clear emphasis on the specific circumstances of foreign policy. Book publications on integration theory are few and far between in any case, and the few anthologies that do exist (O'Neill 1993; Nelsen and Stubb 1998) do not pay any special attention to EU foreign policy. While there is a much greater abundance of theoretical writing in journals, the picture there is the same. Most integration theorists – to the extent to which they study policy-making at all – are concerned with the internal development of the EU rather than with its external relations.

When, however, EU integration specialists do focus upon the international capacity of the Union they are immediately faced with the same fundamental questions that underpin any study of the Union: are we looking at something that is comparable with other social institutions such as the state or international organisations, or are we looking at something wholly unique for which no rule book currently exists? Something that is, in the jargon of the discipline, *sui generis*?

This issue is one which underscores much analysis in EU studies generally but is, perhaps, overplayed. The task of this text, which the authors have undertaken with some enthusiasm, is to set aside these meta-debates about the comparability of the Union's foreign policy and instead to attempt to analyse it using a range of newer analytical tools.

The puzzle of European Union foreign policy

How can we describe, explain and foresee the development of a process that was originally conceived and constructed as being strictly intergovernmental and yet which now aspires to the creation of a 'common defence'? Moreover, in what spatial context is this occurring – is it a policy emerging from amidst the

cooperation of distinct national agents or should it be viewed as a policy deriv-
ing from an emerging single polity? In addition, that aspect of EU foreign policy
that is defined as CFSP is unique in terms of its process and nature. As Jørgensen
notes in his contribution to this volume, '*communication* and *argumentation* are
essential features of the system' (original emphasis). Thus a large part of what
passes for European foreign policy is about the way in which information is
gathered, analysed and shared, the way in which member state representatives
interact and debate issues amongst themselves and, finally, the ways in which
language is used to give effect to the conclusions of those deliberations.

This contrasts – as highlighted by Larsen (chapter 5 of this volume) – with
the extent to which a significant part of the Union's foreign policy can be dismissed by rationalists who often decry it as being 'just words' or 'declaratory
diplomacy.' This text seeks to offer a reflection upon an EU foreign policy
complex that seeks both to address the major definitional issues surrounding
the nature and direction of the EU's external relations but which also draws our
attention to contemporary theoretical debates in both international relations
and European integration. The text might have developed in a number of directions but the choice has been made to establish the subject in terms of a debate
between different approaches and disciplines. This chapter offers one reading
of the theoretical debate based, first, on the differences between IR scholars
and Europeanists and, second, on the epistemological grounding of the respective approaches.

Subsequent chapters illuminate a number of theoretical and analytical
frameworks that can be brought to bear on the vast empirical material of EU
foreign policy. Most of these do so from a constructivist vantage point, not so
much as *deux ex machina* but as something of a redressed balance against the
rationalist-based approaches which predominate in the field.

EU foreign policy: a novel regime in international relations?

While the 1993 Treaty on European Union (TEU) declared unambiguously that
'A common foreign and security policy is hereby established which shall be governed by the following provisions' (Treaty on European Union, Article 11),
there is considerable and obvious distance between that ringing political declaration and the reality of subsequent policy formulation (Hill 1993a; Peterson
and Sjursen 1998). If one can, however, restrain a naturally resulting scepticism,
it is striking to consider the empirical development of this policy-making
regime along at least three axes: bureaucratic structure, substantive policy remit
and decision-making capacity.

First, we have witnessed a significant strengthening in the policy-making
structures underpinning EU foreign policy. Since the inception of EPC there has
been an ongoing debate as to how firmly this process needed to be grounded in
bureaucratic structures and how closely such structures needed to be linked

with those of the central institutions in the European Community/ European Union (Nuttall 1992). The trajectory of such development has been – and continues to be – towards greater institutionalisation and greater coordination. The development of a complex political/military committee structure, the establishment and growth of the political secretariat, the increasing coordination between Community instruments and broader foreign policy goals, and the introduction of a policy planning cell and the office of High Representative for CFSP are all testament to this increased institutionalisation (Keatinge 1997b). Moreover, this has occurred alongside much greater coordination/integration with other Community institutions and policies.

The committees that underpinned much of the work of both EPC and CFSP, for example, have now been integrated with those that operate within the Committee of Permanent Representatives (COREPER). The Commission, which participates at all levels of policy planning within CFSP, is now closely associated with the revised Presidency Troika and may propose foreign policy initiatives to the Council. Indeed, in broad swathes of foreign policy implementation, the Commission is the key interlocutor and focus of policy development. For its part, the Parliament is consulted on policy issues, its views must be taken into account and it must accede to certain foreign policy-related budgetary expenditures. With greater coordination across policy portfolios (e.g. development, trade, economics, human rights and security) it is therefore less than surprising that participants in this policy-making system sometimes see themselves as operating within an EU 'foreign policy' (White 2001).

Second, the remit of policy discussion within EU foreign policy has expanded considerably over time. From a point at which member states were unable to discuss formally any aspect of security issues in the early 1980s, debates now include 'all questions related to the security of the Union, including the progressive framing of a common defence policy which might lead to a common defence' (Treaty on European Union, Article 17). This broadening of the EU thematic agenda has been accompanied by an extended agenda for action. Policy tools at the disposal of the Union include a range of options from diplomacy to economic and trade mechanisms. Following the Amsterdam Treaty, they also include military options within the rubric of the so-called 'Petersberg Tasks' (Keatinge 1997a).

Third, decision-making procedures have also evolved. A hierarchy of decision-making procedures linked to 'common strategies', 'common positions' and 'joint actions' has replaced an earlier formalistic and ritualised intergovernmentalism. These procedures include an expanded scope for the use of qualified majority voting within CFSP, the introduction of 'constructive abstention' and participation as-of-right in military decision-making for those member states outside the framework of the Atlantic Alliance but which choose to participate in a military action of the Union. In all instances these developments are predicated upon the fact that the decision-making processes of CFSP remain distinct from those in operation under the 'Community' pillar of the European Union.

While there is therefore no formal 'communitarisation' of CFSP decision-making, a system is under construction that is certainly moving way from formal intergovernmentalism and which seeks to forge a coherent and effective foreign policy.

A key question thus arises from this evolution in the structure, policy remit and decision-making capacity: 'What is the nature of this foreign policy-making and decision-making regime?' This is the puzzle for which a cognitive approach may offer some considerable assistance.

At least three options are open. First, it has been analysed as a power-based regime based upon a straightforward neo-realist calculation (Pijpers 1990). In this zero-sum analysis, the rules and purpose of the game are established by the most powerful players (i.e. France, Germany and the United Kingdom). Smaller member states have no choice other than to play at the margins of the game and to adapt themselves to it (Mouritzen 1991). It will be the hegemonic impulse of larger players that will determine policy outputs while smaller players can only be consoled – at best – by various side-payments (Mouritzen 1993). Within such an analysis EU foreign policy can only be conceived of as the expression of lowest common denominator politics that can challenge no state's core foreign policy interests. Should it do so, the system must, by definition, collapse. It can therefore only operate through a strict adherence to forms of intergovernmental decision-making.

Employing an interest-based regime approach provides an alternative perspective (Moravcsik 1993). Such a neo-liberal model looks at EU foreign policy through the lens of absolute gains. Participating states arrive at the negotiating table with a pre-established hierarchy of preferences and proceed to bargain these interests against those of their EU partners. A more or less complex incentive structure is then established in which member states trade foreign policy interests but these may also entail cross-policy bargains in the wider EU policy agenda. The most useful analogy of this situation is that of an especially complex poker game – where the member states bring their cards to the table and must then deal amongst themselves to construct the best possible hand. Policy outputs can be characterised as median-interest bargains – beyond the lowest common denominator but falling short of a truly 'common' foreign and security policy.

While debate between these two perspectives is ongoing – especially at the margins of the absolute and relative gains debate – both these approaches share an inherent rationality. Rationality makes important assumptions about the way in which the world works. It begins by assuming that what exists is material, concrete, observable and measurable. Reality is therefore composed of things that we can perceive and that are external to ourselves – reality is 'out there' to be discovered. This assumption about what exists (ontology) is, in turn, based upon a particular philosophy of science (epistemology) that argues that we can only claim to know that which we can measurably observe. This kind of positivist science makes it difficult – if not impossible – to consider 'ideas, norms, culture

– the whole socially constructed realm – [which] are inaccessible to an empiricist form of knowledge' (Williams 1998:208). These rationalist/positivist approaches both see state interests and identity as having been exogenously given that is, an opening set of conditions/parameters for which no explanation is provided and which – crucially – remain sealed off from external influence. In other words, little or no scope can be provided for the evolution of interests or identities resulting from contact, negotiation or even partnership with other states/actors.

The rationalist/materialist approach leads to questions that focus upon why certain decisions, leading to certain courses of action, were made. It searches therefore for explanations of choice and behaviour. In terms of foreign policy these explanations may be found in global structures or in the choices made by individual policy-makers. By contrast, a cognitive approach may ask how such decisions are possible – what are the bases (in dominant belief systems, conceptions of identity, symbols, myths and perceptions) upon which such choices are made (Doty 1993: 298)? In getting behind the rationalist/materialist questions – by lifting the metaphorical 'Wizard of Oz' curtain – we can then begin to understand how it is that the range of 'possible' policy choices is defined and, crucially, how these may be limited by a dominant belief system. All of this underlines a sense that ideas have a directional power or that '. . . very frequently the "world images" that have been created by ideas have, like switchmen, determined the tracks along which action has been pushed by the dynamic of interest' (Weber cited in Goldstein (1989)).

This approach to the study of social phenomena and its utility in the broader study of European integration have been well documented (Christiansen et al., 2002). Moreover, there are a number of debates that relate to the precise relationship that exists between material and social structures, of which a cognitivist approach is just one (Price and Reus-Smit 1998).

By taking a cognitivist approach we can consider ways in which the interests, values, ideas and beliefs of actors are themselves explanatory variables. This does not necessarily exclude rationalism. In other words it might not *just* be about side-payments but it might *also* be about the origins, dynamics and evolution of actors' beliefs and interests. EU foreign policy might also be seen not to be about rationalist calculation at all but be understood as being all about identity creation. In the case of the EU this entails looking at the creation not simply of a foreign policy system but of a foreign policy society – a European diplomatic republic (Jørgensen 1999). This post-positivist turn need not necessarily go so far as some post-structuralist approaches: those far countries of postmodernism where language is everything and there are no material constructs, only discourse. It does, however, offer a fundamental challenge to rationalistic accounts with which several of the authors in this text engage. It is thus our contention that the European Union's foreign policy is an ideal empirical testing ground for what might be called a hard-core cognitivist or *constructivist* approach.

Conclusions

In the early twenty-first century, the EU is making massive leaps to expand both geographically and sectorally. The accession of ten new member states in 2004 is accompanied by moves forward on a new constitutional treaty which in parts codifies previous practice in the Union, but also pushes the boundaries of integration forward. The EU's management of foreign policy has been one of the key issues in this constitutional debate, not only because the negotiations in the Constitutional Convention coincided with the EU's very public display of disunity before and during the 2003 Iraq war, and thus the need for a more effective handling of foreign policy issues was apparent to many, whether supporters or critics of the war. But foreign policy would have featured in the constitutional debate in any case because of the intrinsic significance of this particular policy area to the constitutional foundations of the European polity. The compromises that have been proposed – the creation of the posts of EU President and an EU 'foreign minister' to represent the Union externally, the dual competence of Commission and Council in this area and the tentative moves towards the greater use of qualified majority voting in this area – are a further development of the trajectory that has taken CFSP from Maastricht through Amsterdam and Nice. And constitutional debate and institutional change will certainly not end here, given the way in which the global context continues to challenge the EU to manage its foreign affairs effectively without neglecting the sensitivities of national governments and the wider public in the member states.

EU foreign policy is in a process of constant evolution, and the recent period is testimony to the fact that this evolution can be both rapid and cumbersome. The scholarly challenge in the face of this evolution is to be able to re-think the models and approaches used to analyse it. The various contributions to this volume offer ways of re-thinking European foreign policy from a number of different perspectives, but based on the shared concern of seeking to study the underlying dynamics and subtleties of this process. Collectively they reveal the multi-faceted and changing nature of foreign policy-making in the European Union today.

KNUD ERIK JØRGENSEN

2

Theorising the European Union's foreign policy

Launched in 1970, Europe's common foreign policy has, to some degree, come of age. Because previous attempts to introduce cooperation in the field of foreign policy had failed, the cooperative enterprise was deliberately launched with very modest ambitions. Its development over the years came to include still more policy areas, and still more modules were added to its institutional infrastructure. When defence policy was included in the provisions of the Treaty on European Union (1993) it became, at least in principle, a *tous azimut* foreign policy institution. Thus, while observers of developments during the 1970s and 1980s noted a somewhat slow beginning (Wallace 1983a; Nuttall 1992; Nørgaard Pedersen and Petersen 1993), observers of the 1990s have noted that European decision-makers during the 1990s significantly accelerated their involvement in common foreign policy-making (Hill 1996a; Piening 1997; Regelsberger, de Schoutheete de Tervarent and Wessels 1997; Flockhart 1998; Peterson and Sjursen 1998; Bretherton and Vogler 1999; Cameron 1999).

What are the most significant areas to have been addressed by Europe's common foreign policy? First of all, to European states' traditional bilateral relations with the US has been added a European–US component, meaning that relations with the US increasingly have been cultivated by means of common European stances. Moreover, the US has largely recognised this change on the European side. Furthermore, US–European joint policies have increasingly been thoroughly coordinated and there have been numerous cases of mutual 'backing' (Featherstone and Ginsberg 1996).

Second, the European Union's relations with what was formerly known as Eastern Europe and the Soviet Union have been thoroughly reconsidered and redesigned. In terms of resources spent on a European *Ostpolitik*, it clearly ranks among the first priorities of the Union. Policies towards the Soviet Union, and particularly towards Central and Eastern Europe, were initiated in the mid-1980s. These policies were somewhat contradictory during their formative years

(Torreblanca Payá 1997) but from the Copenhagen Summit in June 1993 they were transformed into a perspective on enlargement of the European Union. A so-called Stability Pact was designed in order to de-escalate potential conflicts in the Central and Eastern parts of Europe. Furthermore, the Eastern enlargement can be regarded as a huge foreign policy initiative significantly increasing the scope of innumerable European regimes, from the entire *acquis communautaire* to administrative practices in the state administrations of future members. In reality, they are currently experiencing a process through which they change from being nation-states to being member states of the European Union.

Third, Europe's relations with developing countries have since the very beginning of the joint European enterprise been a significant feature of Europe's external relations. Until the June 2000 signature of the Cotonou Agreement, the regularly up-dated Lomé Conventions (until 1975 called the Yaounde Convention) framed EU relations with the developing world for nearly fifty years, with other policy tools adding to the overall picture (Ravenhill 1985; Grilli 1993; Cosgrove-Sacks 1999).

Fourth, a common trade policy has been in place for several decades. It has been tested during various rounds of the General Agreement on Tariffs and Trade (Grieco 1990), including the so-called Uruguay round, which resulted in the World Trade Organisation (WTO). Furthermore, it has been tested within specific trade issues, such as the EU–US banana dispute (Stevens 1996), Commissioner Karel van Miert's effective intervention in the Boeing–McDonnell Douglas merger, and innumerable other cases since.

Fifth, although Europe's policy on ex-Yugoslavia came close to being a policy failure, it has, nevertheless, also been a remarkable sign of international 'actorness' on the part of the EU, with the Union functioning for three years as the primary external crisis manager (Owen 1995; Jørgensen 1996). This involvement also tells us something about the aspirations of policy-makers concerning the international role of the European Union.

Sixth, Europe has been involved in numerous other geographical and thematic areas, ranging from the EuroMed initiative (Gomez 1998), Central America (Smith 1995) and China (Yahuda 1998), to the well-established so-called group-to-group dialogues with groupings such as the Association of Southeast Asian Nations (ASEAN), the Gulf Cooperation Council and Mercosur (Edwards and Regelsberger 1990); to negotiations on the Non-Proliferation Treaty and policy-making within the UN General Assembly (Brückner 1990), the Organisation for Security and Cooperation in Europe (OSCE) and other international organisations.

This brief overview is merely meant to serve as an appropriate point of departure leading to the following three observations. First, while the overview is necessarily brief it indicates that it is a worthwhile activity to conduct research on EU foreign policy. Furthermore, the processes producing the foreign policy in question are markedly different from traditional state foreign policy-making. They can be perceived as a Janus-face – being both arena and actor. Determining which 'face' is predominant depends on the issue-area. Sometimes the EU *is* the policy arena, sometimes it is an *actor*, and this seems to change over time. Finally, the relationship adds to the complexity of the matter since in foreign policy-making, the relationship between member states and the European Union is primarily non-hierarchical. Even a casual reading of the practice of collective policy-making reveals some illuminating features.

Communication and *argumentation* are, for example, essential features of the system. The actors exchange views, argue and aim at reaching a consensus. According to the Danish Foreign Ministry, 'a small Member State has good possibilities of influencing the decision-making procedure with the right argument. That is what experience shows' (Interview, Danish Foreign Ministry, March 1998). This suggests that research informed by Habermas' theory of *communicative action* is possible, worthwhile and holds the potential of powerful explanations (see Risse 1998; Lose 2001; Müller 2001). Obviously, parts of communicative action consist of pointing out *reasons* for action, something – as Ruggie (1998a) has pointed out – fundamentally different from *causes* of action. *Intersubjective understandings* are what diplomats' calendars and agendas are full of, whether in the context of *procedure* (as when the Dutch Presidency in September 1991 was politically punished for transcending unwritten rules or when 'The Member States . . . progressively developed disciplines, in written and unwritten rules and procedures, with a view to improving their cohesion in the UN through the various modes of expression, in particular joint statements, voting, and common explanations of vote' (Brückner 1990: 177; see also Jørgensen 1997a), or whether in the context of *policy-making*.

A prominent example of the latter is Jacques Poos' famous, or infamous, remark in July 1991 that international crisis management vis-à-vis the break-up of Yugoslavia showed that the 'hour of Europe' had come. By this remark he simply expressed a widely held intersubjective understanding among European policy-makers and analysts that the absence of the Cold War almost automatically would elevate the EC into a new and significant actor in international politics and, moreover, an actor with considerable diplomatic and political clout. It was a short-lived understanding but at the time it had a significant impact on policy-making.

Contemporary European foreign policy is full of *aspirations*. Policy memos with reference to a desired stronger presence in areas ranging from the Far East to the Middle East are legion. In general, key policy statements more often than not present the Union as 'a strong and credible partner on the international arena'. Furthermore, it is of significant interest that one of the very first EPC declarations was entitled 'Declaration on European Identity' (1973), and that the issue of a European *identity* in international relations has been among the permanent features of European foreign policy ever since. In fact, it is difficult to imagine that it could have been otherwise, and competing notions of European identity have been employed, ranging from the notion of a 'civilian power Europe' to a 'superpower Europe'. This feature makes pre-theories like Alex Wendt's (1994) about *collective identity-formation* highly relevant and interesting.

The issue of *legitimacy* is a second permanent feature of foreign policy, a feature that surely exists in different versions. One version concerns the legitimacy of the common enterprise; that is, whether foreign policy constituencies in member states find the common enterprise legitimate or not. Another issue with regard to legitimacy concerns the practice of European foreign policy; that is, whether – to take an example from current international affairs – military operations without explicit UN authorisation are considered legitimate or not.

A third permanent feature concerns *interests*. Even if policy-makers have been reluctant in making explicit principled statements about common European interests (see Burghardt 1997: 330), such interests can presumably be deducted from foreign policy practice. When policy-makers seek to exert a pressure for change in global politics they in part do so by thinking on the basis of world views. A Dutch analyst neatly describes one such world-view when he describes the EU as 'a civilian power in an uncivil world' (Pijpers 1990: 171). Other views are associated with the image of foreign policy as a civilising mission. Still other views are associated with conceptions of *rights* or *responsibilities*. It is thus significant that the German Presidency in 1988 summarised EC *Ostpolitik* during the autumn of 1988 with the words, 'We want to address central questions of the Twelve's *regional responsibility* for peace. Let us not underestimate the new Europe, with its inner dynamism and its invigorating power' (*European Foreign Policy Bulletin online*, Document 88/168) (author's italics).

Scholars familiar with social constructivist perspectives will recognise from the above outline many of the features well known from the rich toolbox of that approach. In other words, Europe's foreign policy appears to be an ideal case for showing the potential and limits of social constructivism. The claim here is not that social constructivism, at all times and in all cases, is the 'better' option and thus by necessity more powerful than its competitors in offering an understanding of EU foreign policy, but rather that it seems worthwhile to investigate the scope of its potential in the selected case. It should be emphasised that the case is not a common European foreign policy *per se* but rather the more narrowly conceived CFSP, meaning that the communautarian aspects of foreign policy are omitted. The following section aims at exploring possibilities of theorising the CFSP 'the constructivist way'. First, I describe how the balance between deductive and inductive theorising is quite asymmetrical. Then I use nine rules for creative theorising – developed by Rosenau and Durfee (1995) – as a point of departure and combine their rules with social constructivist ways of framing research questions and designs. For each rule there is consideration of how theories would have been, had Rosenau and Durfee's prescriptions been informed by a social constructivist perspective.

Theorising CFSP

Most theory-informed research on the CFSP employs the deductive method and a large number of theories or frameworks of analysis have been applied in research on the CFSP. By now, more or less every imaginable theory has been applied: realism, neo-liberal institutionalism, regime theory, world systems theory, and so on (Pijpers 1990; George 1991; Lucarelli 1998). Unfortunately, these applications have been conducted in a 'single shot' fashion and more often than not they focus on case studies of selected policies or institutional aspects. We are thus far from having reached a critical mass of applications and thus are unable to fully assess the potentials of each theory.

Inductive theorising can imply that we begin from scratch; that is, we act as if we were naive empiricists simply looking at data in front of us. Or we can move on by means of selecting aspects of various theories and then combining them in a new framework. Surprisingly, perhaps, very few theoretical studies of the CFSP have been conducted in such an inductive exploratory fashion. One reason for this absence might be that, among foreign policy analysts, the CFSP is widely considered an appendix to national foreign policy and why waste time on theorising an appendix? A second reason is probably that the CFSP is a topic beyond the attention of scholars with an interest in international theory. After all, we are dealing with a regional not a global phenomenon and even in the regional European context, the CFSP is only one aspect. A third reason may be that the CFSP has been primarily analysed by European scholars and, for some reason, they generally theorise less than their North American colleagues. When Europeans employ theories, they primarily do so by means of the deductive method, meaning that they contribute to the art of testing theories developed elsewhere and sometimes reflecting other experiences and often serving other purposes. These reasons may explain why an inductive, exploratory approach has been somewhat neglected.

For the purpose of theorising the CFSP I have, as mentioned above, selected two manuals in theorising (Rosenau and Durfee 1995; van Evera 1997). I use Rosenau and Durfee's rules for creative theorising and, when appropriate, add some ingredients from van Evera's recipe for theorising. As I proceed I include theoretical reflections from constructivist perspectives and consider which issues could be added to the current research agenda.

Rule 1. Avoid treating the task as that of formulating an appropriate definition of theory (Rosenau and Durfee 1995: 129–30). Certainly, they have a good point here. Many attempts at theorising have stalled at the very beginning because they turn into a definitional exercise, in that the act of definition becomes a hindrance to developing abstract knowledge about world politics. Rosenau and Durfee acknowledge that it is preferable to have a precise conception of theory rather than a vague one and they emphasise features of the demanding art of theorising, an art they associate with 'a set of predispositions, a clutch of habits, a way of thinking, a mental lifestyle, a cast of mind, a mental set' (pp. 178, 180). While I do not know how many scholars can live up to these requirements, I do think it is a well-intended rule, and to some degree also a helpful one. It is, nonetheless, important to note that they consistently refer to theory in the singular, as if the category 'theory' does not include different types of theory. Such a reduction is most unsatisfactory and, as it turns out, Rosenau and Durfee are soon forced to point out that the rules they formulate only apply to what they call 'empirical theory'. While I cannot but disagree concerning the applicability of their rules, their delineation leads to the second rule.

Rule 2. One has to be clear as to whether one aspires to empirical theory or value theory (Rosenau and Durfee 1995: 120–2). Their reasoning is built on the classic distinction between 'is', leading to empirical theory, and 'ought', leading to value theory. As they explain, this distinction underlies entirely different modes of reasoning, a different rhetoric and different types of evidence, leading them to a significant second delineation: 'Aware that our own expertise, such as it may be, lies in the realm of empirical theory ensuring discussion makes no pretence of being relevant to thinking theoretically in a moral context' (p. 181). Van Evera (1997) has chosen a much similar delineation, as he informs his readers that rational choice, critical, postmodern and constructivist approaches have been left out of his guide. We are thus dealing with two manuals, both of which theorise on the basis of narrowly defined conceptions of what it implies to theorise.

One path to follow from this observation could be to make a plea for more value theory in our theorising about the CFSP, or more empirical theory. However, the exact balance between the two types of theorising in studies of the CFSP is irrelevant for my present purposes. I want to follow a different path which, as its point of departure, realises that the very *distinction* is an immensely important part of Rosenau and Durfee's conception of what constitutes theory and derived from that what theorising is all about. In line with arguments within political theory as presented by Ball (1995), I do not share the view that the distinction between 'is' and 'ought' and, hence, between empirical theory and value theory, is valid. Furthermore, I want to include more in my theoretical exploration of the CFSP than what Rosenau and Durfee call empirical theory. However, I will nonetheless henceforth use their rules as reference points and point out how an incorporation of other types of theory makes a difference, leading to a different research agenda, and hopefully to a better understanding of common European foreign policy.

What other types of theory are available? According to Chris Brown, theory at its simplest is reflective thought: 'We engage in theorising when we think in depth and abstractly about something' (1997: 13). From this rather broad conception, he proceeds by emphasising that it is helpful to make a distinction between at least three different types of theory – each associated with a class of questions. The first class of question is: Why do things happen? – leading to *explanatory* theory. An example from the field of CFSP could be why the European

Union did not intervene in Albania in the spring of 1997. A second class of question is – What should we do? – where action can be either instrumental action or morally right action, leading to *normative* or *prescriptive* theory. Examples from the field of CFSP could be what 'we' should do concerning 'failed' states in Africa, for instance the falling apart of Kenya? When should 'we' intervene in international or domestic crises? The third class of question is oriented towards meaning – What is the meaning of this or that? – leading to *interpretive* theory. Examples from this area include the following: What does 'common' in the common foreign and security policy mean? Equally important, what does 'foreign policy' mean, given that we are dealing with an actor like the European Union, characterised by its specific type of polity? Most often such questions are not even raised; the meaning is simply taken for granted: foreign policy is foreign policy is foreign policy.

No matter which type of theory we have in mind, a theory consists of a number of assumptions, a set of definitions and concepts, and an explicitly described area of applicability. A theory includes assumptions about actors, structures, institutions, processes and the relations between these four components. Theories are always embedded in a certain metatheory or a certain philosophy of the social sciences. In this light, Wendt (1987, 1991) argues that a given metatheory privileges certain theoretical constructions and makes others less likely.

In contrast to theorising within a positivist or behavioural framework, there are unfortunately no manuals about theorising within the constructivist perspective. The absence of such a manual makes the task more difficult but not impossible. To begin with, we can note that constructivism is not itself a substantive theory of international relations. Rather, at the highest level of abstraction, it is a philosophy of science category that has a number of consequences for theorising international relations (see further in Jørgensen 2001). If constructivism is not a theory, how can we describe possible links between constructivism and first order theory? Are there any constructivist theories available? Once again Wendt (1994) has something to offer. He explains that his constructivist (pre)theory of collective identity formation makes the following core claims: 'states are the principal units of analysis for international political theory; the key structures in the state system are intersubjective rather than material; state identities and interests are in an important part constructed by these social structures' (Wendt 1994: 385).

Useful or not, it is only one example of constructivist theory. Let us therefore examine an alternative proposal. According to Checkel (1998), one challenge lying ahead for constructivists is to theorise. In my view, Checkel is right in pointing out that theory-building is among the key challenges for constructivists. In more specific terms, he suggests that constructivists should 'specify more clearly the actors – structures *and* agents – and the causal mechanisms bringing about change, the scope conditions under which they operate and how they vary cross nationally' (1998: 348). The language is very eloquent, facilitating dialogue about theory-building and, furthermore, the approach has the potential for bringing about contending theories. However, I have certain reservations concerning his explication of what it means to theorise from a constructivist perspective.

Checkel proposes that theories should be able to explain change, but why privilege factors bringing about change? While I think Checkel has a point and is right in believing that structural leanings among constructivists can be explained by reference to their opposition to methodological individualism, I find it equally important that many social constructions actually are characterised by stability and therefore are relatively enduring or static. In principle that could be a second reason for constructivists to favour elements of structure in their studies. Furthermore, why should we explain why and how constructions vary across countries? It puzzles me that social constructions are assumed to be neatly country-specific; obviously some are but that is far from being the complete picture. One example where it is possible to conduct comparative studies, across countries, is Anderson's (1983) approach to research on processes of nation-building.

I believe it is equally self-evident that a whole range of social constructions are anything but country-specific, and then it does not make sense to ask theorists to use a design that makes comparisons across countries possible. Finally, it is puzzling that Checkel finds the need for theory especially evident at the domestic level. He explains that constructivists theoretically operate most strongly at the systemic level because they draw on what he calls systemic sociological literature. Here he seems to assume a certain congruity between the systemic level of international relations and systemic sociological theory. This assumption is quite misleading as systemic sociological literature can equally be applied at the domestic level and, besides, we also have other currents of constructivism. Why favour one over the other? In conclusion on this point, Checkel seems to believe that the choice of a constructivist theoretical framework has few consequences for key questions such as, What is theory? What can theory do for us? and, consequently, How can we engage in theory-building? In summary, instead of ending up opting for either empirical or normative theory, we can draw on Brown's three types of theory. Furthermore, Checkel has sharpened important tools for constructivist theorising.

Rule 3. One must be able to assume that human affairs are founded on an underlying order (Rosenau and Durfee 1995: 182–3). They explain that this rule implies that theorists should assume that everything is potentially explicable; that is, presume that nothing happens by chance, capriciously, at random; that for every effect there must be a cause. Theory is based on the law of probability, hence it purports to account for key tendencies. The rule can be read in both an open and a critical strict fashion. An open interpretation would emphasise the law of probability; – that is, the view that not every single incident needs to be theoretically explicable and, furthermore, that to theorise is to be concerned with central tendencies. The element of 'capriccio' is to accept that things can actually happen by chance and will thus be theoretically inexplicable. Alternatively, we can imagine that certain apparently inexplicable developments may be explicable with reference to a *competing* underlying order – an order analysts hitherto have been unaware of. A strict interpretation of the rule will read it as yet another aspect of so-called 'normal' science. Van Evera has a clear preference for studies of cause/effect relations, which means that his book contains many useful hints concerning this particular type of analysis: causal analysis. However, I want to engage in something different, suggesting that other types of theory are possible and ought to be explored.

In contrast to van Evera, Ruggie points out the possibility for noncausal explanation, suggesting that ideational phenomena such as aspirations, legitimacy and rights 'fall into the category of *reasons for action*, which are not the same as *causes of action*' (Ruggie 1998a: 22, original emphasis). Wendt describes the contrast between causal and constitutive explanation in the following terms:

> To say that 'X [for example, a social structure] constitutes Y [for example, an agent]', is to say that the properties of those agents are made possible by, and would not exist in the absence of, the structure by which they are 'constituted'. A constitutive relationship establishes a conceptually necessary or logical connection between X and Y, in contrast to the contingent connection between independently existing entities that is established by causal relationships. (Wendt 1995: 72)

Clinton (1993) asks the interesting question, 'International Obligations: To Whom Are They Owed?' and answers that obligations can have at least three sources: (1) They can be owed to others, (2) to a set of rules, or (3) 'first and foremost' to oneself. In my view, it is clear that both the 'open' interpretation and Ruggie, Wendt and Clinton's way of reasoning are of significant relevance to studies of the CFSP. In order to point out how, I will present three examples that lead to different types of theorising.

In the case of the CFSP, we can actually identify an underlying order, in this case a set of formal and informal rules and norms; an ever expanding set of treaty provisions; reproduced policy practices; an ever expanding scope of policy areas, engagements, commitments; ever higher aspirations; a policy area which because of subsequent enlargements of the Union, increasingly deals with relations between Europe and the rest of the world. Yet, we also have a dimension of order that we can characterise by apparently unavoidable instances of inaction, lack of consensus, lack of impact on external actors, events and developments. How can we explain this dialectic between unity and diversity when dealing with common European foreign policies? Can we perhaps say that the CFSP has had a significant impact on the ontological dimension – 'who are *we*'? If so, this would lead to the conclusion that collective intentionality is far more predominant today compared with situations ten, twenty or thirty years ago.

The second example begins with the fact that, according to a narrow formal conception, the CFSP actually is an archetypical example of intergovernmental cooperation. It functions at different levels, from junior officials to senior ministers and diplomats; it makes use of a range of foreign policy instruments and has certain outputs in the form of declarations, demarches, statements and military deployments. The CFSP is nothing less than shorthand for the modern European foreign policy system; thus we can here potentially establish links with research conducted within the tradition of foreign policy analysis (FPA) (Smith and Carlsnaes 1994; White 1998). In this regard, a mathematical formula is helpful:

$$p = \frac{n(n-1)}{2}$$

The original 'Six' made a system of fifteen bilateral relationships. 'The Nine' constituted a system of thirty-six bilateral relations and 'The Twelve' had sixty bilateral relations. The current system, 'The Fifteen', makes 105 relationships possible.[1] A twenty-state Union makes a system of 190 bilateral relations. Needless to say, the cultivation of such an impressive number of relations would be very costly in terms of time and manpower resources. So, clearly, the CFSP is a subsystem of some sort but is it more than that?

Example number three. In *The Expansion of International Society* (1984), Hedley Bull emphasises in the introductory chapter that the expansion and development of Europe's international society was a co-constitutive process, meaning that Europe did not first develop international society and then embark on a huge system-export operation. Most of *The Expansion of International Society* is devoted to studies of how non-European states joined international society. The book is thus a typical product of the English School and, as such, it has a pronounced blind spot on European integration. Apparently, the honourable members of the School suffered from a well-developed phobia concerning European integration. In a sense, studies of the CFSP describe what happened to Europe's international society *after* its expansion. Given Bull's acknowledgement of co-constitutive processes, I assume that the ever expanding society is of importance for the original (European) international society, also after the Second World War, during decolonisation and during the decline of the Western European great powers. In other words, though I find the themes analysed in *The Expansion of International Society* interesting, I find it at least as equally interesting to analyse what has happened to international society in Europe during the last three to four decades. It seems to me that CFSP practices constitute a significant part of contemporary international society.

Rule 4. One must be predisposed to ask about every event, every situation or every observed phenomenon. Of what is that an instance? (Rosenau and Durfee 1995: 183–5). They encourage us to search for patterns, generalisations and abstractions, suggesting that we avoid treating phenomena as unique and propose that we cultivate our impulses to always search for more general theoretical insights. This rule is absolutely splendid and hence a very fruitful component of any research strategy. Of course, once again, the nomothetical ideal lurks in the background and some of the explanations are more purist nomothetical than I find necessary. The problem is, in Denzin and Lincoln's words, that 'too many local case based meanings are excluded by the generalising nomothetic positivist strategy. At the same time, nomothetic approaches fail to address satisfactorily the theory and value-added nature of facts, the interpretative nature of enquiry and the fact that the same set of facts can support more than one theory' (1994). Constructivism focuses on local (emic) rather than on general (etic) phenomena; on middle range rather than grand theory, implying that it is a great paradox that we have so few constructivist middle-range theories. Middle-range theorising should be to constructivists what Old Trafford is to Manchester United. According to Ruggie (1998a: 34) 'concepts are intended to tap into and help interpret the meaning and significance that actors ascribe to collective situations in which they find themselves.' The huge gap in the literature is ready to be filled, and I think it is a fairly reasonable prediction that this will be one of the most busy construction sites in the near future.

Rule 5. One must be ready to appreciate and accept the need to sacrifice detailed observation for broad observations (Rosenau and Durfee 1995: 185). This rule is explicated by Rosenau and Durfee with the following words: 'Theory involves generalizing rather than particularizing and requires relinquishing, subordinating, and/or not demonstrating much of one's impulse to expound everything one knows' (p. 185) as such, the rule is interesting and fruitful for my purpose. Presumably, failures in observing this rule led Keohane and Hoffmann to their assessment of European research as being 'longer on detailed description than analysis' (1990: 276).

The relevance of the rule for studies of the CFSP is considerable. Not uncommonly they are rich in detailed observation and somehow lack broad, generalised observation. Two things are relevant in this context. First, if we consider the passage suggested by Rosenau and Durfee, it does not necessarily imply that we enter analytical modes that depend on large n data-sets that may lead to correlations and identification of possible cause–effect relationships. In van Evera's discussion of large n data-sets, he points out some of the weaknesses: either that we have to assemble data (may be difficult or costly) or, if we rely on existing data-sets, they may prove inadequate for our research question. The obvious example within studies of the CFSP is the use of statistics on European governments' voting behaviour in the UN. The good news is that such statistical data are available. The bad news is that these statistical data cannot serve as exclusive data if we want to understand voting in the UN. The most illustrative and interesting things about voting in the UN are to be found in the explanations for voting; that is, in *reasons* for voting rather than in the votes themselves. Second, it has been an implicit or explicit axiom among CFSP analysts that it is best seen as a unique phenomenon. Consequently, it has been regarded as futile to examine similarities and differences between, say, CFSP, WEU, OSCE and NATO. The CFSP is certainly a unique phenomenon but one could and should ask whether it is also an example, among others, of multilateral intergovernmental forms of cooperation. In other words, how different is intergovernmental cooperation in the CFSP from intergovernmental cooperation within NATO? Such a comparison, to my knowledge, has not been attempted by anyone, meaning that we are unable to specify differences between the two institutions and, in turn, to *specify* how different or similar processes of collective identity formation work in the two institutions.

The absence of such comparative studies is unfortunate because we cannot reach general conclusions about intergovernmental cooperation or something about the specifics of each of the institutions mentioned. Concerning the specifics of the CFSP, the body of knowledge that is constituted by actors' self-reflectivity has seldom been analysed systematically (for exceptions, see Andersen 1998; Glarbo 1999). In other words, we arrive at the classic triangle including author, reader and text; and thereby arrive at equally classic issues such as author intention, original intent and the role of the reader (see Collini 1992; Ball 1995).

Rule 6. One must be tolerant of ambiguity, concerned about probabilities and distrustful of absolutes (Rosenau and Durfee 1995: 186). They emphasise that 'To be concerned about central tendencies, one needs to be accepting of exceptions, deviations, anomalies, and other phenomena that, taken by themselves, run counter to the anticipated or prevailing pattern' (ibid.). Furthermore, they emphasise that theories have to live with or work with uncertainty. This rule is as if tailored for CFSP studies. Doing research on the CFSP requires a high degree of uncertainty. We should therefore not be too concerned about fluctuations between substance and empty rhetoric in CFSP policies, about the fact that probabilities live a prominent life in the world of CFSP policy-makers or that uncertainty continues to reign concerning the significance and influence of European foreign relations. Instead, we should accept that knowledge about the CFSP is produced as a product of continuous dialogue between *the CFSP and its critics* and *the critics and their CFSP*. Exceptions have long played a prominent role in research on the CFSP, primarily because analysts for various reasons have attempted descriptions that take realism in art as inspiration; that is, they feel that every single detail ought to be present.

Rule 7. One must be playful about international phenomena (Rosenau and Durfee 1995: 187–8). They point out that the core of theorising is creative imagination. Only deep penetration into 'a problem discerning relationships that are not self-evident and might even be opposite to what seems to be virtually apparent can produce incisive and creative theory. Good theory ought never be embarrassed by surprises, by unanticipated events' (p. 187). They also suggest that we play the game 'as if'; that is, engage in counter-factual analysis. An obvious example of being playful about the EPC/CFSP is to ask what would have happened had the EPC/CFSP not existed; that is, whether European foreign policies, state identities, state relations, Europe's influence on non-European affairs and so on would have been any different had the EPC/CFSP not existed during the last thirty years. If this is not the case it would obviously be a waste of time to do research on the CFSP and even more futile to theorise about it. It is, therefore, a key assumption that the CFSP actually makes a difference, meaning that the task is to specify the differences it makes.

A second example is even more playful. Pierre Hassner provides the clue of this example raising, back in 1987, a very provocative question. Even if it is a lengthy quote, in the present context it makes sense. Hassner asks: 'Does any Western power have an East European policy, or are all *Ost Europa Politiken* both more and less than policies towards Eastern Europe in the sense that they usually involve more than Eastern Europe but amount to less than policies?' (p. 189). The question is relevant for all Western states but, according to Hassner, for none more than France. He adds,

> Once upon a time this attention could even have been called a policy; the French case illustrates even better than the others that Western interests in Eastern Europe are more indirect than direct and more declaratory than effective. Most of the time France has needed Eastern Europe for its strategy aimed at Germany, Russia or the United States; this vision of the future of Europe or this self-presentation as the champion or the spokesman for small nations or human rights. (ibid.)

And then he ends, 'from de Gaulle to Francois Mitterand French leaders were cast more than ever as specialists in vision rather than policy, in words rather than deeds' (ibid.). Many are inclined to take it for granted that France has a policy towards Eastern Europe but it appears not to be as simple as that. Maybe we should be aware of more subtle levels of policies or visions.

The third example is based on pure behavioural observation. The EPC/CFSP experience covers a period of thirty years. Junior diplomats, senior foreign ministers, European commissioners, and heads of state and government are all engaged in the EU's external relations. A lot of work, time, travelling, meetings, declarations, consultation take place, implying that a significant number of diplomats devote a considerable part of their time to CFSP issues and considerable financial resources are spent on the CFSP. We can add that the EU has more diplomatic representations around the world than most middle or great powers have embassies. While we professionally know that politics and diplomacy can function rather well, even at a long distance from a common-sense reality, it, at least to me, is somewhat difficult to imagine that all these people, engaged in all this activity, would do so if it did not serve a purpose or if it did not make a difference. I therefore take practices as a hint that we are dealing with an important aspect of modern European diplomacy. In line with this, one could ask whether an analysis of CFSP's output really is futile. By 'output' I am not only thinking of the about 5000 documents adopted during the last decade[2] but also of hypothetical output in the form of changed foreign ministry organisation, state identities and interests, and diplomatic practices.

The tentative findings gained from the three examples suggest that the CFSP actually makes a difference and thus seems to be an important aspect of modern

European diplomacy, but also that certain key features of states' dealings with foreign affairs seem to have changed during thirty years of increasing interaction.

Rule 8. One must be genuinely puzzled by international phenomena (Rosenau and Durfee 1995: 188–9). According to Rosenau and Durfee, we should be 'as concerned about asking the right questions . . . as one is about finding right answers . . . . Genuine puzzles are not idle, ill-framed, or impetuous speculations. They encompass specified dependent variables for which adequate explanations are lacking' (p. 188).

Bridge-building between different perspectives seems possible here, particularly because constructivists are inclined not to take things or concepts for granted. It thus seems to me that constructivists are well armed to meet this challenge of asking the right questions. Reconceptualisation is an important part of constructivists' research agenda, an agenda that can be motivated both by normative and analytical concerns. Following Berger's (1986) advice, constructivists do not do research on a phenomenon's function before they have done research on its meaning. In Berger's words, we should not put the cart before the horse. In other words, this is where meanings, understandings and ideational factors come in.

Let us examine three examples. The first example concerns Germany's role in world politics. German debates during the 1990s on participation in peace support operations (PSOs) and permanent membership of the UN's Security Council demonstrate the importance of state identities. Obviously, such debates can be reduced to debates about means and ends but they can also be analysed from the perspective of identity politics, raising questions such as, Is Germany a great power? Ought Germany be represented in the Security Council? Is Germany a civilian power? Is an engagement in PSOs compatible with perceptions of Germany's role in world politics? (see further, Zehfuss 1998).

The second example concerns contemporary conceptions of states. Current hegemonic ideas about what constitutes a modern European state mean that the European Union has become a centre of gravity, that the Union has established itself as the prime institution representing what is widely considered *modern* Europe. Previous alternatives such as the Council for Mutual Economic Assistance (CMEA or Comecon) and the Nordic model have all vanished, or declined into romantic dreams about the past. Ideas about modernity combined with the so-called 'magnet effect' mean that non-member states know in which direction they have to move if they want to become members and thereby be recognised as modern, as non-marginalised, as premier league players. The Austrian slogan of the late 1980s – '*Wir sind Europareif*' – was among the first expressions of this new balance of ideational power.

The third example is a bit more abstract and concerns the relevance of Habermas' theory of communicative action. Risse (1998) points out that

> Communicative action oriented toward mutual understanding is necessary to achieve endurable solutions in the following problematic situations, (i) to change

zero sum into mixed motive games and to establish the common knowledge necessary to achieve cooperative arrangements in the absence of a hegemonic enforcer;
and (ii) to establish new international norms to socialise actors into existing ones'
(1998).

These observations are very relevant for our understanding of the CFSP. Why?
Because contrary to NATO, the CFSP does not include a hegemonic enforcer.[3]
Risse (1998) expects pockets of discursive and argumentative processes in world
politics: 'I hypothesise that international institutions can serve as a substitute for
the absence of a common life world . . . they provide a normative framework
structuring interaction in a given issue-area. They often serve as fora or arenas
in which international policy deliberation can take place'.

In contrast, it is significant that van Evera (1997: 26) reduces the importance
of actors' views and perceptions: 'the insights of the actors or observers who
experienced the event one seeks to explain can be mined for hypotheses' because
they 'often observe important unrecorded data that is unavailable to later inves-
tigators.' Again we see limited ambitions: the aim is merely to explain an event –
and insiders' insights are reduced to a means for hypothesising. In contrast,
in constructivist approaches 'the inquiry aims . . . are oriented to the production
of reconstructed understandings, wherein the traditional positivist criteria of
internal and external validity are replaced by the terms *trustworthiness* and
authenticity' (Denzin and Lincoln 1994). Because practitioners *have* been associated with research on the EPC/CFSP, no matter which strategy one chooses,
there is a rich literature to 'mine for hypotheses' or to use for the reconstruction
of understandings (see Andersen 1998; Glarbo 1999).

According to Ruggie, constructivist theories represent a 'commitment to
the study of the world from the point of view of the interacting individuals'
(1998a: 85). In the case of the CFSP, it follows that three groups of people are of
interest: diplomats, politicians and observers (journalists, commentators and
academics). Diplomats and politicians produce texts (statements, declarations,
speeches) and observers interpret these texts in their way – which is sometimes
far from the intention of the text producers. Nevertheless, they (we) contribute
in the exercise that gives meaning to discursive practices. Ruggie (1998a)
emphasises that ideational factors shaping actors' outlooks and behaviour
include culture, ideology and aspirations.

Rule 9. One must be constantly ready to be proven wrong (Rosenau and Durfee
1995: 189–90).

Conclusions

Instead of hard-rock conclusions, I reach a number of hypotheses. Could it be
that the CFSP actually is 'better' than the rumours about it? Among the reasons
for not knowing could be that we have analysed the CFSP in the wrong way and

for the wrong things. A second reason for the CFSP's bad publicity could be that many analysts are over-ambitious on behalf of the object they study. The third reason could be that drama, failure and disagreement are what make good newspaper stories that subsequently are read and distilled by foreign policy analysts, specialising in the CFSP. A fourth reason could be that analysts do not tend to care about actors' self-reflections about the CFSP's weaknesses and strengths. The fifth and final reason could be that analysts tend to think that knowledge acquired during the Cold War still applies. Could it be that the world has changed and the CFSP has changed with it? Let me summarise my view in a rather unusual way.

I think the relationship between the CFSP and national foreign policies can be described in a way very similar to how the Danish painter, Asger Jorn, painted *The Disquieting Duckling*. In the background we see the well-known world, the world people feel comfortable with, well described and viewers are not uneasy about it because it gives them comfort to think in a rather kitschy way. Then enters the disquieting duckling, an instance of *The Shock of the New* (Hughes 1991), something we are not used to, not familiar with and not comfortable with. We are uncertain about precisely what it means and what it implies. After some thirty years, we still do not know precisely how to make sense of the CFSP. So we choose between neglecting it, meaning that we study national foreign policies of European states as if the CFSP were of no significance whatsoever – or we analyse the CFSP as if it were the embryonic foreign policy of a state in the making, sort of Italian foreign policy in the nineteenth decades of the last century (on this, see Chabod 1996). Maybe, if we are interested in the significance and impact of the CFSP, we have been looking for the wrong things and used the wrong instruments.

Notes

Previous versions of the paper on which this chapter is based have been presented at conferences in Aberystwyth, Washington and Mannheim. I am grateful for comments I received from the discussants at those meetings, Roger Norgan and Jennifer Sterling-Folker, and other participants.

1   However, note that whereas it was common to talk about 'The Six', 'The Nine' and 'The Twelve', nobody actually talks about 'The Fifteen'. Rather, current everyday *parlance* is the 'EU', the 'European Union', or just the 'Union'. The formula to calculate the number of relations in various systems was found in *International Relations*, 1972: 278.
2   Needless to say, the creation of the *European Foreign Policy Online Database* is helpful for any analysis of CFSP text production.
3   Concerning NATO it is wellknown that the US has played, and continues to play, the role of a hegemon; cf. Brenner (1993).

Jakob C. Øhrgaard

3

International relations or European integration: is the CFSP *sui generis*?

The study of European integration has in the past been plagued by the so-called *sui generis* problem: 'the EU is considered somehow beyond international relations, somehow a quasi-state or an inverted federation, or some other locution' (Long 1997: 187). At the empirical level of analysis, few would deny that the EU does indeed display unique characteristics, be it in its scope, institutional design, decision-making procedures or supranational legal identity. Yet many students of international relations would probably instinctively echo Moravcsik's claim that 'although the EC is a unique institution, it does not require a *sui generis* theory' (1993: 474).[1] The danger perceived by students concerned with global trends in international relations is that theories developed specifically to explain one particular manifestation of a more general phenomenon become so embedded in the more unique characteristics of their object of study as to seriously limit their range of general applicability. It is in this space between the richness of empirical observation and the parsimony required by theoretical generalisation that the *sui generis* problem arises.

Long has suggested that 'the *sui generis* problem . . . is at one level less acute with the CFSP', given that 'the CFSP is intergovernmental and is probably better characterized as a process rather than as an institution' (1997: 188). Pijpers takes this argument one step further when arguing, with reference to realism and the study of CFSP's antecedent, EPC, that 'the traditional paradigm demonstrates that EPC is a less unique phenomenon than some integration theorists prefer to believe' and that 'considering the record of EPC so far, or its cooperation procedures, it is difficult to discover original aspects of the Twelve's approach in world politics' (1991: 31–2). Yet few analysts of European foreign policy cooperation, even those working within international relations theories, would probably go as far as Pijpers. Thus, Long concedes that, when analysing the CFSP, 'the *sui generis* problem does not disappear altogether', mainly because 'the CFSP is not an ordinary multilateral institution or process' (1997: 188).

In fact, one might even argue that the *sui generis* problem is exacerbated in the case of the CFSP: not only is the CFSP a unique form of *international* cooperation, it is also a unique form of *European* cooperation. While it may therefore fit uneasily into existing theories of international relations because it is *too unique*, it fits equally uneasily into traditional European integration theory because it is *not as unique* as the Community. In other words, the supranational institutions, majoritarian decision-making procedures and legal character on which traditional integration theory relies are not present in the CFSP, nor have national foreign polices been superseded by a single European foreign policy. As Regelsberger noted with reference to EPC, 'supporters of the more traditional concept of integration, where competence in foreign policy was expected to transfer from the national to the supranational level may be little satisfied with the evolution of EPC' (1988: 4). The same, of course, applies to analysts working within the framework of traditional integration theory.

It is this double *sui generis* problem that this chapter aims to address. To do so requires identifying the defining characteristics of CFSP which emerge from the numerous contributions of participants in and analysts of European foreign policy cooperation which have appeared over the years, and which any theoretical explanation of the phenomenon must, as a minimum, address. Naturally, this is a considerable task that would require more space than provided here. However, the aim is not to provide an empirically neutral and comprehensive account of CFSP, but rather to highlight issues of theoretical relevance, and it will therefore be done with the various theoretical alternatives in mind. Hence the discussion will be structured around the following key issues of relevance to the main theoretical debates: the key actors and the institutional framework for their cooperation; the nature of their interactions and their style of cooperation; and the possible impact of participation in CFSP on national interests and foreign policies. It will be argued that while the *sui generis* nature of CFSP presents an acute problem for international relations theory, it is less pronounced with regard to traditional integration theory. The conclusion is, thus, that traditional neo-functionalist integration theory, while in some respects problematic when applied to intergovernmental cooperation, nevertheless provides the most promising basis for further theorising about CFSP.

CFSP: a unique phenomenon

It appears natural when analysing European foreign policy cooperation to take as a starting point its intergovernmental nature. The key features of the original EPC framework – separate institutional framework, exclusion of autonomous supranational institutions, consensual decision-making, absence of legally binding commitment and enforcement mechanisms – are still present in the provisions of the CFSP, despite the introduction of a number of 'federal detonators' (Hill 1993b). And although the initially strictly observed institutional separation of

EPC from the Community has been relaxed somewhat over the years, mainly through gradual codification of informal practice, the pillar structure of the TEU (retained in the Amsterdam and Nice Treaties) bears witness to the persisting desire of most member states to resist any formal supranationalisation of their foreign policy cooperation. Thus, 'at the formal level of reasoning it seems difficult to question CFSP's inherent intergovernmentalism' (Jørgensen 1997a: 167).

Yet CFSP participants and analysts alike have long warned against simplistic application of such a general term to as complex and unusual a process as European foreign policy cooperation. As one practitioner has put it, CFSP 'may be called "intergovernmental" [but] the connotation of 'normal international practice' is grossly misleading' (Von der Gablentz 1979: 694). Thus, 'even if EPC shares ... conceptual elements with historically familiar forms of diplomatic cooperation, the intensity and quality of EPC activities, however, go beyond these accepted concepts in the way that makes this characterization appear no longer applicable in any satisfactory way' (Wessels 1982: 14). CFSP may be intergovernmental at the level of formal institutional arrangements, but the practices of European foreign policy cooperation which have emerged over the years, and the impact which they have had, even at the institutional level, are not easily captured by this term as traditionally defined in opposition to supranationalism (Jørgensen 1997a; Øhrgaard 1997). Before embarking on the task of explaining CFSP, it is therefore necessary to try to understand the main features of this unusual, and perhaps unique, phenomenon.[2]

Actors and institutional framework
CFSP is often described as an instance of intergovernmental cooperation. As noted by Jørgensen, 'intergovernmentalism typically implies that member states continue to control decision-making' (1997a: 169), and a cursory glance at the formal institutional arrangements for European foreign policy cooperation appears to confirm this characterisation of CFSP. In the original EPC framework laid out in the 1970 Luxembourg Report, all decision-making powers were invested in the foreign ministers, who were also to act as the main public representatives of the European Union in international affairs through the rotating Presidency. In their work, the foreign ministers would enjoy the support of the Committee of Political Directors in the national foreign ministries, but mainly at the logistical and preparatory level of cooperation. No central institutions were created, the Community's supranational institutions were given no formal powers in EPC, and foreign ministers would meet as the Conference of Foreign Ministers in the capital of the Presidency rather than in the Council in Brussels.

EPC did, however, rapidly evolve into an unusually dense process of cooperation. The Luxembourg Report foresaw two annual meetings of foreign ministers and four annual meetings of the Political Committee (Part Two, Articles II.1(a) and III.1). In these early days of EPC, European foreign policy cooperation was still at an experimental stage, and 'in November 1970, when the Foreign Ministers of the then six EC member states met for the first time to discuss matters of

foreign policy, there were strong doubts that similar meetings would follow'
(Regelsberger 1988: 3). Yet the workload of EPC soon increased to a level which
could not be adequately dealt with on such a relatively limited basis. Little more
than a decade on from its inception, foreign ministers would meet formally more
than once per month, and in times of international crises might find themselves
consulting with each other on an almost daily basis.[3]

The density of cooperation was not, however, limited to the ministerial level
of EPC and 'on a practical, day-to-day basis, governments could not ignore the fact
that delegation and communication below the European Council/Presidency level
were required, especially in the absence of an EPC bureaucracy' (M. E. Smith
1998a: 313). In 1973, the Copenhagen Report noted that the Political Committee
had met nine times in the preceding year and, as a result of its increasing workload,
had established a number of sub-committees, specific working parties and expert
groups, and increased consultations between member state embassies and within
the UN (Annex, Article 2). In addition, it sanctioned the establishment of a Group
of Correspondents charged with monitoring the implementation of political
cooperation and the running of the '*correspondance européenne*' (COREU) telex
network linking national foreign ministries (Part II, Article 3).[4] A mere three years
into its existence, EPC had thus developed into an 'inter-diplomatic structure
which does not simply limit cooperation to the highest level, but anchors it firmly
in the diplomatic machinery of [member states]' (Wessels 1980: 23). Furthermore,
in recent years we have been witnessing 'the beginnings of staff exchanges among
foreign ministries and shared embassies' (Hill and Wallace 1996: 6).

To be sure, none of these developments alter the fundamental fact that CFSP
has remained essentially intergovernmental at the formal level of the institutional
distribution of power. Indeed, no formal supranationalisation of European foreign policy cooperation has taken place. One can detect a process of what Allen
has termed 'Brusselisation' – 'a gradual transfer, in the name of consistency, of
foreign policy-making authority away from the national capitals to Brussels'
(1998: 54) – but this has essentially been a matter of logistical rationalisation:
meetings of working groups previously organised in the member state holding
the Presidency were switched to the rooms of the Brussels-based Secretariat established with the Single European Act (SEA) in 1986 (Regelsberger 1997: 71–4).[5]
Similarly, while the Commission has seen its formal role upgraded from a right to
be consulted to sharing the right of initiative and having co-responsibility for
consistency and external representation, it has not acquired Treaty powers akin to
those it enjoys within the Community, nor has it hitherto been very successful at
expanding its limited competences under the CFSP (Allen 1998; Peterson 1998).
The 'federalist detonators' contained in the CFSP provisions (Hill 1993b) have,
as far as the institutional distribution of power is concerned, been left untouched
by member states, mainly, it would appear, as a result of their 'fear that any new
decisions will set precedents for the CFSP that may bind them later or that will
involve the Commission or [the European Parliament] to a greater degree than
they desire' (M.E. Smith 1998b: 154).[6]

From this observation, however, 'it does not necessarily follow that the CFSP is a typical example of intergovernmental cooperation' (Jørgensen 1997a: 168) in the traditional sense of tight governmental control with policy-making. Intergovernmentalism is a term used to describe cooperation between governments, but because of the intensity of cooperation within EPC, 'governments did not monopolize the system to the extent assumed by intergovernmental approaches' (M. E. Smith 1998a: 308). Without necessarily accepting that 'transgovernmentalism was *the* key feature of EPC from the beginning' (ibid.: 313),[7] it is safe to say that transgovernmental interaction and interpenetration certainly have been *a* key feature of CFSP. This becomes abundantly clear when one examines the nature of interactions and style of decision-making within CFSP.

Interactions and decision-making

One consequence of the growing density of the CFSP agenda was the emergence of a strong transgovernmental network of national diplomats sharing 'professional expertise and professional pride' (Hill and Wallace 1996: 11). Through its regular meetings, it provided 'a constant European training on the job for an important branch of government in finding European solutions for their problems' (Von der Gablentz 1979: 694), resulting in 'an important group of actors, as well as maintaining national loyalties, orient[ing] itself towards the development of common European positions' (Wessels 1982: 15). At the level of individual relationships, according to Nuttall, 'the Political Directors [were] on first-name terms' and among the European Correspondents, 'the *esprit de corps* of the group [was] even stronger than that of the Political Directors and many of them [became] personal friends' (1992: 16 and 23). As the intensity of the process increased, so more and more officials, whether based in national foreign ministries, at embassies in third countries or on secondment to foreign ministries of other member states, would come into contact with each other and gradually come to see each other as 'no longer 'foreign' but as colleagues' (Hill and Wallace 1996: 12). Thus, as CFSP developed, 'the more 'Europeanised' became the diplomats, including even those who had never dealt directly with European affairs before' (Regelsberger 1988: 36).

The socialisation (or Europeanisation) effect to which this gave rise was further helped by the initial absence of formally specified procedures, providing participants in the process with the freedom to establish the 'rules of the game' as they went along, thus creating a sense of 'ownership' of the process. As Michael E. Smith points out, 'CFSP insiders consistently stress the value of habitual processes of socialisation, building trust, and the adoption of pragmatic working habits in a decentralised system with no real compliance mechanisms' (1998b: 151). Perhaps the most significant of these working habits was an unusually high degree of communication and information exchange which gradually contributed to the emergence of a '*communauté d'information*' (de Schoutheete de Tervarent 1986: 49). This was given its most tangible expression in the 'coordination reflex', a phenomenon which participants in EPC all claim rapidly became a significant factor in the definition of national positions and in the search for common positions (Von der Gablentz 1979; Hurd 1981; de Schoutheete de Tervarent 1986; Nuttall 1992; Tonra 2001) and which was formally recognised as early as the Copenhagen Report (Preamble). Naturally, the coordination reflex did not exclude the possibility that a member state might ultimately decide to pursue its own objectives unilaterally, regardless of the views of its partners; but it did increase the cost of such actions as they would inevitably come to be viewed as resulting from open and direct disregard for partners' views and could not be explained away as misunderstandings resulting from lack of information (Hurd 1981: 389; Hill 1997: 9). As Wessels points out, despite the absence of formal enforcement mechanisms, 'the habit of cooperation and the self-obligation (coordination reflex) imply sanctions which are not based on legal rules but on group expectations of mutuality' (1980: 23).

The initial lack of clearly specified procedures, and the development of a strong transgovernmental network, had a significant impact at the level of decision-making. In line with intergovernmentalist principles, and in contrast to cooperation within the Community framework, the formal rule of the process was that decisions taken were to be based on consensus. The corollary of this rule was often assumed to be that decisions reached would inevitably reflect the 'lowest common denominator' of national positions, given that any member state could, in principle, at any time prevent the emergence of a consensus by reference to its particular national interest. This was not, however, the case. As Wessels has pointed out, 'the regular reference to unanimity points to only one aspect of reality; the consensus principle does not mean a stiff inflexibility of national positions, but it leads to dynamic adaptations' (Wessels 1980: 23). Two former participants put it more directly: 'it would be erroneous [. . .] to conclude that a compromise reached after lengthy deliberations would only reflect the lowest common denominator of national briefs' (Von der Gablentz 1979: 698); 'a lowest common denominator would only result if the procedure followed were that all the national positions were put on the table and whatever coincided became the European position', but 'this [was] not the case' (Nuttall 1992: 314).

Instead, EPC operated 'by talking incessantly' (Nuttall 1992: 12) with a view to achieving common positions. At least two factors facilitated this approach. First, although formal decisions were taken during meetings at ministerial level, these meetings were not conducted in a vacuum, but were preceded by extensive preparatory work at sub-ministerial level. Thus, 'decisions [were] made after painstaking and frequently long drawn-out processes of consultation, negotiation and coordination which [were] characterized by a complex inter-bureaucratic network between the member-states' (Wessels 1982: 13). The inter-diplomatic socialisation effect and coordination reflex described above further reinforced this decision-making style as 'the preparatory stages of national policy-making [would] already [be] infused with shared information and consensus building' (Hill and Wallace 1996: 12). The 'special code of conduct among Community diplomats' which emerged included, in addition to the commitment to inform, a commitment to consult with a flexible attitude, of which 'to face partners with a *fait accompli* [was] considered to be a particularly grave contravention' (Von der Gablentz 1979: 691). The result was that, at all levels, 'EPC [did] not operate under the perpetual threat of veto', but instead participants would make 'genuine efforts to reach a positive outcome' (Nuttall 1992: 12).

The second important factor in facilitating consensus-building within EPC was the role played by the Presidency. As in the Community, the Presidency was expected to look after the interests of the group as a whole and to 'raise its horizons beyond the pursuit of immediate national interests' (Wallace 1983b: 5). The Presidency offers the holder, particularly when a small member state, the opportunity to achieve 'enhanced visibility and presence on the international scene' (Lorenz 1996: 236) as a representative of the European Union as a whole, but this depends on the ability to ensure backing from one's partners and thus avoid paralysis. In CFSP, the successful President would therefore, first and foremost, need to 'acquire the confidence and understanding of its partners', then 'endeavour to know the precise limits of possible concessions of each partner' and, eventually, 'identify the areas of possible agreement and seize upon them quickly in order to achieve common action' (de Schoutheete de Tervarent 1988: 79). The weak institutional framework and relatively undefined scope of CFSP made this both an easier and a more delicate task. The absence of a neutral mediator such as the Commission could, potentially, make agreement more difficult to achieve, but it also meant that there was 'no Commission to act as a scapegoat for failure or alibi for inaction' (Wallace 1983: 4). Similarly, the absence of a predetermined agenda could be a paralysing factor, but it also enabled member states to agree implicitly that some sensitive issues, for domestic or historical reasons, were the '*domaines réservés*' of member states and thus not a subject for deliberation. On balance, however, both factors probably played a positive part in ensuring the commitment of member states to a process which, due to its flexibility, was unlikely to pose a direct threat to any perceived national interests.

National interests and CFSP

In principle, the institutional design of CFSP, with its core unanimity requirement and lack of legal obligations,[8] protects its members' national interests. While the original commitment to work 'for a harmonisation of views, concertation of attitudes and joint action *when it appears feasible and desirable*' (Copenhagen Report, Part Two, Article I(b))[9] has been upgraded to an obligation on member states to 'ensure that their national policies conform to the common positions' (TEU, Article J.2(2)) and a provision that 'joint actions shall commit the Member States in the positions they adopt and in the conduct of their activity' (TEU, Article J.3(4)), nothing in the CFSP provisions can in practice prevent a member state from unilaterally pursuing its national interests, even if in contradiction of agreed common positions. The existence of such national interests has often been seen as the most serious obstacle to the emergence of a truly common European foreign and security policy. Before EPC had even been established, Hoffmann (1966) warned that a 'logic of diversity' in the sphere of foreign policy would not only prevent the integration process from spilling over into this traditional area of 'high politics' but would also, ultimately, put a brake on economic integration. While this prediction has yet to come true, in the wake of CFSP's perceived failures in a number of areas, most notably the Gulf crisis and the disintegration of Yugoslavia and in its marginalisation during the US-led airstrikes against Afghanistan, this concept continues to attract the attention of analysts of European foreign policy cooperation (Hill 1997; Zielonka 1998).[10]

There can be little doubt that national interests have continued to coexist within CFSP instead of being replaced by a distinctly 'European' interest. As Ifestos has warned, 'an observer should avoid searching for the existence of an autonomous 'European interest' and instead examine where, when and how the national interests of the member states converge, or at least are not in conflict' (1987: 106). On the other hand, if CFSP decisions rarely reflect the lowest common denominator of national positions, and if the high degree of socialisation has had an impact on the actors' perceptions of their interests, then it should be possible to detect even subtle changes in member states' definitions of these interests. Thus Michael E. Smith identifies a number of areas in which this appears to have taken place, both on regional issues such as the Middle East, Central America and South Africa, and on substantive issues such as nuclear non-proliferation and security issues more generally (1998c: 30–8).[11] While the substantial policy impact of CFSP has undoubtedly been stronger in the small member states, at times compelling them to create foreign policy in areas where none previously existed,[12] even the larger member states have at times, more or less enthusiastically, adapted their national foreign policies to common CFSP positions.[13] And once these common positions have been more or less formally codified in the '*acquis politique*' member states have, to a large degree, found themselves bound by them in their subsequent actions, thus adding to the '*de facto* binding quality' (Wessels 1982: 15) of their commitment in CFSP, increasing the expectations of third countries and creating 'a certain knock-on effect from one issue to another' (Hill 1983: 199).[14]

Perhaps the most tangible evidence of this knock-on effect is the gradual widening of the scope of European foreign policy cooperation to include, first, 'the political aspects of security' (London Report, Preamble), then 'the political and economic aspects of security' (SEA, Title III, Article 30.6(a)) and, eventually, 'the progressive framing of a common defence policy . . . which might lead to a common defence, should the European Council so decide' (TEU, Article J.7(1)). The European Union – even with its Rapid Reaction Force – is arguably still some way from having an operational security policy by comparison with, say, NATO, in whose shadow it remains. However, from an internal and historical viewpoint the very acceptance of security and defence policy as a core policy competence marks a significant development. As noted by Kirchner with reference to the

SEA, 'considering that the subject was taboo for such a long time, the explicit reference to security cooperation in the EC [was] a big step forward' (1989: 8). Admittedly, the dynamics behind this development were essentially external, with developments in the international system in the 1980s initially putting security considerations firmly back on the agenda and the end of the Cold War redefining European security interests. But pressures also came from within, especially in terms of a British determination to re-assert leadership within the European Union and seeing defence and security as an area of comparative advantage for so doing (White, 2001: 118).

Somewhat paradoxically, the key to understanding these adaptations appears to lie in the very fact that CFSP has been perceived by its members to serve a number of useful functions for the pursuit of national foreign policies (Hill 1983a, b; 1996b). CFSP has at various times served as 'amplifier', 'cover'/ 'alibi' or 'legitimiser' for member states in the pursuit of their national foreign policies.[15] Yet while this instrumental, or functional, value of CFSP to member states would initially appear to confirm the intergovernmentalist interpretation of European foreign policy cooperation, a commitment such as this, based as it is on self-interest, need not make CFSP peripheral, let alone subordinate, to national interests. Indeed, the very fact that CFSP has proved so useful for its member states has transformed it into an interest in itself. In other words, because CFSP has been a key, and for some member states *the* key,[16] instrument in the pursuit of national foreign policy, maintaining this system has come to be widely seen as a prerequisite for a successful national foreign policy. As Wallace pointed out almost two decades ago, 'in little more than ten years, [EPC] has become an accepted and indispensable part of the national foreign policies of every member state' and 'its value to *all* member governments . . . is now clearly established' (1983b: 14–15).[17]

This does not, of course, imply that foreign policies have become totally subordinated to CFSP, nor should it conceal the fact that the CFSP faces an ongoing crisis of commitment.[18] Indeed, just a few years ago a trend was detected towards what Hill termed the 'renationalisation' of foreign policy, even in traditionally committed member states such as Germany and Italy (Hill 1997: 2). Since then the CFSP's institutional structures and policy capacity have grown significantly. The installation of the High Representative, the development of military policy-making structures and the construction of the Rapid Reaction Force all point towards something more than just the 'European rescue of national foreign policy' (Allen 1996: 288) but something less than a quasi-federal EU foreign, security and defence policy (White 2001).

CFSP: *a* sui generis *phenomenon?*
It is clear from the above that CFSP presents a serious challenge to mainstream international relations theory. This challenge is two-fold. First, traditionally dominant strands of international relations theory, such as (neo)-realism or neo-liberal institutionalism, appear ill-equipped to account for some of the

defining characteristics of CFSP. The traditional realist paradigm, with its emphasis on differing national interests and an overriding concern with sovereignty, may provide at least a partial explanation of why member states have resisted the supranationalisation of their foreign policy cooperation. Yet it cannot account for the density and quality of cooperation within CFSP, nor the significant impact this appears to have had on member states' perceptions of their national interests and their growing commitment to the enterprise as evidenced in the Amsterdam Treaty and subsequent agreements on the creation of a European Security and Defence Policy (ESDP). This problem becomes even more acute in the structural version of realism (or neo-realism), which has traditionally rejected any notion of an institutional impact on national interests and behaviour on the grounds that the anarchic structure of the international system compels states to focus on their individual security at the expense even of potential mutual benefits from institutionalised cooperation.[19] By contrast, neo-liberal institutionalists, while recognising the constraints on cooperation created by the anarchic structure of the international system, argue that international institutions can nevertheless help states realise some of the benefits of cooperation by reducing mutual suspicions and increasing behavioural predictability through the promotion of negotiations on the basis of shared information and commonly agreed rules within a stable framework.[20] However, while international institutions may in this sense constrain and clarify the strategic options open to essentially self-interested sovereign states, neo-liberal institutionalists do not assume that they will seriously affect the fundamental interests and preferences of these states. In other words, they are essentially instrumental in states' pursuit of their exogenously defined national interests.

More recent strands of international relations theory, such as multilateralism and social constructivism, attempt to address this problem of institutional impact on national interests. Multilateralism focuses on the generalised principles of conduct which are embedded in international institutions and which can, at times, compel states to sacrifice individual short-term interests for the greater mutual benefits involved in the very participation in multilateral cooperation.[21] In other words, institutionalised cooperation becomes an interest in itself, coexisting alongside and competing with other national interests. Social constructivists take this argument one step further by arguing that interest formation must be seen as endogenous to institutionalised cooperation; that is, in part resulting from the process of cooperation itself.[22] According to constructivists, states do not merely use international institutions as arenas or instruments in the pursuit of their interests, but are influenced by them to the extent of internalising the norms of behaviour that are embedded in them. These norms, in turn, affect the way in which states perceive their social identity, and thus their interests. However, whereas these theoretical frameworks may initially appear well suited to capturing the defining characteristics of the CFSP experience – and have indeed been shown to be so (Long 1997; Jørgensen 1997a; Jakobsen 1995; M. E. Smith 1998c) – they illuminate the second problem faced by international relations theory in explaining CFSP: while drawing attention to a key aspect of institutionalised cooperation, they often suffer from 'empirical ad hocism' in the sense that they have difficulties in generalising about 'when, how, and why [social construction] occurs, clearly specifying the actors and mechanisms bringing about change [and] the scope conditions under which they operate' (Checkel 1998: 325).[23] These approaches therefore hardly help move the study of CFSP beyond the rich empirical descriptions and generalisations which already abound and towards a coherent theoretical explanation of the phenomenon.

As far as international relations theory is concerned, the *sui generis* problem in CFSP thus remains largely unresolved. Should the multilateralist or constructivist approaches develop into something resembling a coherent theoretical framework, then they would surely offer a promising way forward. In the meantime, however, it would appear worthwhile examining whether traditional integration theory, with its well-developed assumptions and causal mechanisms, might not offer a better starting point for any attempt at explaining the phenomenon of CFSP. In other words, although CFSP remains a *sui generis* problem for both international relations theory and integration theory, the problem may be less acute for the latter, given the proximity of CFSP to the Community and the identity of the individuals involved in the two institutions. The purpose of the following section is to examine this proposition.

CFSP: integration through intergovernmentalism?[24]

Neo-functionalist integration theory has traditionally been rejected as a useful framework for conceptualising the CFSP experience. At the heart of this rejection lies an often implicit supranational–intergovernmental dichotomy that posits a trade-off between intergovernmental *cooperation* and supranational *integration* (Jørgensen 1997a; Øhrgaard 1997). To be sure, if one accepts Haas' formal definition of integration as 'the process whereby political actors in several distinct national settings are persuaded to shift their loyalties, expectations and political activities toward a new centre, whose institutions possess or demand jurisdiction over the pre-existing national states' (Haas 1958: 16), then clearly it is difficult to conceive of CFSP as a process of integration. In CFSP, no central institutions have emerged which possess jurisdiction over member states' foreign policies, nor has CFSP led to the emergence of a political community defined as 'a condition in which specific groups and individuals show more loyalty to their central political institutions than to any other political authority' (Haas 1958: 5). Despite the commitment of its participants to the process, in CFSP 'a pronounced shift of loyalties to a new centre of decision-making with jurisdiction over the national level cannot be identified' (Wessels 1982: 13). As put rather starkly by Ifestos, 'seen in terms of traditional integration theory, [EPC] is malintegrative, if it reinforces inter-governmental cooperation rather than supranational integration' (1987: 208).

Yet one should be careful not to dismiss neo-functionalism merely on the grounds that CFSP has failed to develop the institutional characteristics associated with Haas' definition of political community. Neo-functionalists, including Haas, were always more ambivalent about the nature of integration than the formal definition quoted above suggests. Even in early neo-functionalist writings there was an ever-present tension between integration as defined by a particular institutional outcome and integration conceived of as a process of cooperation and decision-making. Thus Haas argued that 'conceived not as a condition but as a *process*, the conceptualisation relies on the perception of interests and values by the actors participating in the process' and that 'integration takes place when these perceptions fall into a certain pattern and fails to take place when they do not' (1958: 11).[25] Similarly, Lindberg suggested that 'collective decision-making procedures involving a significant amount of political integration can be achieved without moving toward a 'political community' as defined by Haas' and thus advocated 'a more cautious conception of political integration, one limited to the development of devices and processes for arriving at collective decisions by means other than autonomous action by national governments' (1963: 5).

As this section will seek to demonstrate, it is possible to distil from neo-functionalism a framework for conceptualising the form of cooperation which has developed within CFSP. The main challenge is to separate the processes that characterise integration from their institutional framework and ultimate outcome. This requires, first, an acceptance of the ambivalence which characterises neo-functionalist writings on this point and, second, that this ambivalence be exploited to relax some of the more deterministic assumptions of neo-functionalism concerning the actors, their motives and the institutional factors which condition their behaviour.

Actors and institutional framework

In terms of the actors involved and the institutional framework for their interactions, CFSP appears to pose at least two problems for neo-functionalism as traditionally conceived: first, 'transnational coalitions which break the national monopolies for taking the final decisions [were] not existing in [EPC]' (Wessels 1980: 22); and , second, 'no parallel has been created within EPC to the role of the Commission as 'motor', 'agent', 'guardian of the treaty' and 'executive body' which can rely upon a bureaucracy with continuity, experience and specialized knowledge' (Wessels 1982: 14). These characteristics would initially appear to correspond more closely with the intergovernmentalist focus on national governments setting the agenda and controlling decision-making than with the neo-functionalist emphasis on social and economic transnational actors as *demandeurs* of integration and supranational institutions serving as a focus for these demands and possessing autonomous powers to deliver the desired integration.

This version of neo-functionalism derives from an understanding of integration as an essentially economic process but, although widespread, this interpretation is too simplistic.[26] Indeed, neofunctionalists always recognised the central importance of national governments in the process of integration. Thus, Lindberg explicitly acknowledged that 'only the positive action of legitimate national authorities (the nation-states) can be the ultimate basis of integration' (1963: 291) and that 'political and economic integration cannot be expected to succeed in the absence of a will to proceed on the part of the Member States' (1963: 11). Similarly, Haas noted that 'the new central institutions depend on the good faith of the old power centres for the realisation of their aims, [in part] because of the real powers retained by national governments' (1958: 58). As a result, in his specification of the relevant political actors involved in the process of integration, Haas explicitly referred to 'policy-makers in government' and 'higher civil servants' (1958: 17). The fact that CFSP remains within an intergovernmental institutional framework, where the main actors are governments and national civil servants, does not, therefore, constitute a valid reason for rejecting, a priori, the potential relevance of neo-functionalism to explaining the phenomenon.

Interactions and decision-making

It is in the interactions and the style of decision-making that neofunctionalists located the main sub-processes driving the overall process of integration forward. Indeed, as Lindberg argued, 'if political integration . . . is going on, then we would expect to find change in the behaviour of the participants (1963: 9). One sub-process to which neofunctionalists attached great importance in achieving such change was 'élite activation' (Lindberg 1963: 9). One important way of achieving such activation was through the growing socialisation resulting from working together on transnational problem-solving. According to Haas, 'as the beliefs and aspirations of groups undergo change due to the necessity of working in a transnational institutional framework, mergers in values and doctrine are expected to come about, uniting groups across former frontiers' (1958: 14). Lindberg made a similar point: 'there is strong evidence that this sort of interaction [between high policy-makers and civil servants] contributes to a 'Community-mindedness', by broadening perspectives, developing personal friendships, and fostering a camaraderie of expertise, all of which come from being involved in a joint problem-solving operation' (1963: 286).[27]

Neofunctionalists foresaw that this growing socialisation among elites with influence on the decision-making process would gradually lead to changes in the style of decision-making. Increasingly, conflict resolution would come to replace simple bargaining. At least three forms of conflict resolution could be distinguished (Haas 1961: 367–9; Lindberg 1963: 11–12). The first, 'lowest common denominator bargaining', resembled the style traditionally associated with intergovernmental diplomacy, with the overall outcome determined by the least cooperative state. The two other forms of conflict resolution both involved some compromise in national positions. Conflict resolution based on 'splitting the difference' involved trading off concessions across issues with a view to finding a mutually satisfactory overall outcome, while 'upgrading of common interests' involved leaving the most controversial issues aside and concentrating on those issues on which agreement could most easily be achieved, in the hope that this would later facilitate agreement on the initially controversial issues. Of these three styles of conflict resolution, the two latter were perceived to have the greatest integrative impact, with conflict resolution based on the 'upgrading of common interests' representing 'the true contribution to the art of political integration' (Haas 1961: 369).

It should be noted, in this context, that neofunctionalists did ascribe a key role to central institutions in facilitating this type of conflict resolution. According to Lindberg, such institutions were necessary 'in order to *represent* the common interests which have brought the Member States together, and in order to *accommodate* such conflicts of interest as will inevitably arise' (1963: 8).[28] However, Lindberg explicitly warned that this should not be mistaken for an argument in favour of supranationalism. What he was referring to were 'Community' institutions, and he was adamant that 'the Council of Ministers clearly considers itself a Community institution and not an intergovernmental body' (1963: 285). It could therefore not be assumed that national governments, acting within the framework of the Council, would always resort to lowest common denominator bargaining in the pursuit of their individual national interests. As Haas warned, 'the supporters of Council powers may be . . . seriously mistaken in thinking that an intergovernmental structure automatically guarantees the prevalence of diplomatic decision-making techniques and thereby controls integration' (1958: 487). Indeed, in a specific reference to the three possible styles of decision-making, Lindberg claimed that 'conflict resolution in the Council usually follows an upgrading-of-common-interests pattern' (1963: 285).

National interests and common policies

Implicit in the two processes described above – socialisation and upgrading of common interests – is the idea that the participants might eventually come to conceive of their interests differently, as a direct result of their participation in the enterprise. However, neofunctionalists did not expect this to happen in a purely random and self-generating fashion. Instead, they argued that these processes would exist in a mutually reinforcing relationship with a third process, that of 'spillover'. This process, the one most often associated with neo-functionalism, operated in the following way: 'earlier decisions . . . spill over into new functional contexts, involve more and more people, call for more and more inter-bureaucratic contact and consultation, thereby creating their own logic in favour of later decisions, meeting, in a pro-community direction, the new problems which grow out of the earlier compromises' (Haas 1961: 369). Thus, participants in the process would become increasingly caught up in the web of their previous decisions, making further decisions in an ever growing number of related areas necessary lest the initial decision become ineffectual. The spillover process could manifest itself either in the expansion of cooperation into another, related area – 'spillover in scope' – or in a strengthening of the commitment to cooperation in the initial area – 'spillover in level' (Schmitter 1969: 162).

One common misinterpretation of neo-functionalism is that the spillover process would eventually gather such momentum as to become automatic, causing member governments to lose control with a process increasingly driven by trans- and supranational actors. While it is true that neofunctionalists did expect increased cooperation to limit somewhat the abilities of member governments to pursue their individual interests in total disregard of the interests of their partners, spillover nevertheless 'assume[d] the continued commitment of the Member States to the undertaking' (Lindberg 1963: 11). In other words, national governments would only allow spillover to occur if it was perceived as necessary to the realisation of their interests. Yet the decision to allow spillover would not necessarily be a conscious, strategic one, but would to a large degree be determined by pressures resulting from the unforeseen consequences of previous decisions, including the socialisation which cooperation to achieve these decisions would have brought about. Thus, while Haas did recognise that 'the primary task of the Council, in its own view, is to safeguard the interests of member states', he also claimed that in the Council, 'national interests are always compromised; they are never maintained in the face of the 'atmosphere of cooperation' which prevails' (1958: 489–90). Thus, national interests would be subtly redefined as a result of participation in the enterprise of cooperation.

According to Haas, the prospects for these three processes – socialisation, upgrading of common interests and spillover – would be further facilitated if a sense of 'engagement' prevailed among the participants: 'if the parties to a conference enjoy a specific and well-articulated sense of participation, if they identify themselves completely with the procedures and codes within which their decisions are made, they consider themselves completely 'engaged' by the results even when they do not fully concur in them' (1958: 522). In other words, a sense of 'engagement' might cause participants to be willing to sacrifice individual, short-term interests in the expectation that mutual commitment to the process of cooperation itself, and the atmosphere of compromise which it had fostered, would facilitate the achievement of greater and more important interests in the long term. This did not imply that participants had generally abandoned their individual interests, or were no longer acting in a self-interested way. Indeed, Haas explicitly recognised this pervading fact when he argued that 'rather than relying on a scheme of integration which posits 'altruistic' or 'idealistic' motives as the conditioners of conduct, it seems more reasonable . . . to focus on the interests and values defended by the major groups involved in the process' (1958: 13). But, as Lindberg noted, while 'there is always the possibility of a calamity . . . it would seem almost impossible for a nation to withdraw entirely from integration' (1963: 291).

CFSP: integration through intergovernmentalism?

In the more flexible version proposed above, neo-functionalist integration theory clearly possesses significant explanatory power when applied to CFSP. The social-isation of participants, including government ministers, with its *engrenage* effect, the style of decision-making based on the upgrading of common interests, and the limited but gradual spillover, in both level and scope, are all evident in CFSP. More importantly, all these processes have been underpinned by a strong sense of *engagement* which has, to a large extent, made up for the absence of any legal obligations and enforcement mechanisms. Even the concepts used, independently of each other, by CFSP participants and analysts, on the one hand, and neo-functionalists, on the other, are strikingly similar: Europeanisation/socialisation, *esprit de corps*/elite activation, *domaines réservés*/upgrading of common interests, *acquis politique*/engagement, knock-on effects/spillover. Neo-functionalism, despite being associated with the supranational experience of the Community and thus often assumed to be of little relevance to explaining an instance of intergovernmental integration such as CFSP, would thus, initially, appear better suited to overcoming 'its' *sui generis* problem than most strands of international relations theory.

Yet even the most flexible reading of neo-functionalism cannot obscure the one difficulty which remains when applying integration theory to CFSP: in the absence of a political community in which *supranational* institutions possess the powers necessary to compel reluctant member states to honour their infor-mal commitments, any process of integration will always remain vulnerable to set-backs, whether in the form of individual cases of veto, parallel unilateralism or defection, or, at a more general level, in the form of a trend towards the rena-tionalisation of foreign policy.[29] As suggested elsewhere (Øhrgaard 1997), one way to overcome this problem is to view the integration process as a three-stage process of socialisation, cooperation and formalisation, where the initial trust and commitment generated through socialisation permit a style of decision-making based on the upgrading of common interests and, eventually, the for-malisation of the spillover in both scope and level to which this gives rise. CFSP would appear to have evolved in this way, with the Copenhagen Report, London Report, SEA, TEU, Treaty of Amsterdam and Treaty of Nice successively codify-ing informally developed practices and gradual policy expansion.[30] Naturally, this conceptualisation of intergovernmental integration leaves the question of the ultimate institutional destination of European foreign policy cooperation unanswered. In this, however, it only reflects one of the most fundamental historical characteristics of CFSP.

Conclusions

More than a decade ago, two leading specialists deplored the failure of an 'acad-emic community unable either to relate EPC into any meaningful system theory, integration theory or international relations theory let alone create a new EPC general theory' (Weiler and Wessels 1988: 229). They noted that 'although there has been plenty of academic discussion and extremely fruitful analysis of many facets of EPC, the term theory as such has, one gets the impression, often been studiously avoided' (ibid.: 232), resulting in 'too many case studies, *ad hoc* 'lessons' from limited experiences and organizational description, but . . . too little theoretical mediation' (ibid.: 230). While acknowledging that 'the illusive [sic!] general theory continues to illude [sic!]' (ibid.: 229), they nevertheless purported to "theorise' unashamedly since we believe that this very sentiment (of the irrelevance of theory) has denuded discussion of EPC in the last decade' (ibid.: 230). Theorising, they argued, would help 'provide a coherent account and explanation' (ibid.: 234) of the phenomenon of EPC.

One decade on from this self-critique, the literature on CFSP reveals that the academic community has made but modest progress towards providing such a coherent account and explanation of the CFSP experience. Arguably, the last decade has witnessed more theorising on CFSP than the preceding two decades.[31] Yet in analyses of CFSP, theorising remains subordinate to case studies and organisational description,[32] with the result that 'the problems in grasping fully the phenomenon of EPC, and in analysing the factors that have led to success or failure' (Pijpers et al. 1988: 259) remain unsolved. This continued failure may, as argued by Hill and Wallace, be put down to 'the elusive character of the phenomenon' (1996: 1) itself or, as suggested by Long, to 'the paucity of things to theorize about' (1997: 184), but these characteristics are not exclusive to CFSP, and the explanation for the failure to theorise is therefore likely to lie elsewhere.

As argued throughout this chapter, the problem lies in the *sui generis* problem which CFSP continues to pose for traditional theories, whether of international relations or European integration. As a result, the study of European foreign policy cooperation remains at a pre-theoretical stage, where individual concepts and partial explanations continue to appear to hold out the best promise for explaining CFSP. As some CFSP scholars have warned, 'attempts to apply *a* theory to the *totality* of CFSP seem to cast the aims too high' (Weiler and Wessels 1988: 237).[33] Others have gone even further and rejected such attempts as 'inappropriate and foolhardy' (Holland 1991: 5), and for these authors, 'the failure to create a [CFSP] general theory . . . is perhaps in fact to be welcomed' (Bulmer 1991: 89–90). However, as suggested by Weiler and Wessels more than a decade ago, the sheer amount of empirical case studies and pre-theoretical analysis available increasingly requires, and indeed deserves, some form of ordering into a coherent explanation. This chapter has suggested one way of seeking theoretical parsimony without sacrificing the most defining empirical knowledge which has been generated about CFSP over the years. As such, it is meant merely as a contribution to an ongoing debate, not as a final answer to what remains, at this stage, a considerable challenge.

Notes

1 It should, however, be noted that despite his claim that 'the EC can be analysed as a successful intergovernmental regime designed to manage economic interdependence through negotiated policy co-ordination', Moravcsik nevertheless concedes that 'contemporary regime analysis requires refinement to take account of the unique institutional aspects of policy co-ordination within the EC' (1993: 474–9). The *sui generis* problem is difficult to avoid indeed.

2 For a discussion of the epistemological and methodological differences between explaining and understanding, see Hollis and Smith (1990).

3 As at the time of the American bombing of Libya in 1986 (Regelsberger 1988: 3) or during the Gulf crisis of 1990 (Hill and Wallace 1996: 15fn15). For figures on the frequency of meetings, see Regelsberger (1997).

4 Figures provided by Regelsberger (1997: 69) put the number of COREUs at 12,699 in 1994 and the number of sub-ministerial meetings at 153 in 1992 alone.

5 The location of the Secretariat in Brussels was itself for many years an issue of contention, with France, in particular, arguing for all EPC matters to be conducted at a safe distance from the Community institutions (not surprisingly, its preferred choice was Paris). For an account of the work of the Secretariat, see da Costa Pereira (1988).

6 This has been most evident in the protracted battle between the Council and the European Parliament over the basis and procedure for financing the CFSP joint action on the administration of the Bosnian city of Mostar in 1994 (Monar 1997b) or in member states' continuing efforts to prevent the Commission from exercising and strengthening its powers within the CFSP more generally (Allen 1998; M. E. Smith 1998b).

7 Emphasis in original.

8 For an enlightening discussion of the legal implications of the SEA for EPC, see Dehousse and Weiler (1991).

9 Emphasis added.

10 On the constraints placed on EPC/CFSP by these crises, see Edwards (1992a), Pijpers (1992) and Salmon (1992).

11 For a slightly more sceptical assessment, see de la Serre (1988). For more detailed accounts of specific policies, see, among many others, the collections of essays in Edwards and Regelsberger (1990), Regelsberger, de Schoutheete de Tervarent and Wessels (1997) and Holland (1997). Several monographs also exist on specific policies, including Ifestos (1987) on the Middle East, Holland (1988, 1995) on South Africa and K. E. Smith (1999) on Eastern Europe. On the impact of EPC/CFSP on national foreign policies, see Tonra (2001) and the collections of essays in Hill (1983, 1996a).

12 This has, not surprisingly, been most evident in the case of Luxembourg (Lorenz 1996), but similar trends can be detected in Denmark, Ireland and the Netherlands (Tonra 2001).

13 It is often forgotten that while the debacle over the recognition of Slovenia and Croatia in 1991 may justifiably be interpreted as resulting from the unwillingness of one large member state – Germany – to stick to the originally agreed common line, the eventual adoption of Germany's policy of recognition as the common policy reflects a willingness on the part of two other large states – France and Britain – to modify their own positions. See Tréan (1991), Stark (1992) and Jakobsen (1995).

14 On the '*acquis politique*', see Ifestos (1987: 261–79). On outside expectations, see Wallace (1978) and, more recently, Regelsberger (1990), Hill (1993a), Monar (1997c) and K. E. Smith (1999).

15 For examples of the amplifier function, see Tonra (1997, 2001), de la Serre (1996) and Hill (1996b). For examples of the cover function, see Haagerup and Thune (1983), Pijpers (1983) and Bonvicini (1983, 1996). For examples of the legitimiser function, see Rummel and Wessels (1983), Rummel (1996) and de la Serre (1996).

16 With respect to the Netherlands, Pijpers goes so far as to claim that the CFSP 'has probably become the primary political reference point for the bulk of Dutch foreign policy decisions' (1996: 265).

17 Emphasis in original.

18 Thought-provoking attempts to explain the current problems facing the CFSP are made by Zielonka (1998) and M. E. Smith (1998b).

19 See, among others, Waltz (1979) Grieco (1988, 1990, 1993) and Mearsheimer (1990, 1995). There have recently been signs that neo-realists may be relaxing this assumption by incorporating the role of international institutions into their otherwise exclusively structural theoretical framework; see, in particular, Grieco (1995, 1996).

20 See, for instance, Keohane (1984, 1986a, 1986b, 1989a, 1989b, 1990, 1993a, 1993b, 1993c), Keohane and Hoffmann (1993), Keohane and Nye (1993) or Keohane and Martin (1995).

21 See, for example, Keohane (1990), Ruggie (1993) and Kratochwil (1993). There are also strands of this line of argument in Keohane (1989b, 1989c) and Keohane and Hoffmann (1993).

22 Among them Wendt (1992, 1994, 1995), Katzenstein (1996), Florini (1996), Legro (1997) and Ruggie (1998a).

23 For similar critiques, see Kowert and Legro (1996) and K. E. Smith (1999).

24 The subheading is borrowed from the title of Wallace (1983a).

25 Emphasis in original.

26 Admittedly, Haas did, at times, appear to focus almost exclusively on the economic aspects and rationale of the integration process (see especially Haas (1964, 1967)). This emphasis on the economic to the exclusion of the political subsequently became the starting point for Hoffmann's challenge to neo-functionalism; see Hoffmann (1964a, 1964b, 1966).

27 This form of socialisation, based on a growing intensity of interactions, has been described as 'engrenage' (Taylor 1983a).

28 Emphasis in original.

29 This problem, with regard to the Community, became the main focus of neofunctionalists following President de Gaulle's challenge to the Community method in the 1960s, resulting in the development of a number of ad hoc hypotheses, such as 'forward linkage', 'output failure', 'equilibrium' or 'spill-back', thus making the original theory increasingly indeterminate. See, for example, Lindberg (1968), Lindberg and Scheingold (1970) and the contributions to Lindberg and Scheingold (1971).

30 This might also partly explain why the CFSP can appear comparatively unsuccessful, given that the TEU introduced institutional reforms to which the participants had not been previously socialised. This argument is pursued further by M. E. Smith (1998b).

31 See, among others, Holland (1987), Weiler and Wessels (1988), Pijpers (1991), George (1991), Bulmer (1991), Long (1997) and Øhrgaard (1997).

32 This is evident in two of the most recent publications on the CFSP: of the nineteen contributions to Regelsberger et al. (1997), not one is dedicated to theorising, or even theoretical discussion, while Long (1997) is the only theoretical contribution among the eleven chapters in Holland (1997).

33 Emphasis in original.

BRIAN WHITE

4

Foreign policy analysis and European foreign policy

This chapter addresses two key objectives of this book identified in the introductory chapter. It makes a case for a new theoretical approach to the study of the European Union as a global actor based explicitly upon an adapted foreign policy analysis. It also seeks to broaden the focus of the analysis from the Common Foreign and Security Policy to the much more broadly based concept of European foreign policy. The chapter begins by reflecting upon the limitations of existing theoretical approaches, the pervasive institutionalist approach in particular, which provides a justification for developing a rather different approach here. Before an FPA framework can be set up, however, two sets of clarifications are needed. First, we need to demonstrate that FPA can be adapted from its traditional state-centric focus which appears to be inappropriate in an EU context. Second, we need to establish the alternative focus of the analysis here. The EU's global role will be analysed in foreign policy terms by reference to the controversial idea of European foreign policy which needs some preliminary discussion. After developing an FPA framework for analysing European foreign policy, the final section of this chapter reports briefly on this author's attempt to apply the framework in a book-length study elsewhere.

Contending approaches to European foreign policy

There are two different approaches in the literature that arguably dominate existing analyses of Europe's global role. The first, the 'European Union-as-actor' approach, concentrates on the impact of Europe on world politics. Working backwards, as it were, from impact, scholars have tried to identify what sort of an 'actor' Europe is that has enabled it to be such an influential global player. Implicitly or explicitly, the working model has been the state, but increasingly scholars have moved beyond a state model to identify a distinctive non-state but nevertheless collective entity, with the European Community and latterly the European Union providing the 'actor' focus of the analysis. This approach has made a major contribution to our understanding of Europe's global role in both empirical and conceptual terms (Whitman 1997; Bretherton and Vogler 1999).

Important though this body of work has undoubtedly been in developing our understanding of Europe's global role, it can be argued that the EU-as-actor approach is limited in two particular respects. First, the focus is on outcomes rather than process. As Bretherton and Vogler admit in their study, they are primarily concerned to assess 'the overall impact of the EC/EU' on world politics (1999: 2–3). They are much less concerned with analysing the processes through which EU foreign policy is formulated. Indeed, they explicitly reject a policy analysis approach to understanding EU foreign policy. A different view is taken and a different policy-oriented approach is offered here. The foreign policy analyst is less concerned with explaining and evaluating policy outcomes and more concerned to understand and to explain the policy process itself – how policy emerges, from whom or what, and why. To the extent that 'actorness' or, in Allen and Smith's formulation, 'presence' characterises the EU in world politics, the assumption here is that this is related to and emerges from elements of a foreign policy system in action, such as the context in which policy is made, the nature of the policy process, the instruments used, the issue in question, and so on (Allen and Smith 1990).

A second problem area with this approach is the assumption that the EU can be appropriately analysed and evaluated as a single actor. The position taken here is that to conceive of the EU as *an* actor, *a* 'presence' or *an* 'international identity' – in short to adopt a holistic approach to analysis which focuses on 'singleness' or 'unitariness' – is to misrepresent what Jørgensen calls the 'multiple realities' that constitute the European Union (Jørgensen 1998: 12). Hence the assumption here is that the EU is more appropriately analysed as a non-unitary or disaggregated entity in world politics.

The other popular approach in the literature is very different from the first in terms of the perspective from which the EU is analysed. This approach can broadly be located within neo-liberal institutionalism which, rather than focusing on actor-generated behaviour, provides an explanation of actor behaviour as a function of the international institutions or other structures within which actors are located (see for example Ifestos 1987 and Allen et al. 1982; Nuttall 1992; Regelsberger et al., 1997). The essential focus of neo-liberal, and indeed neo-realist, approaches is on structures rather than actors; hence they have also been characterised as 'structuralist' approaches (Hill 1996a: 6). Though not initially developed in a European context, the relevance of institutionalist thinking to the increasingly institutionalised process of European cooperation and integration is evident. Indeed, institutionalist ideas have stimulated the integration process in Europe, and the EU is an important test case of institutionalist expectations about regional and international cooperation. EU foreign policy has not been a major preoccupation for institutionalists but they too have made a significant contribution to our understanding of Europe's global role. First, as their label suggests, they have been fascinated by the growth of EC/EU institutions and the extent to which decision-making has become institutionalised. They have analysed the ways in which institutions like the European Commission have constructed their own agenda and developed their own capabilities, enabling them to act increasingly independently of states.

Second, the new institutionalists have become increasingly interested in analysing member state behaviour, identifying ways in which states have adapted their behaviour as a result of operating within an EU institutional context. They have noted that the broadening agenda of European integration has tended to strengthen institutional and weaken governmental control. Third, institutionalists have been well placed to observe that the EU is not simply an intergovernmental system of states but is characterised by a wider range of policy processes, including transnational, transgovernmental and supranational processes. Finally, the regional/global perspective of institutionalists has highlighted the relationship between Europe's global role and global processes like interdependence and globalisation. From this perspective, institutionalised European integration can be seen as a regional response to important global trends.

But structuralist approaches also have their limitations, stemming largely from the level at which they analyse the behaviour of states and other actors. What might be called the 'actor problem' is the first in a set of interrelated problems. The assumption that systemic imperatives (whether the system is conceived of in global or regional terms) determine the behaviour of the actors within the system leaves little room to explain those occasions when the state or some other actor does not behave in accordance with the dictates of the system. Clearly, for those occasions at least, some other, more actor-centred perspective is required which investigates the particularity of the actors. As Christopher Hill notes, this is an important illustration of the collective action problem that has concerned political theorists for many years. He suggests that states 'find it genuinely difficult both to reach agreement on group strategies and then to hold to these strategies once agreements are reached'. Significantly, he adds, 'solidarity is the exception rather than the rule – even in Western Europe' (Hill 1996a: 7) An analytical focus on states themselves (or other actors) is required to make sense of what may be called a predisposition to defect or 'free ride'. This is a major problem for institutionalists who are concerned primarily to explain international cooperation from a systemic perspective.

If structuralists are weak on agency, it follows that their conception of the foreign policy process within states and their understanding of the role of domestic factors in that process will also be underdeveloped or understated at best. Certainly a focus on structural imperatives leads to a simplified view of policy processes. If the behaviour of states and other actors is essentially determined by international structures, the assumed reaction of those actors will be limited to recognising what they are required to do by the system and adapting their behaviour more or less effectively. While acknowledging important work by structural theorists who seek to introduce domestic factors into their analyses, what has emerged is a reintroduction of the 'rational actor model' of state behaviour described in the next section (Moravcsik 1991; Buzan et al. 1993). The resulting picture of an integrated political elite in one state bargaining with similar elites in other states by manipulating the interests or 'preferences' of the state according to rationalist principles may capture important elements of the foreign policy process but, as Hill argues, this focus offers 'a somewhat impoverished view of politics in general and the domestic environment in particular' (Hill 1996a: 11).

There is a problem relating structuralist imperatives to an understanding of Europe's global role and there is a need to complement the 'macro' approach of institutionalism–structuralism with some form or forms of 'micro', actor-centred analysis but which, unlike the EU-as-actor approach, do not make inappropriate assumptions about single 'actorness'. The central question is whether FPA can be adapted to fill this role in a European context.

The adaptability of foreign policy analysis

One of the main arguments of critics of FPA is that despite the transformed nature of contemporary world politics, FPA is outdated because it is still locked into 'state-centric realism' with, as Michael Smith puts it, 'the state and governmental power' still providing the 'central conceptual building block of the field' (Smith 1994: 22). Marjorie Lister's study of the European Union illustrates a view that FPA is unable to throw any light on the EU's external relations. Not only does the EU not have a foreign policy, in Lister's view, but 'the tools of traditional foreign policy analysis add relatively little to our understanding of the EU. The EU is best understood as a unique type of institution rather than an embryonic state' (Lister 1997: 6).

A response to these criticisms requires some understanding of the development of FPA as a field of study. In the 1970s, Jo Nye labelled the traditional foreign policy analysis approach, 'state-centric realism' (Nye 1975). Three assumptions underpin this approach. First, *state-centricity* captures the assumption that states are the most important actors in the international system; consequently, it is their foreign policy behaviour rather than any other actors that interests foreign policy analysts. Second, the idea of the *state-as-actor* denotes the assumption that states act in the international arena as unitary, rational actors (Allison and Zelikow 1999). State behaviour, in other words, is assumed to be analogous to that of a rational individual. Third, reference to *realism* in this context denotes the idea that assumptions about the state are in turn linked to realist assumptions about the nature of the international system. In particular, given assumptions about the anarchic nature of that system, states are assumed to be preoccupied in their foreign policy behaviour with military–security and with issues and instruments associated with security. From this perspective, *security politics* conceived of in military terms defines the essence of state behaviour and, indeed, of world politics.

The development of FPA as a field of study can be seen as a response to challenges to these traditional assumptions (Clarke and White 1989; Halliday 1994). The first major challenge came in the 1950s with the introduction of decision-making analysis which led to foreign policy behaviour being analysed less as a response to a hostile, anarchic international environment and more as a process essentially internal to the state. Building upon the work of Graham Allison and others, analysts developed a solid body of knowledge about the way foreign policy processes work and the relationships between process and output. A behaviouralist approach with a focus on trying to explain the behaviour of decision-makers rather than the abstract 'state' appeared to constitute a major attack on realist assumptions (White 1978).

With hindsight, however, we may argue that the decision-making approach offered a limited critique only of traditional assumptions. While both the idea of the unitary, rational 'state' and realist assumptions were undermined, the state-centric focus of FPA was left relatively unscathed. Indeed, critics of FPA argued that the decision-making approach was leading foreign policy analysts into an excessive preoccupation with the domestic context of foreign policy-making and, consequently, predisposing them to take insufficient account of important changes in the international environment (Light 1994). While foreign policy analysts were indeed focusing on domestic policy processes, major transformations in the international environment were being analysed by other IR scholars.

The cumulative impact of these changes was to undermine all the traditional assumptions of FPA including, critically, the assumption that states and governments remain the only important actors in world politics. In broad terms, these changes, conveniently organised here in terms of actors, processes and issues, challenged traditional FPA assumptions as follows.

State-centricity has been challenged by an evident increase in the forms and variety of states in the international system, the changing roles and functions of developed states in particular, and the emergence of a range of non-state actors operating at different levels of activity. What has been characterised as a more complex 'mixed actor' international system (Young 1972) raises fundamental questions about the nature of statehood and poses a major challenge to foreign policy analysts. State-centricity is further challenged by related processes like interdependence and transnationalism which directly challenge the autonomy of states and their ability to control outcomes (Keohane and Nye 1977).

Significantly, both *state-centric* and *state-as-actor* assumptions have been undermined by what Keohane and Nye refer to as transgovernmentalism. This denotes the predisposition of subunits of governments to form international coalitions across national boundaries and to operate on the basis of shared interests which might undermine the operation of 'national interests' in policy-making processes (Keohane and Nye 1974).

Security politics assumptions derived from a traditional realist account of international relations have been directly challenged by the new agenda of world politics, an agenda which is itself a product of both the changing role and function of the state – in particular the growing welfare functions of the modern state – and a changing international environment. This agenda consists of a far wider range of issues than military–security; indeed, security itself has been redefined in much broader terms that go beyond the military–defence arena (Buzan 1983). One of the defining features of newer processes like interdependence and integration is that they are less conflict-oriented and more geared to achieve cooperation between states and other actors.

If we consider the overall challenge to FPA that these changes represent, we might reach one of two conclusions. One conclusion is to accept the view of critics that these changes fundamentally undermine FPA to such an extent that it is no longer a helpful way of understanding world politics. Many IR scholars have indeed concluded either implicitly or explicitly that states and the governments that represent them no longer constitute a useful level of analysis from which to make sense of world politics. The key structuralist assumption, as we noted above, is that the structure of the international system effectively determines the behaviour of its constituent units, therefore the international system itself is the appropriate level from which to analyse the workings of the system. Hence, various types of structuralist accounts of IR have predominated in recent years to the partial exclusion at least of explanations like FPA.

The other, less radical conclusion advanced here rejects the idea that FPA is anachronistic but recognises that FPA must be further adapted to take account of a transformed international system. The importance of the European case here is that the global changes outlined above are more clearly illustrated in Europe than in any other region in world politics. It might be argued, therefore, that if foreign policy analysts can use their analytical techniques to make sense of European foreign policy, this will not only throw light on an important new area of foreign policy activity but will also make a major contribution to the development of FPA as a field of study.

Clearly, much hinges on the extent to which FPA is still wedded to 'state-centric realism'. Looking first at state-centricity, there appears to be no obvious reason why the perspective of, and the analytical techniques associated with, FPA cannot be transferred from the state to other significant international actors or, indeed, mixed actor systems. After all, FPA emerged as a major field in IR during the early post-war period when there were no serious challengers to the state and it was logical to base a 'micro' analysis of international relations upon the state, evidently the most significant actor within the international system. But, arguably, it was always the actor perspective rather than a specific actor or actors that was important to the foreign policy analyst (Hill 1974).

If replacing 'state' with 'actor' appears to do no fundamental damage to an FPA perspective, what of the associated focus on government and governmental power? Clearly, the emergence of what Stephen Krasner has called 'authority structures that are not coterminous with geographic borders', whether territorially or regionally based (like the EU) or issue based, has to a greater or lesser extent posed problems for all political scientists (Krasner 1995: 116). The solution elsewhere has been to substitute the term 'government' with the term 'governance' to facilitate a study of government-like activities. As with replacing state by actor, it does not obviously damage the essence of an FPA approach to replace government with governance. Indeed, if governance is taken to subsume government, it can provide a framework for analysing policy-making and policy outcomes that emerge from a political system like the EU which is constituted by interactions between traditional 'authority structures' (i.e. states and governments) and newer forms of non-state authority (Rosenau 1992: 3–6). The focus on policy at the international level is arguably what is important to the foreign policy analyst rather than whether the actor is a conventional government or not.

Finally, what of the relationship between FPA and realism? The brief overview of the development of the field presented here suggests that there is no necessary connection. Certainly, foreign policy analysts have not been content to accept uncritically the idea of the state as a unitary, rational actor struggling to survive in an anarchic international environment or the associated simplicities of a traditional power analysis of state behaviour. Stimulated by the introduction of a decision-making approach, analysts have persistently looked within the 'billiard ball' state to identify key decision-makers and to unravel the domestic processes of foreign policy decision-making. While the now conventional attempts, following the pioneering work of Graham Allison, to disaggregate the state-as-actor and to 'domesticate' foreign policy have attracted criticism for understating the extent to which state behaviour is constrained by the international system, it would be difficult to maintain that FPA at the beginning of the twenty-first century is hopelessly tied either to state-centricity or to a realist agenda.

Reflections on European foreign policy

Having made a case for the adaptability of FPA as an approach but before taking a look at how an FPA framework might be developed in a European context, it is important at this point to clarify exactly what we mean by 'European foreign policy', the putative focus of the analysis here. Why 'European' rather than 'EU' foreign policy? Problems with the holistic EU-as-actor approach have already been discussed. Another reason for staying with 'Europe' rather than 'European Union' as the qualifying adjective is to capture more effectively developments in Europe since the end of the Cold War. Prior to the 1990s, the process of integration in Europe was limited by ideological East–West divisions to Western Europe. The end of the Cold War has now resulted in the inclusion of states formerly Eastern Europe in the integration process. Whether or not all these states eventually join the European Union, a Europe-wide foreign policy is now at least a theoretical possibility that should not be ruled out by unnecessarily restrictive language.

But we do need to recognise that the notion of a *European* foreign policy is a controversial idea subject both to sharp intellectual debate and to the same passions and emotions that the whole process of European integration evokes (Hill 1992: 109–10). Any discussion of European foreign policy, in short, is part of the wider debate about European integration and, as such, is a very live political issue. Intellectuals, politicians, journalists and the 'attentive public' in Europe and elsewhere take at least three different views on the possibility and the desirability of a European foreign policy:

One view is that European foreign policy already exists though that term may not be used. From this perspective, it is an integral part of the process of European integration which increasingly – particularly since the Single European Act, the Treaty on European Union and the subsequent treaties signed at Amsterdam and Nice – has a strong foreign, security and defence dimension to it.

A second view is that a European foreign policy does not yet exist but it should. Problems illustrated by the inadequate collective European performance in the succession of crises in the Balkans are taken as a clear indication that a common or even a 'single' European foreign policy is needed to deal effectively with such issues.

A third view is that European foreign policy does not exist, it never will and, moreover, it never should! Proponents of this view are wedded to the idea that the ability to control foreign and defence policy is a fundamental, defining characteristic of the nation-state. Accepting both the concept and the reality of a European foreign policy would mean nothing less than member states giving up both independence and sovereignty and must lead inexorably to the early demise of the nation-state.

This last view, it should be noted, is linked theoretically to a 'state-centric realist' perspective which maintains that foreign policy is essentially the preserve of states and governments. If EU member states wish to retain national foreign policies they cannot also be a party to something called European foreign policy. The latter is a contradiction in terms at best and a myth at worst. David Allen, for example, argues that 'the determination to preserve national foreign policies is ultimately at odds with the ambition to create a European foreign policy' (Allen 1998: 42; see also Allen 1996). Quite simply, the EU is not a state – it may well never be – and therefore it does not qualify as a foreign policy actor. Indeed, from this perspective, the very concept of a '*European* foreign policy' is an intrinsic part of an ideological, federalist vision of Europe and the logical corollary is that a 'European foreign policy worthy of the name' must await a federal European state (Hill 1993a: 316).

What might constitute European foreign policy from a broadly state-centric realist perspective is the sum of member states' foreign policies studied as a limited set of cases in an exercise (implicit or explicit) in comparative foreign policy analysis (Hill 1983; Stavridis and Hill 1996). At first sight, Roy Ginsberg's influential work on foreign policy actions in the EC looks like a useful model to build upon, with foreign policy defined as 'the process of integrating policies and actions of the member states' (Ginsberg 1989: 1). That definition and the ensuing analysis make it clear, however, that Ginsberg's ostensibly state-centric approach is essentially locked into a structuralist perspective. He looks first to integration theory and global interdependence to explain foreign policy, invoking what he calls 'self-styled logic' (internal decision-making and political dynamic) only when actions are not taken in response to outside pressures (Ginsberg 1999).

Ginsberg is unusual, nevertheless, in including *all* of the external relations of the Community within his analysis of 'foreign policy actions'. Much more typically from an institutionalist perspective, as Hazel Smith points out, European foreign policy has been rather narrowly defined both in scope and level by the way 'foreign policy' is defined at the level of the European institutions themselves (1998: 154–7). Thus, European foreign policy viewed through the lens of the standard institutionalist literature is synonymous (since 1993) with EU foreign policy. It refers to the process of foreign policy coordination known as European political cooperation which began in the 1970s and was upgraded by the Maastricht Treaty into a Common Foreign and Security Policy in 1993 and subsequently amended by the Amsterdam and Nice Treaties.

From an institutionalist perspective, moreover, EPC/CFSP is 'real' European foreign policy (despite the resistance to actually using the words 'foreign, and 'policy' until 1993) which can be contrasted with the external powers or 'competences' originally established by the Treaty of Rome which are generally labelled 'External Relations'. If this narrows the scope of European foreign policy to the processes and the outcomes of EPC/CFSP with significant political implications, the contribution of individual member states' foreign policies to European foreign policy is either downgraded by the institutionalists, with their focus on cooperative, integrative behaviour at the European level, or passed over almost entirely by adherents of the 'EU-as-actor' approach.

The foreign policy analyst, on the other hand, concerned both to track and to analyse actor-directed policy at the international level, can and arguably should offer a less restrictive definition of European foreign policy. The position taken here is that to be useful for analytical purposes, the concept has to encompass the fragmented nature of agency at the European level and the variety of forms of action. Observation of foreign policy activity in Europe reflecting what Hill calls 'the sum of what the EU *and* its member states do in international relations' (Hill 1998: 18) should lead us to conclude that defining European foreign policy as 'member states' foreign policy' or as 'EU foreign policy' or, indeed, as 'EC foreign policy' (H. Smith 1998) is too restrictive. European governance in the foreign policy field appears to take all three forms which can be differentiated for analytical purposes, though, it should be stressed, a key research task that the foreign policy analyst can undertake is to establish the extent to which these types have become interwoven over time (Peterson 1998). Clearly, the more extensive the interrelationships between them, the more justified we are in using the label 'European foreign policy'.

An FPA framework

We have argued so far that existing approaches to understanding Europe's global role are limited. Institutionalist analyses of European foreign policy in particular are limited by a set of weaknesses, the most serious of which are the absence of a developed view of state/actor behaviour, a simplified view of policy-making processes and, as highlighted in the last section, a restrictive definition of foreign policy in a European context. The possibility of FPA providing an approach that fills those gaps is dependent upon the adaptability of traditional FPA. If FPA remains tied to state-centric realism, its value is clearly limited, though this should not be taken to imply that states are not important actors in European foreign policy. The argument here is that FPA is not necessarily tied to state-centricity nor is it dependent upon a realist paradigm. To summarise the rest of the argument, the essence of FPA is that it offers an actor rather than a state perspective and, equally important, it provides a policy focus at the international level. Building upon these premises, this section outlines and develops an appropriate analytical framework. A starting point is provided by posing six standard FPA questions:

1   Who makes European foreign policy?
2   What is the nature of the European foreign policy process?
3   What issues constitute the European foreign policy agenda?
4   What instruments are deployed by European foreign policy?
5   What is the context within which policy is made?
6   What are the outputs generated by the policy process?

It is assumed that the elements of this framework – actors, processes, issues, instruments, context and outputs – are interrelated and constitute a foreign policy system in action. Thus, the nature of the policy process is affected by the identity of the actors involved, the issues being dealt with, the policy instruments available and, not least, the context within which policy is made. These interrelationships in turn generate the outputs from the system (Clarke and White 1989).

Before the elements of the analytical framework can be further specified, however, we need to underline the conceptual analysis in the last section by clearly identifying the different types or 'subsystems' of European foreign policy.

'Community foreign policy' refers to the foreign policy of the European Community which emerged as a direct consequence of the establishment of the original European Communities in 1957. These powers established by the Treaties of Rome codify the external consequences of the Common Commercial Policy and cover principally trade and development relations with third parties.

From an adapted FPA perspective, this form of policy-making is uncontentiously foreign policy and can be regarded as constituting the foreign economic policy dimension of European foreign policy.

'Union foreign policy' refers to the more overtly political dimensions of European foreign policy and consists of the coordination of the foreign policies of member states in a process that, until the Single European Act of 1986, was pursued outside the legal framework of the Community. This type of policy was established in the early 1970s as an intergovernmental process known as European political cooperation. The TEU upgraded this process and replaced EPC with a commitment under the terms of TEU to establish a Common Foreign and Security Policy. CFSP was established as a separate 'pillar' of the European Union; hence the label adopted here despite its prescriptive, federalist connotations (Smith 1996a).

'National foreign policy' refers to the separate foreign policies of member states which have continued to exist and indeed to thrive. What is important in the context of establishing the parameters of a European system of foreign policy, however, is the extent to which the foreign policies of member states have been transformed by the process of operating within the EU institutional context. Hill and Wallace offer an initial description of the transformed context in which member states operate. 'Habits of cooperation, accepted advantages of shared information, responses to common threats, cost saving through increased collaboration, have all significantly altered patterns of national policy-making' (1996: 12).

Their conclusion offers a useful but, from an FPA perspective, limited characterisation of the relationship between the three types of European foreign policy. 'This is an intensive system of external relations in which the cooperating actors which constitute the system intertwine' (1996: 12). While the problem with the term 'external relations' has already been noted, if the various elements of a European foreign policy system are interrelated we must assume that the system includes but extends beyond the 'cooperating actors'. Having identified different types of governance in this field, we can begin to explore the extent to which each type attracts a different cluster of actors, is characterised by a different policy process, operates within a distinctive context and across a specific agenda, utilises different sorts of policy instruments, and generates different outputs.

Actors and policy-making
The first and possibly the most important element in our integrated FPA framework attempts to relate actors to policy-making by a sustained focus on the nature and dynamics of the policy process or, more accurately, policy processes given the different types of European foreign policy identified here. For analytical purposes, this element naturally subdivides into studying the different stages of the policy process from policy-making/formulation through to policy implementation via policy instruments. We can assume that the nature of the policy process – and the identity of the key actors involved – depends upon

the type of European foreign policy being analysed. If foreign policy in this context is defined in political terms as Union policy, then European foreign policy can be described and analysed as essentially an intergovernmental process. This suggests that the governments of the member states effectively control a process where unanimity is the rule.

The problem with this model of policy-making is that the notion of intergovernmentalism also implies that member states remain the 'classical sovereign states of realist theory', independent and autonomous in the defence of their respective national interests (Hill and Wallace 1996: 11). But, for many institutionalists like Wessels and Edwards, this understates the degree to which member states are locked into a 'complex network of institutions and procedures' at the European level. Constant interaction within that network serves to limit the autonomy of any member state, even the most powerful (Wessels 1991; Edwards 1996). This point is again neatly summarised by Hill and Wallace. 'Intergovernmentalism in theory does not erode sovereignty; in practice, over time, it too has ties that bind' (Hill and Wallace 1996: 11).

While the nature of the Union policy process can be debated, other types of policy appear to show even more clearly the limits of state power. If European foreign policy is defined as Community policy, the process of policy-making can be assumed to be more akin to the Community model of decision-making, with the European Commission in theory at least playing the role of principal actor at the European level. Once again, however, a simple characterisation of the policy-making process is likely to be deceptive with respect to establishing who controls what. As Michael Smith notes, some areas of foreign economic policy, like monetary policy and investment, have never been subject to a Community-level policy-making process (Smith 1996: 249). And even in areas like trade policy where in theory the Commission has exclusive competence, a careful reading of the relevant Articles of the Treaty of Rome shows that there is a division of powers between the Commission and the Council of Ministers.

Capabilities and instruments

The critical link in the foreign policy literature between policy process and output is the existence or otherwise of capabilities, resources which can be converted into usable policy instruments. Reflecting and to some extent defining its limited actor status, the EU as a whole appears to have had an incomplete set of policy instruments of varying effectiveness. While a powerful set of economic and financial instruments has been developed over time in Community policy, policy instruments deployed in Union policy are either much weaker or nonexistent. With respect to diplomacy, a growing dissatisfaction with the effectiveness of diplomatic statements led to the adoption of 'common position' and 'joint action' mechanisms in the 1993 TEU. That Treaty also finally addressed the significant absence of a military capability/set of instruments at the European level. The replacement of European political cooperation by a commitment to a Common Foreign and Security Policy and the subsequent development of the

European Rapid Reaction Force signalled a determination at least to move forward on that front, initially through the mechanism of the Western European Union but ultimately through the creation of a European Security and Defence Policy. We need still to explore whether these aspirations have been converted into a substantial and effective European military capability.

The effectiveness of policy instruments may well reflect the issue being addressed. Two related analytical concerns have dominated the FPA literature on issues, and both are equally relevant to a discussion of issues and policy areas in a European foreign policy context. The first relates to the range of issues that constitute the foreign policy agenda and how different issues attract different sets of actors and are handled by different policy processes. The central point in that literature is that for a variety of reasons the agenda, particularly for 'modernised' states, has dramatically expanded. This raises questions about the effectiveness of what might be called systems of policy management. A related focus is the extent to which an expanded agenda of issues creates 'boundary' problems. These boundaries are of two types, broadly between economic and political issues – or, as Edward Morse (1970) described it – between 'high' and 'low' policy issues and second, issues which cross the 'boundary' between domestic and international politics. The boundary problem dimension also raises questions about policy management but, in addition, introduces problems relating to the political sensitivities of member states.

The European foreign policy agenda has clearly expanded, particularly in recent years as a result of the end of the Cold War. Since 1989, the 'new Europe' has been confronted by a host of new issues and old issues in a new form that raise broadly the same analytical questions as those familiar to foreign policy analysts. Maintaining coherence across an expanding agenda and dealing with boundary problems demands for the EU as for developed states, a constant search for new instruments and new institutional mechanisms to manage policy. One example of the former are the Europe Agreements reached with Central and Eastern European countries, while the succession of institutional reforms in the European Commission through the 1990s illustrates a continuing attempt at a European institutional level to manage more effectively both the growing politicisation of EU activities and the ever more blurred boundary between economic and political issues.

Policy context

An important set of variables used in foreign policy system models relates to the context within which policy is made, often referred to in that literature as the 'setting' or 'environment' of policy-making. These variables are generally conceived of from this perspective as constituting important 'inputs' into the foreign policy system, helping to define the parameters within which the system can operate. If context is subdivided into internal and external elements, this aspect of the analytical framework can be further elucidated. The 'internal' setting though is more complex in a multi-level European policy context than in a state. Account has to be taken of intra-EU factors as well as the traditional 'domestic' intra-state setting to the extent that they impact upon European foreign policy.

At the EU 'internal' level, analysts might focus on, for example, the constitutional context – broadly who is given what powers or competences to do what in foreign policy-making. Like many other contextual elements, constitutional provisions are a dynamic, changing element in the policy process. Not only have we seen a series of treaties refine and expand the constitutional provisions established in the 1957 Rome Treaties but European Court of Justice interpretations can also change the context of foreign policy-making in the broadly defined sense in which the term is being used here. Another dynamic element of the internal environment is the development of a burgeoning diplomatic machinery controlled by the Commission. This extends a permanent network of representation abroad together with a growing number of diplomatic missions accredited to the EU/Commission. This element links to the multi-level nature of the decision-making process which not only helps to shape the policy process(es) but should also be regarded as part of the context within which policy-making takes place. As summarised by William Wallace, multi-level governance denotes *inter alia* 'complexity and the contested character of policy-making' which in turn 'makes for dispersed and disjointed decisions, and for incomplete implementation' (Wallace 1996: 445).

From an external perspective, similarly, different factors can be identified and built into the analysis. The obvious example that has been dealt with at length in the literature, though not necessarily from this analytical perspective, is the impact of the end of the Cold War on the foreign policy process in the new Europe. As Michael Smith notes, underlining the interrelationship between the elements of our analytical framework, the transformations in Europe have dramatically 'reshaped both the context and the agenda' of what he calls 'the EC's external relations'. One important element within this transformed policy environment, though ostensibly part of the internal policy agenda, has been the establishment of the Single Market which has major ramifications for European foreign policy (Smith 1997: 280ff).

It should not be forgotten at this point that FPA can also provide a framework for analysing member states' foreign policy as well as the other subsystems of European foreign policy. The 'Europeanised' context within which national foreign policy is made and implemented is a particularly important element within that framework. While there is a need for more comparative research here on foreign policy, the indications are that this dynamic policy context poses major problems for national governments in terms of constructing an effective machinery for coordinating policy at different levels of activity (Wright 1996). On the other hand, there is some evidence with respect to smaller member states that operating through EPC/CFSP has, in Ben Tonra's conclusion, 'improved the effectiveness, broadened the range and increased the capabilities of foreign policy-making' (1997: 197 and 2001).

Applying an FPA framework to European foreign policy

If the previous section is taken as an indicative attempt to flesh out an appropriate FPA framework, the final section of this chapter reports briefly on the attempt to test out the framework in a book-length study of European foreign policy (White 2001). Summary conclusions are drawn here with respect to the utility of the framework in analysing the development of European foreign policy. The first and arguably the most important substantive conclusion that can be drawn from the study is that, from a thirty year perspective, the progress made towards a common European foreign policy, given the strengths and divergence of interests, has been remarkable – even if there is still a long way to go. It is argued that an FPA approach focused on the relationship between policy processes and policy output over time does effectively highlight evolutionary trends at work in European foreign policy (Peterson 1998: 14–15).

Second, the three subsystems of European foreign policy identified earlier remain separate and European foreign policy can appropriately be characterised as 'subsystem dominant'. But, as the study shows, there has undoubtedly been a growing interaction between these subsystems over time. Community, Union and national foreign policies are increasingly intertwined at both policy-making and policy implementation levels. Union and national foreign policies may still be described as intergovernmental in form – apparently reinforced structurally by changes following the Amsterdam Treaty – but the development of transnational policy networks operating increasingly across both the pillar framework and our subsystems makes control of the process by governments, individually or collectively, difficult though not, of course, impossible (indeed, following the Treaty of Amsterdam, the national veto appeared explicitly in treaty form). The more established these networks have become, the more the members of them have become socialised into accepting particular sets of values and norms. This means that there is a more or less collective commitment to reach agreements and to push the process of coordination further forward.

Growing linkages across different foreign policy systems are perhaps most apparent at the operational end of the process. In this context, it will be particularly interesting to track the development of 'common strategies' which were designed explicitly to link cross-pillar decision-making to capabilities and instruments drawn from all three types of European foreign policy. A useful way of characterising the impact of piecemeal changes to the policy process over time, particularly at the 'subsystemic' or 'policy-shaping' level of decision-making (Peterson 1995), is to deploy the 'ratchet' metaphor. Peterson (1998: 16), for example, gives the establishment at Amsterdam of the Policy Planning and Early Warning Unit as an illustration of the 'ratchet effect' on foreign policy coordination. The more recent formal establishment of the various political and military committees in Brussels as a result of developments in European defence policy since St Malo might serve as examples from the defence/security field of institutional mechanisms that are likely further to 'rachet up' cooperation and foster incremental change.

Third, within European foreign policy, the individual foreign policies of member states remain very important, possibly still more important than either Community or Union foreign policies in terms of their overall impact on world politics. Clearly, member state foreign policies have not been replaced by European foreign policy. However, as illustrated in the study by a detailed chapter on Britain, the foreign policies of member states are scarcely recognisable as traditional foreign policy. The context in which they operate, the processes through which they are made and their outputs all show very clearly the growing impact of Europeanisation.

Fourth, despite the focus in much of the literature and the media on specific policy failures and the ineffectiveness of European foreign policy more generally, it is now possible to review policy output over time and begin to talk of some policy successes which might be set against a more negative appraisal. Though, consistent with our FPA approach, the study concentrates more on process than outputs, European foreign policy (EFP) and specifically CFSP have arguably had a number of successes, though criteria for establishing success and failure are not easily established (Jørgensen 1998). One obvious candidate from the case studies undertaken in the study is European policy towards South Africa since the 1970s (White 2001). Certainly, the study reinforces Peterson's view that member states have moved from 'nominally' adjusting their foreign policies in the 1970s and 1980s to a point 'where something which deserves the name "common" has been created in the 1990s' (1998: 4).

Fifth, though progress is being made, albeit haltingly, towards a common European foreign policy, there are continuing pressures from within the EU and without to present a united face to the outside world and thus to move further, beyond a common and towards a single European foreign policy. These pressures are unlikely to go away; indeed, they are likely to be reinforced by precisely the issues that currently preoccupy the EU. In particular, economic and monetary union has major implications for the future of EFP. The physical circulation of the euro as the single currency from 2002, as Bonvicini argues, means that the EU 'will inevitably be forced to play a bigger international role. As a "global currency", the euro will require a [single] policy towards the dollar and the yen, with unavoidable repercussions for the Union's foreign policy' (1998: 73).

Finally, the study concludes that the use of the term 'European foreign policy' rather than any of the more commonly used alternative concepts has been justified as a focus of description and analysis. European foreign policy is not simply a convenient shorthand for the collective foreign policies of member states. Nor is it simply 'EU foreign policy', which appears to be the preferred label of most commentators. The study establishes that there are different types of foreign policy systems in the European Union and that these different types increasingly overlap. We therefore need a term which encompasses them but goes beyond a narrow focus on any one of them. There are, of course, different ways of conceptualising European foreign policy.

One possible criticism of the particular way EFP is conceptualised here is to say that it is too EU-centred or possibly too 'Eurocentric'. Hill develops the argument that European foreign policy gets 'made' in a variety of ways that increasingly involve what he calls a 'mixity of organisations and actors' that extend beyond the EU family of players. These other actors – non-EU states, non-European states like the US, other non-EU organisations (governmental and non-governmental) all overlap the EU's areas of activity. His general point is that contemporary world politics as a whole is characterised by 'overlapping institutionalism' and that separating out the activities of different regional players for analysis is increasingly problematic (Hill 1998: 43–6). This is an important argument and there are examples throughout the study of the role played by non-EU actors in ostensibly European foreign policy activities. But, as Hill himself comments, he is talking about 'foreign policy in Europe;' rather than 'European foreign policy' and, to the extent that these terms have different connotations, his argument does not undermine the way that European foreign policy has been conceptualised here with an FPA focus on the different actors and policy processes within the EU.

If, as has been suggested, the study of CFSP remains at a 'pretheoretical stage', the same comment is even more justified with respect to the study of European foreign policy (Ginsberg 1999: 429). At this stage, a variety of theoretical approaches is to be welcomed. A strong case has been made here that a foreign policy analysis approach suitably adapted has a useful contribution to make to an understanding of European foreign policy and, more widely, to an understanding of Europe's global role.

Notes

This chapter is adapted from B. White (1999), 'The European Challenge to Foreign Policy Analysis', *European Journal of International Relations*, 5:1, 37–66.

Henrik Larsen

5

Discourse analysis in the study of European foreign policy

Social constructivist discourse analysis has, since the early 1990s, become increasingly popular across the social sciences, including international relations. The aim of this chapter is to outline the possibilities for the use of discourse analysis in the study of European foreign policy. Pure rationalists often dismiss EU foreign policy as 'just words' or 'declaratory diplomacy' as it is often labelled contemptuously: 'Even in this area [the Middle East] . . ., although EC policies were fairly well coordinated, they were primarily declaratory and had little actual effect' (Gordon 1997: 84). According to this view, what really matters in an analysis of the effects of EU foreign policy is implicitly or explicitly seen to be the effects of clearly identifiable non-discursive practices. In general terms, the argument in this chapter is that the study of EU foreign policy lends itself well to an analysis of discourse. Because a discourse approach sees language as a material part of social reality it can analyse aspects that, in particular, rationalists, downplay. Language is seen as a rich source of analysis rather than 'just' words. Struggles over social meaning as they are played out in declaratory diplomacy are seen as just as central to international relations as they are to other domains of social life. Something happens when social meaning is produced in texts and talk. Discourse analysis is a theory and a method for analysing this. This does not, of course, rule out the study of power or of 'policy effects'.

Neither does it necessarily lead to a neglect of the study of other than discursive practices (if such a distinction is relevant). But it means that language is seen as having an important independent status. It is not just a mirror of other social practices or a smokescreen covering up what is 'really happening'. The focus in this chapter is on the research potential of discourse analysis rather than on a comparison of discourse analysis with all other possible approaches to analysing European foreign policy. The main point is that there is ample scope for the use of discourse analysis in the study of European foreign policy, and that much work remains to be carried out drawing more directly on the insights of discourse analysis.

The empirical focus of this chapter is EU foreign policy. EU foreign policy is understood as the foreign policy of the EU as a whole (i.e. as a 'negotiated order'; Smith, 1996a). In certain places I do, however, distinguish between the pillars when this is relevant in the context. I do not directly address the issue of the analysis of the national foreign policies of European states, although this is clearly also a way of understanding 'European foreign policy' and applying discourse analysis (for this see for example Larsen 1997b). However, the link between national and European foreign policies from a discourse perspective is briefly addressed.

In the first part of the chapter, I briefly introduce the main features and assumptions of discourse analysis within the general field of social constructivism, and present the main implications of discourse analysis for concrete empirical research. I end by describing the main dimensions of discourse analysis using the categories of Milliken (1999): *representation, policy practice* and *play of practice*. In the second part of the chapter I highlight the use, and potential use, of discourse analysis in relation to four different aspects of EU foreign policy: *is the EU constructed as an actor, as what kind of actor, what kind of values does it draw on, and how are EU foreign policy decision-making procedures constructed?* I refer to research that has already been conducted, including research that does not explicitly draw on a discourse framework but which lends itself to a discourse analytic interpretation of the results. The last section includes the concluding remarks.

Discourse analysis and social constructivism

In the following, I introduce the main assumptions of discourse analysis, locating it within the wider field of social constructivism, and I present the implications for concrete analysis. The section argues for the use of discourse analysis as a research methodology based on the assumption that language constitutes meaning.

Social constructivism

The self-understanding of social constructivists within the academic discipline of international relations is that it is a position that can clearly be distinguished from discourse analysis and post-structuralist approaches (see for example Adler 1997b: 320–332; Jeppeson, Wendt and Katzenstein 1996: 46).[1] However, contrary to this but in line with the tendency in many other disciplines, I see discourse analysis as a particular theoretical and methodological position *within* the general perspective of social constructivism[2] and not a fundamentally different position. I will therefore outline what I see as the main features of social constructivism, and subsequently go into discourse analysis in more depth.

A central point in social constructivism as it is broadly used across disciplines is that the social world is only accessible to us via our ways of categorising it. Our knowledge about the social world is not a mirror image of the world, but a product of our ways of categorising it. The general point of departure is thus anti-essentialist, although social constructivist approaches vary widely with respect to whether they include essentialist elements. Human knowledge is seen as historically and culturally specific, which means that it is basically contingent: it could be different under other historical or cultural circumstances and could give rise to other identities and social relations. Moreover, the construction of intersubjective views has concrete social consequences: different views on the social world lead to different social actions and different forms of social organisation (Burr 1995: 2; Jørgensen and Phillips 2002: 13–14). Whether this is to be understood in terms of constitutive effects, causal effects (see for example Wendt 1999) or social phenomena of a different and more complex nature (see for example Alker 1999: 148; Smith 2000a: 156–60) is a question on which views diverge. Of special relevance for the study of politics, a general point in constructivism is that interests and derived policies are shaped within a particular framework of meaning and are not exogenously given. Actors do not have preferences and interests that are external to their understanding of the social world and their own identity and place therein (see for example Weldes 1996).

However, constructivist approaches differ over how this central meaning dimension of social life is to be conceptualised and analysed. The approach taken depends, to a large extent, on whether language is seen as a transparent conveyor of meaning or not. If language is seen as a neutral conveyor of meaning (as is mostly the case in phenomenology and symbolic interactionism), this naturally leads to little interest in the systematic study of linguistic practices and the language in texts.

Discourse analysis

Social constructivist approaches drawing on discourse analysis, in contrast, take as their point of departure that we need to focus on the language used in social life as a central and independent object of study. The background for that is the view that there is no meaning residing outside language or that, even if there is meaning outside language, there is no way of studying the meaning 'behind' language. No investigation can therefore take place directly at the level of ideas. We are always, strictly speaking, studying the dynamics of language.

The discourse approach to language questions the idea of an abstract and general structure of language as assumed by the founder of linguistic structuralism, Saussure. As soon as we enter into the substance of social language, we do not find one general system of meaning, but rather special systems of meaning whereby meanings of words differ from system to system, that is from discourse to discourse. Expressed in theoretical terms close to Foucault (1989 [1972]; cf. Norris 1982), the impact of words derives not only from the differences between them, as Saussure argued, but also from the social values given to them (or more correctly to the social values given to the different signifiers). Language is, therefore, more fluid and flexible.

It is important to note that definitions and usages of the term 'discourse' differ considerably from one approach to the other. In traditional linguistics and social psychology, discourse is often used as a micro concept, for example as a way of analysing the pattern of everyday conversations among individuals in different situations (families, jobs, and so on). Contrastingly, discourse is widely used in social research (including interdisciplinary approaches in linguistics and social psychology) as a macro concept to analyse how language both constrains and constructs social processes; that is, how language constrains the choices of agents and how it more fundamentally generates agents and social processes. This latter usage is particularly associated with Foucault. Here I only deal with social constructivist approaches to discourse analysis. The focus here is therefore on the second kind of approach (discourse as a macro concept).

Along the lines of Foucault (1989 [1972]), I understand discourse as a limited range of possible statements promoting a limited range of meanings. When I employ the term 'discourse analysis' in the following to discuss its use in European foreign policy, I take as the point of departure macro approaches which fall into the categories of discourse theory (Laclau and Mouffe) and critical discourse analysis (as for example represented by Fairclough) (see below). Within these macro approaches a central distinction is between text-oriented approaches that engage in detailed analysis of individual texts to show how the meanings of broader discourses are promoted, and approaches which do not engage in detailed textual analysis but focus on broadly based discourses which are identified in relevant texts. Critical discourse analysis (CDA) belongs to the first group whereas the discourse theory of Laclau and Mouffe belongs to the second.[3]

Discourse analysis versus other social constructivist approaches

How, in general terms, is a discourse approach distinct from social constructivist approaches which assume that language is transparent? There are four main implications for concrete studies as compared with studies which see language as transparent.

First, the strong social and transsubjective character of the beliefs identified is stressed via the focus on language as the concrete social medium. Discourses are not seen as the product of individual language users' brains or psychology. Rather, individual views and identities are constructed by discourses which are formed and changed in social interaction and thus are fundamentally social. An analytical focus on the views of an individual or a politician is therefore only relevant as expressions of broader societally shared discourses (contrast this with, for example, Wendt's tendency to focus on Gorbachev in Wendt 1992: 420–2[4]).

Second, since language constitutes meaning, the analytical focus is not on what is 'really' meant by a particular text or statement. What is really meant is not something the researcher can know since we do not have access to meaning outside language. We therefore stay at the 'surface' of the text and pay attention to the narrative structures and vocabulary in the text. Tactical/rhetorical use of language is certainly seen as important within discourse analysis. It is, however, seen as constrained by the discourses in which the strategic actors are embedded. This is in contrast to those social constructivist approaches which consider language as transparent and which are often drawn towards inquiring about what is 'really' meant by a text because there is no concept of what the level for studying meaning is (how 'deep' we need to go). This can lead to a neglect of the transsubjective, constraining and productive character of texts and to a focus on individual and social meaning as something outside the text. Discourse analysis, in contrast, has a relatively clear view of how and where meaning is to be studied – at the level of the language.

Third, discourse approaches see language as inherently unstable, fickle and fluid as meanings are permanently being defined and redefined as an integral part of the social process. They are not a permanent property of individuals or groups. This does not mean that elements of stability may not be identified. A central goal is indeed to show how meanings are temporarily fixed in discourses, and where there are dominant discourses where one would not *a priori* expect them. There might be both an interest in continuity and change (see for example Larsen 1997b; Wæver 1998). Simplifying maybe more than is fair, non-discourse approaches tend to focus more on stability, but when they do identify change it is often seen as a total change.

Fourth, instead of the focus on what is 'really' meant in a particular text, the focus is on the discursive structures cutting across texts, or the way discourses dominate or compete in particular texts. The question asked is how the individual text is an articulation of broader discursive structures rather than the concrete message or argument in the text. One is interested in narrative structures and vocabulary in the language used.

Implications for empirical research

It is important to stress that social constructivist discourse analysis is a theory (and a method flowing from that) about the shaping of the social world through the process whereby meanings are produced and reproduced. It contends that the social is, at least to a large extent, constructed in language. But as a theory, it does not say anything about the substance or content of the construction. The ontology is empty. It says that the social world is constructed, not *what* kind of social world is constructed. What we can say is that the language used plays a central part in constructing social life (and is not a derived phenomenon) and that language therefore is a central object of study. But discourse theory itself cannot say anything about what kind of discourses are present and fix meaning in particular contexts. This is an empirical question. We have to formulate our questions about a particular area from our knowledge of the field (interpreting them, of course, within the terms of discourse analysis sketched out above).

Milliken (1999) has attempted to formulate the central elements of research from a discourse analysis perspective within international relations, arguing that there is by now something that amounts to a discourse analysis research programme. Good scholarship in this area, she argues, is built upon a set of theoretical commitments that organise discourse studies and restrict appropriate contexts of justification and discovery. Among the most important commitments of this research programme are three 'analytically distinguishable bundles of theoretical claims' (Milliken 1999: 228, 231). These three key claims are:

1   Discourses are systems of representation (the general constructivist understanding of meaning). Discursive studies must empirically analyse how discourse constitutes the world in meaning.
2   Discourse produces subjects and objects defined by the discourse. Discourses make intelligible some ways of acting towards the world and exclude other possible modes of identity and action. The analytical focus should be on how discourse produces this world, including its policies.
3   Discourses are changeable and historically contingent. Discourse analysis should analyse the indeterminate play of practice between discourses and how efforts are made to stabilise and maintain dominant meanings. This also leads to analytical attention being paid to whether there are alternative discourses which are silenced by the hegemonic discourse or whether there are open discursive antagonisms (Doty 1997: 375–9; Milliken 1999: 229–31).[5]

Discursive dynamics and struggles are central in social change. I return to these categories below when I look more closely at the use of discourse analysis in the study of European foreign policy.

Discourse analysis and European foreign policy

A central question in the literature and political debate about European foreign policy is the issue of whether one can talk about a common understanding of EU international actorness in or outside the EU. This question can be said to lie behind many other issues of EU foreign policy. Is there a common understanding of EU actorness at the EU level which shapes general policy? Or is there, rather, a battle over the content of European actorness in relation to every single policy issue which means that we are really closer to the realists' conception of EU foreign policy as the lowest common denominator of the national views or national cost/benefit considerations? (See for example Gordon 1997; Bretherton and Vogler 1999). The representation of EU actorness is a central issue to approach from a discourse perspective. If there is no joint representation of the EU as a foreign policy actor of some kind at the EU level among the central EU actors or outside the EU, it may not make sense to inquire further into the issue of the foreign policy of the EU from a discourse perspective focusing on the EU level (whereas it might be interesting to inquire into the discursive dimension of various national European foreign policies and how these make sense of and shape European foreign policy; see for example Larsen 1997b). In this case the basic realist approach to EU foreign policy would seem to be confirmed as the policy stances taken by the EU vis-à-vis the outside world are a function of nationally generated views.[6] However, if the EU is found empirically to be con-structed as an actor, the next general analytical step from a discourse perspec-tive is to ask what kind of actor is constructed, including what kind of values are articulated as an inherent component of actorness. Also part of this general focus of analysis, although at a lower level of abstraction, is the issue of how the actors involved construct and reproduce the decision-making procedures linked to this international actor. Rationalists including neo-functionalists assume these to take a particular character given the nature of the actors involved (states and institutional actors). For discourse analysis, it is an empirical question how these actors construct their mutual relations in language. Key questions in rela-tion to EU foreign policy from a discourse perspective, then, include the fol-lowing: (1) Is the EU constructed as an international actor? (2) If it is, what kind of actor is constructed? (3) What kind of values is this actor based on? (4) How are its decision-making procedures constructed by the actors involved?

In the following, I will suggest preliminary avenues of inquiry into these issues of European foreign policy, partly drawing on the work that has been done in these areas, including my own work (Larsen 2000a, b).[7] The aim is to suggest avenues for future research from a discourse perspective, rather than attempting a comprehensive presentation of these issues. In presenting these issues, I have structured the presentation along the three dimensions of dis-course research suggested by Milliken (1999) outlined above, although I do not deal with them in the same order (I merge the first and the third dimensions). I then discuss the four substantive issues identified in relation to EU foreign policy along the dimensions of representation and play of discursive practice and then social practice (policy). It is important to stress that the distinctions between the three dimensions are analytical rather than ontological. In general terms, it is part of a constructivist understanding that all social practice is mean-ing-based. Policy (part of the social practice) is therefore always constructed in meaning through a system of representation. An analytical distinction between representation and policy does not therefore imply that policy is of a different ontological order.

The analytical distinction is relevant, however, because the relationship between representation and policy is not simple (Larsen 1997; Hansen 1998: 87–97; cf. Wæver 1998).[8] Even if policy is understood solely as an articulation of discourse,[9] the challenging question is *what* discourse(s) are articulated within this particular field, including in the process of implementation (Milliken 1999: 240). Moreover, I am only concerned with indicating the possible extent of this discursive shaping of policy practices, not in a comparison with possible effects of other practices of a different ontological order, let alone attempting to com-bine different approaches. Discursive representations are assumed to constitute an enabling framework for certain policies and to exclude other policies. The focus in the play of discursive practice is the discursive struggle which is played out between competing discourses. To a large extent the discursive struggles in relation to the shaping of EU foreign policy can be seen as struggles between states[10] and instititutional actors adhering to different discourses. The interesting analytical question in this context is which and whose discourses, if any, become hegemonic or dominant in EU foreign policy. Power (which can be understood as both constitutive of actors and as constraining actors) and dominance of particular discourses are in a Foucauldian perspective two sides of the same coin. Finally, for reasons of space, I do not cover all the aspects which discourse analysis can be used to illuminate (as suggested by Milliken).[11]

The EU as an international actor

REPRESENTATION AND PLAY OF DISCURSIVE PRACTICE

As mentioned above, representations of actorness are central for the study of the EU, since they can be said to constitute the point of departure for further inquiry into EU foreign policy from a discourse perspective. Across EU documents a discourse can be identified according to which the Union is constructed as a unit which defends its own interests and has an obligation to take on responsibilities in the light of international challenges (Larsen 2000a). Expressions such as the following from Article 2 and Section V on the CFSP in the Amsterdam Treaty are common in EU documents: 'The Union shall [. . .] assert its identity on the international stage' and, 'To safeguard the common values, fundamental interests, independence and integrity of the Union' and 'The Union shall define a CFSP' (in the TEU it was 'The Union and its Member States'). They are statements belonging to a common discourse on EU international actorness.

Within rationalist approaches, EU actorness is mainly treated as a question of what they see as the non-discursive impact on the world (see for example Gordon 1997: 84). Clear policy effects are the key to establishing whether the EU has actor status, often based on the identification of some hard capabilities. A discourse approach starts from a different analytical position. According to this perspective, the Union is an international actor if it constructs itself as one vis-à-vis the rest of the world and if other international actors conceive of it as such. The crucial point therefore is that there is a dominant EU discourse which articulates the EU as an international actor. To a large extent other international actors also conceive of it as such (Bretherton and Vogler 1999).

That the Union constructs itself as an international actor does not, however, mean that it does not also construct itself as belonging to other international entities. For example, the EU clearly constructs itself as a part of the West. But it does not equate itself completely with the 'West'. It is a separate political actor which promotes Western values (Larsen 2000a).

In Union documents (in the Council context) there is, surprisingly, a hegemonic, unitary discourse on the assertion that the EU is an international actor with its own interests and policies. This is the discourse which shapes the EU's policy practice (see below). The discourse that contests this point is a discourse according to which the Union cannot be an actor because there are seen to be no 'real' European interests. According to this discourse, if the Union has actor features it is because it has taken on powers which rightly belong elsewhere, mostly to the states (as right-wing adherents to this discourse would mostly claim) or to more broadly based international and democratic organisations (as some on the left and some Greens would argue). It is presented as on its way to becoming a superstate. The language within this discourse is therefore one of misuse of power rather than just power (strong sceptics usually want the Union to be less of an actor and more of a loose forum for coordination). This discourse, however, is, unsurprisingly, not present in official EU documents and does not shape EU policy practice. Rather, it is part of the discursive battle at the national levels and, to a much lesser extent, in the European Parliament, about the future construction of the EU as a whole vis-à-vis the member states. At the national levels, this discourse has a strong position in Britain and in Denmark (Larsen 1999) but can also be identified among the so-called *souveraintistes* in France.

POLICY PRACTICE

The dominant discourse on the Union as an international actor with its proper interests is reflected in the Union having a policy line across a whole range of functional and geographical areas, although of varying intensity and detail. Union policy is clearly most uniform in relation to trade, fisheries and agriculture. In terms of geographical scope, Union policy is most intensive and detailed with respect to the areas around Europe, the Central and Eastern European countries (CEEC) in particular. In these policy areas, the Union's policy practices can be said to have contributed to shaping international policy processes. This is particularly clear if the scope of the inquiry is not just taken to be the CFSP but Union policy as a whole. The exceptions to this so far have been strategic and military affairs in the sphere of high politics and crises management (with the possible exception of Cyprus), although this might be changing (see below). Moreover, the Union is considered as a significant actor by important sections of the international community in many policy areas (Bretherton and Vogler 1999). Whether there is seen to be a gap between the expectations (internal and external) for the Union's ability to act and the Union's impact on international political processes (Hill 1993a, 1998) is to a large extent a question of what is the base of comparison or what stories/expectations are used to evaluate the actions of the Union (Jørgensen 1998). In some cases, the EU can be said to have more policy instruments than states or other organisations (K. Smith 1998a), in other cases fewer. What is clear is that the discursive practice constructing the Union as an international actor is also a series of political practices across different policy fields.

What kind of international actor?

REPRESENTATION AND PLAY OF DISCURSIVE PRACTICE

In the dominant discourse, the Union is presented as a unique and complex construction; it is not presented as taking the place of the member states but is an inseparable counterpart to the member states (Reflection Group 1995: I–III). In this light, the frequent use of the term 'identity' or 'genuine identity' in Union discourse in relation to the need to strengthen the EU in the international context is significant. The Union is articulated as an international actor, but not as a state or a future state (Larsen 2000a; cf. Wæver 1995, 1996). Along the same lines, Wæver (1995) has labelled the understandings of the Union 'post-sovereign'.

An important issue in the literature in relation to EU actorness is the issue of whether the EU is a civilian power (Duchêne 1972, 1973; Hill 1990). The debate about whether the EU is and should remain a civilian power was launched by Duchêne's work in the early 1970s which argued that there were international and internal factors that pulled the EC towards remaining a civilian power and that it was in the EC's interest to remain one (Dûchene 1972, 1973). From the perspective of this chapter, the question of whether the EU is by its nature a civilian power can be recast in discourse terms: it would not be seen as a question of what the Union in essentialist terms *is*,[12] but rather what kind of actor is constructed in the discourses articulating the Union's actorness. This approach, on the one hand, means that the nature of the Union is not given once and for all since discourses are never stable. On the other hand, it also means that access to particular means – military means of course being the most interesting in this context – does not *per se* make the Union into a particular kind of actor. Rather, the decisive element is how these means are articulated as part of Union actions. After the entry into force of the TEU in 1993, the Union formally gained access to military means through the WEU, at least on a very small scale. And yet the dominant discourse within the Union did not articulate the Union as a military power in relation to concrete international issues until the second part of 1998 (see below). Until 1998, the dominant EU discourse was one which stressed the role of civilian means in the foreign policy of the Union in relation to solving concrete international issues (Larsen 2000a). In the original formulations of the concept of civil power (Duchêne 1973; Hill 1990), the emphasis on persuasion remained an important part of the concept. While persuasion remains an important element in the way the Union conceptualises its political actions, there is little doubt that the Union in the 1990s has constructed itself as a *political* power which should draw on its political, economic and military means to further its political goals (Larsen 2000a: 224).

While the dominant discourse in Union documents until the late 1990s, then, has been a discourse which has stressed the civilian power character of the Union in relation to concrete issues in international relations, including conflict resolution, the presence of another discourse can also be identified in Union documents. According to this discourse, access to military means is central to asserting the international identity of the international (diplomatic) standing of the Union as an actor. This discourse coexisted with the civilian power discourse in the 1990s in official Union documents (Larsen 2000a), although the civilian power discourse dominated policy practice until 1998. The division between these two discourses could also be found in relation to the treaty changes in the 1990s.

But from 1998, the hitherto dominant civilian power discourse mentioned above has been challenged by another discourse which has since been gaining dominance in Union documents. Within this discourse, the civilian power discourse elements have been articulated with the element that the Union's access to military means might be beneficial in responding to international crises and in contributing to international peace and stability, so that the Union has access to the full scope of instruments. This new dominant discourse could be called the 'full instrumental power discourse'. The element that the Union's use of military means may be beneficial in responding to international crises and in contributing to international peace and stability is now articulated as part of the dominant discourse:

> [The Council] should have the ability to take decisions on the ... Petersberg Tasks ... To this end, the Union must have the capacity for autonomous action, backed by needs to develop a capacity for autonomous action backed by credible military forces ... in order to respond to international crises without prejudice to actions by NATO. The EU will thereby increase its ability to contribute to international peace and security in accordance with the principles of the UN Charter. (Declaration by the European Council in Cologne, 3 June 1999, on strengthening the common European policy on security and defence)[13]

From a discourse perspective, the articulation of the EU as an actor that may also draw on military means for instrumental purposes within the 'full instrumental power' discourse might be seen as a change in the nature of the EU as an international actor. The discourse which stresses access to military means as central to asserting the Union's status and identity can, however, still be identified in EU documents. So while a new dominant discourse articulates civilian and military elements as part of an instrumental whole, elements of a more identity- based discourse continue to exist (e.g., the Conclusions from the European Council in Cologne, 3–4 June 1999 read: 'The members of the European Council are convinced that the EU shall play its full role on the international stage'). Meanings at the EU level concerning the nature of EU actorness can therefore not be said to be fixed.

POLICY PRACTICE

The policy activities of the EU have so far concentrated on the civilian aspects of foreign policy (stability pacts, trade and cooperation agreements, political conditionality, declaratory diplomacy, etc.) and excluded military instruments (apart from the joint action according to TEU J.4.2 in 1998 consisting in training mine clearers) in line with the dominant civilian power discourse. It might be argued that this is because the Union has lacked the means to conduct such operations. In the 1990s, however, the Union did in principle have access to military means, although small scale, through the WEU, but only drew on them to a negligible extent. It can be argued, then, that the 'civilian power' discursive practice shaped the use of policies and policy instruments used (see below). The articulation of the new military elements into the dominant discourse from 1998 has enabled a new momentum for the Union in the field of defence and the shaping of the new institutional structures in the Union which will increase the Union's ability to use military means and the likehood of it using them. It is within this framework of meaning that it has been decided that the EU should have access to military forces earmarked for this purpose by 2003 at the latest.

The EU's values

REPRESENTATION AND PLAY OF DISCURSIVE PRACTICE

Across EU documents the Union's (foreign policy) identity is articulated with liberal values, as in the following example: 'The Union is founded on the principles of liberty, democracy, respect for human rights and fundamental freedoms, and the rule of law, principles which are common to all member states' (TOA Article 6).

These are presented as the values that the Union is meant to defend internationally[14] and international conflict resolution is linked to furthering these values. These liberal values are linked in chains of equivalence. (Within the framework of Laclau and Mouffe (1985) a chain of equivalence is a linking of concepts whereby the difference between concepts disappears). Within discourses, elements are interconnected and mutually supportive, so that one concept is presented as leading logically to the other (Laclau and Mouffe 1985: 127–34) which contribute to constructing the identity of the Union: 'The European Council recalls the contribution of human rights to the establishment of conditions which are more conducive to peace, security, democracy and social and economic development' (European Council, Presidency Conclusions, 1997). There can thus be said to be an EU discourse on joint values, and not just on decision-making procedures, as is sometimes suggested (see for example Forster and Wallace 1996).

Discourse approaches consider identities as relational rather than as given attributes of actors. They therefore focus on how identities are constituted as a mirror of an 'other' or a threat.[15] An important focus in relation to EU foreign policy is therefore who is constructed as Europe's other and hence contributes to constituting the liberal values as central in the dominant discourse of the Union. Campbell (1992), more generally, sees the articulation of threats as an essential part of establishing a foreign policy identity. Articulation of threats is also an important part of creating the inside–outside distinction between the domestic and the international which is arguably necessary for the establishment of a foreign policy identity (Walker 1990, 1993; L. Hansen 1995: 118–19). In establishing who is constructed as threats to Europe as an 'other', the 'securitization' approach is central from a discourse perspective. The core of this approach is to analyse the language used in a particular context to establish what is constructed as an existential threat in relation to a particular referent (e.g. a country or an organisation) – that is, the focus is on the use of a *grammar of security.* The grammar of security allows the actors to break the normal rules of the game (Wæver 1996; Buzan, Wæver and de Wilde 1997). Along the lines of Campbell (1992), the identification of a concept of security in the EU discourse is also interesting because the articulation of threats, an 'other', is a crucial part of establishing a foreign policy identity. The question then is, what elements are constructed as threats to European or EU security?

Wæver (1996: 122) argues that the threat to European security is not found in space but rather in time: Europe's past of wars, genocide and dictatorship. The threat to European security, he argues, is constructed as threats to European integration. Within the dominant discourse, EU integration is therefore articulated as security (Wæver 1996). One could argue, then, that what is 'othered' is Europe's past so that the emphasis on the liberal values in the Union can be seen as a negation of Europe's dark past (Larsen 2000a; cf. Wæver 1996: 122).

Conversely, Neumann (1998) argues that Europe's 'other' (if not a direct threat) is to be found in space in the form of Russia or the 'East'. Russia or the East, Neumann argues, has historically and up until today constituted a defining pole for what Europe is not – that is, barbaric, authoritarian and Asiatic. Although Russia has at times been presented as becoming more European, it has always been discursively constructed as in between Europe and Asia, or on its way to Europe. The main metaphor used in the discourse has been one of transition. This is arguably also the case today (Neumann 1998: 111–12, 160, 207).[16] Along the same lines, the Central and Eastern European countries' non-Easternness becomes defining for the EU's enlargement policy and hence for EU foreign policy directed against this region.

On the basis of an analysis of EU documents in the 1990s (Larsen 2000a), I have argued elsewhere that the values constructed as part of European (foreign policy) identity can be seen as constituted with reference to internal *as well as* external dangers to European security. The internal dangers are seen as a cessation of EU integration and a failure to complete enlargement, which are closely linked. They can be seen as constituted by a negation of an 'other' in the past as argued above, and thus constitutive of the liberal values. The external dangers are presented as instability in Russia (unstable democracy), the Mediterranean area (unstable democracy and Islamic fundamentalism) and non-geographical dangers (environmental risks, crime, etc.). These dangers can also be seen as constitutive of the liberal values at the core of the EU's foreign policy identity. The complex multitude of dangers and risks in EU discourse does not lead to a clear-cut binary othering in relation to European security (Wæver 1996: 122). But it reinforces the liberal values at the core of European identity, since it is the negation of these values which is part of the construction of dangers (Larsen 2000a).

No challenge has been mounted to the discursive construction of the core values of the Union as a foreign policy actor – these are universally accepted to be liberal values. There do not seem to be other general discourses in EU documents which draw on something different from a liberal chain of equivalence. Rather, disagreements about the shaping of policies can be found *within* this discourse.[17]

POLICY PRACTICE

What kind of policy practices are enabled by the dominant discourse on the liberal values? An important aspect of the Union's policies consists in pronouncing itself on human rights globally, and not least in Africa (e.g. in relation to the situations in Niger, Nigeria and around the Great Lakes).[18] Political conditionality, which in the 1990s has been an integral part of the Union's policy towards demandeur countries, consists in linking improvements in conditions in the liberal values of the countries in question to economic support or conclusion of trade agreements, positively or negatively (K. Smith 1998b). The main part of the Lomé agreements also contained clauses on human rights from 1989. Political conditionality in some form can be seen as an element in the Union's policies globally from the Central and Eastern European countries to Africa. However, the way it is applied varies considerably. Countries that are important to the Union for commercial or political purposes generally suffer less from negative sanctions and there are often disagreements about what policies to adopt within the general liberal discourse, (K. Smith 1998b: 274). But the liberal discourse identified contributes to the EU's policy articulations in many fields. The question is, with what kind of other discourses is the liberal discourse co-articulated?

Policy practices relating to management of conflicts and furthering regional stability can be seen as based on the central role of the liberal values (Larsen 2000b). The Stability Pacts for Central and Eastern Europe and for the Balkans can be seen as policy elements shaped within the discourse whereby the liberal values play a central role in conflict resolution.

In a broader sense, the ways in which other regions around Europe can be seen as contributing to constituting EU identity in EU discourse through 'othering' is manifested in EU policies towards these regions. The significant issue is whether the policies take the form of integration with 'us', aiming at membership, or whether the policies are rather an expression of 'othering' and are not leading up to membership. The policies towards the CEEC can be said to be inclusionary to such an extent that it is debatable whether it can still be said to be foreign policy, based as it mostly is on Pillar One instruments and extensive cooperation about 'domestic' issues (M. Smith 1996b). The policies towards the Mediterranean and Russia, although highly institutionalised (Barcelona Declaration, joint strategy/ partnership agreement with Russia), are arguably about managing relations with someone outside (with the aim of preventing instability), not with bringing prospective insiders or members closer to the EU (Larsen 2000a).

EU decision-making

REPRESENTATION AND PLAY OF DISCURSIVE PRACTICE

Discourse analysis asks whether there is a common procedural (decision-making) discourse which cuts across actors and institutions which might mean that intergovernmentalism (in the case of the CFSP) is not the defining feature of EU foreign policy decision-making. This is a different avenue of research from approaches which study the European foreign policy decision-making process based on the formal structures (intergovernmentality for the CFSP) or the character of the participating actors (primarily states but also supranational actors).

A significant amount of empirical and theoretical work on the CFSP has been published which includes considerations about common procedural understandings (less has been done on the external relations of the EU) and even aspects of language which cut across state actors (Jørgensen 1996, 1997a; Tonra 1996, 1997, 1998, 2001; Ekengren 1997). Although the method and the analytical frameworks used are not discourse analytical, many of the findings lend themselves to an interpretation drawing on discourse analysis. For example, the 'consultation reflex', and the identification of a pull towards the median in relation to forming common positions (as identified by Nuttall 1992: 312, 314), can be seen as part of a CFSP discourse. This discourse can be identified in the numerous reports on the EPC/CFSP since 1970.

The understandings identified by Tonra (1996, 1997, 1998, 2001) in particular can be understood as discursive representations of CFSP procedures present in the EU institutions and member states. Tonra stresses, for example, that socialisation has led to a primary coordination reflex with the EU partners for new policy initiatives. The language used in the CFSP has increasingly become a language shared by all partners (Tonra 1997: 187) and the national foreign policy-making process is increasingly driven by the EPC or European agenda. European political cooperation has become the central forum for the delineation of foreign policy interests in each of the three states he examined (Tonra 1997: 190). There is a procedural EU discourse of consultation and cooperation which shapes the decision-making process. 'Side payments' or 'trade-offs' are not the order of the day when formulating CFSP stances. Rather, policy-makers understand themselves as being engaged in a process of collective policy-making which contributes to formation of their foreign policy identity (Tonra 1997: 186–7; Tonra 1998: 11–12).

It is interesting to compare a discourse approach to the issue of common procedural understandings with a more phenomenological/symbolic interactionist approach, since the latter approaches are often implicitly drawn on in analyses of the CFSP. A phenomenological approach will tend to see the development of these CFSP norms as a result of interactions between individuals involved, particularly the political directors. The informal, clubby atmosphere of this group is a key object of study, and biographical and personal evidence are treated as important sources. Distinctions such as the effects of socialisation versus what individuals willingly concede to and which might therefore involve an understanding of a rational calculus are drawn on (see for example Glarbo 1999). Social 'learning' is seen as central for identity formation (Checkel, 1998: 344).

A discourse approach, in contrast, will tend to see the understandings developed as results of socially shared discourses produced and transformed through social interaction. The informal clubby atmosphere, which has characterised the EPC and to a lesser extent the CFSP and which is often credited with being the hot-bed for developing common understandings, is seen as an expression of a particular CFSP discourse – perhaps a hybrid of traditional diplomatic discourse and community discourse; it is not the result of individuals' isolated views, but of socially shared discourses that individuals draw on as strategic resources in text and talk in the CFSP. A discourse approach would focus more on patterns and constraints than phenomenology. These patterns and constraints would be understood in terms of discourses which construct objects and subjects in particular ways and thus shape and constrain action. A discourse approach would, for example, note how the consultation reflex language was present already from 1973, and study how the EPC/CFSP developed within this discursive framework. Support for this approach is provided by the fact that, although individual civil servants get to know each other in the EPC/CFSP working groups and in the political committee, in diplomacy individuals are generally very mobile, continually being replaced. There is not the personal continuity which would provide for a person-based 'communaute de vue'.

There is a conflict between a hegemonic discourse which assumes a supplementary European forum for foreign affairs and another discourse which argues that such a decision-making forum is an aberation, and breaks with the national model of foreign policy-making which is seen as the natural one (as outlined under 'international actor' above). Most adherents to the latter are to be found on the political wings, and not within the political/administrative elite (with the UK as a possible exception). This discourse is predominantly articulated within some EU member states, Britain and Denmark in particular (Larsen 1999), and not at the EU level.

In a broader perspective, the key questions are whether one can talk about a discursively constructed European (political) identity, and among which actors – states and institutions – such a discourse might be dominant. The questions relate the issue of meanings in European foreign policy procedures with the framework of meaning of the rest of the European polity. Fundamentally, this is linked to the issue of whether there is a European demos or a European public sphere and how this might affect EU foreign policy (Guénno 1998, 2000; Hix 1998; Peterson 1998: 3). Here is an issue where much more research from a discourse perspective is needed, research which cannot, of course, be limited to EU foreign policy.

POLICY PRACTICE

The discourse on intensive cooperation in foreign affairs in relation to the CFSP outlined above produces and reproduces political practices in EU foreign policy: there has been a Europeanisation and a Brusselisation of national foreign policy-making, although this does not necessarily manifest itself in the same way in all EU member states (Whitman 2000b). A recent study of the foreign policy of EU member states concludes that 'it now seems more appropriate to suggest that EU Member States conduct all but the most limited foreign policy objectives inside an EU context' (Whitman 2000a: 271). Most departments in member states' foreign ministries are now in some ways involved in EU foreign policy-making (Spence 1999: 262), and national political/administrative decision-making is to a large extent adapted to the calendar of EU decision-making (for an example see Ekengren 1997). At the EU level, the fact that many EU policy positions arrived at can be seen as the median of the many national stances rather than the lowest common denominator (Nuttall 1992: 314) can be seen as a policy practice produced by the discourse which cuts across the actors in EU foreign policy-making and ascribes a special status to EU foreign policy coordination.

The policy practice of the CFSP cooperation discourse can also be said to consist in the way it produces and reproduces the role of legitimate actors in EU foreign policy decision-making (member states' diplomatic and other representatives, the High Representative of the CFSP, the Commission). The European Parliament, for example, is not taken very seriously as a political actor by the Council, contrary to the situation in external trade affairs which fall under the Community pillar. In external trade affairs, the European Parliament is increasingly taken seriously, linked, of course, to its stronger role provided in the treaties in this field. Although the low legitimacy of the European Parliament in the dominant CFSP discourse could be seen as a simple reflection of the role accorded to the different institutional actors in the treaties with regard to foreign affairs, it can be interpreted in an alternative way from a discourse perspective: treaty changes in the field of EU foreign policy have to a large extent been codifications of already developed policy practices and arguably take place within the framework of the dominant discourse on the CFSP.

Concluding remarks

In this chapter, I began with a brief introduction to discourse analysis. I then presented three central dimensions of discourse analysis, along the lines of Milliken (1999): representation, policy practice, and play of practice and attempted to show how these three dimensions can serve to shed light on what I see as central aspects of EU foreign policy (actor status, actor attributes and values, decision-making procedures). The focus was on how these issues can be approached from a discourse perspective. I described work which has been carried out in this field, partly from a discourse perspective, partly from perspectives that lend themselves to interpretation in terms of the discourse perspective.

My conclusion is that there is wide scope for drawing on discourse analysis for analysing European foreign policy. But the conclusion is also that little research has been done which has explicitly and systematically drawn on a discourse analytical framework. From the perspective outlined here, the recommendation is for research which more directly uses a discourse analytical theory and method. In this respect, it should be stressed that there are many different approaches to social constructivist discourse analysis. Which one is chosen has important consequences for the way the analysis is conducted, since some approaches lend themselves more easily to being combined with other kinds of theoretical framework than others. The post-structuralist discourse analytical approach of Laclau and Mouffe, for example, cannot easily be combined with other non-discourse approaches since the point is that all societal phenomena are discursive. The critical discourse analysis of Norman Fairclough, on the other hand, can more easily be used in combination with other theoretical approaches since it operates with societal phenomena other than discursive phenomena (Jørgensen and Phillips 2002).

Notes

1   It is, however, rarely clear what the precise criteria for this demarcation are. In some respects, social constructivist approaches might for example draw on a rather rationalist/ modernist epistemology, while in other respects dealing with the same foci or ontology as post-structuralists, such as identity, language and discourse. It seems more appropriate to say that there are many social constructivist approaches which in some respects might be more or less close to rationalists, while in others they are more or less close to the assumptions and foci of oststructuralists/deconstructivists (for a distinction between different strands see Ruggie 1998b: 880–2. For the distinction between constructivists and deconstructivists see Wæver 1997. See also Larsen 1997a: 244).

2   For this point in sociology see Bertilsson and Järvinen (1998: 10). For philosophy see for example Collin (1997), who does not distinguish between linguistic and non-linguistic approaches to social construction.

3   For a description and a comparison between these two approaches see Jørgensen and Phillips (2002).

4   Wendt relies heavily on symbolic interactionism (1992; 1999: 1, 170–1, 336).

5   One weakness in Milliken's categorisation is that she seems to suggest that discourse analysis is basically one unitary school.

6   For the issue of whether national or common understandings shape national policy see Wendt (1992: 423).

7   This builds on empirical analysis of a corpus of EU documents from the 1990s. For a list of these see Larsen (2000a: 240).

8   For an attempt to distinguish analytically in an empirical study see Larsen (1997b).

9   The question is whether there are social practices other than discursive practices. This is where macro approaches to discourse analysis vary, CDA assuming that there are social practices other than discursive practices, the theory of Laclau and Mouffe assuming that there are not.

10 For an analysis along these lines concerning general EU policy, see for example Larsen (1997b) and Wæver (1990).

11 Most notably I do not go into the issue of genealogy in relation to European foreign policy. Neither do I go into deconstruction, where very little work has been done (see, however, Wæver 1994: 248).

12 Not least because Duchêne's argument for why the EU *is* a civilian power is, to a large extent, based on the circumstances of the early 1970s (see for instance Duchêne 1972: 38).

13 See also the Presidency's conclusions from the European councils in Helsinki (1999) and Feira (June 2000) (European Council, Presidency Conclusions 1999 and 2000).

14 See for example TOA Article 11.

15   Recognition by other international actors as a necessary component of actorness from a discourse perspective is not a given. Neumann has argued that there is a difference between the role of 'the other' within constructivism and post-structuralism. The 'other' in constructivism contributes to constituting the ego by recognising ego. In post-structuralism the 'other' is part of ego's self-definition through a kind of mirror function, what ego is not. The recognition aspect is not stressed (Neumann 1998: ch. 8). The position in this chapter, however, is that the recognition aspect can be contained within a discourse perspective.

16   Neumann (1998: ch. 2) also describes how Turkey has previously had this defining 'othering' function for Europe, particularly when it was politically strong.

17   The focus on liberal values is of course a common Western focus, in particular after the Cold War.

18   See K. Smith (1998b: 267).

LISBETH AGGESTAM

6

Role identity and the Europeanisation of foreign policy: a political–cultural approach

> The foreign policy process has become Europeanised, in the sense that in every international issue, there is an exchange of information and an attempt to arrive at a common understanding and a common approach – compared to how things were in the past, where most issues were looked at in isolation without addressing the attitudes of other member states or a European dimension.

These words of a senior British foreign policy-maker reflect the experience of foreign policy cooperation between member states of the European Union for more than a quarter of a century.[1] Over the years, the level of ambition to speak with 'one voice' in foreign affairs has steadily increased to include even security and defence questions. The Maastricht Treaty clearly stipulated that the Union's Common Foreign and Security Policy should aim to assert the EU's identity on the international stage. This progressive deepening and widening of European integration in foreign policy raises a number of interesting questions, particularly regarding the significance and future role of the state in foreign policy: Are states no longer the most important organisational actors in foreign policy? Is the realist idea that states ultimately seek to preserve their national independence in foreign policy still relevant to international relations in Europe?

The precise implication that the CFSP has for national foreign policy is a matter of contention in the academic literature. Yet, few analysts would probably disagree with the observation that it has 'moved the conduct of foreign policy away from the old nation-state national sovereignty model towards a collective endeavour, a form of high-level networking with transformationalist effects' (Hill and Wallace 1996: 6). How we conceptualise these changes in foreign policy is a major challenge and provokes us to look anew at the theories and categories with which we go about our research on foreign policy in contemporary Europe. A central research problem is to explore the relevance of the state and investigate whether the agency of foreign policy is now increasingly conceived on the European level by policy-makers.

This chapter sets out to explore this research problem using a political–cultural approach and seeks to illuminate the cognitive mind-maps with which policy-makers interpret their political 'realities'. Culture is here defined as the broad context in which individual and collective identities are linked, producing shared meanings that influence the framing of political action. In foreign policy, the concept has been characterised as 'broad and general beliefs and attitudes about one's own nation, about other nations, and about the relationships that actually obtain or that they should obtain between the self and others in the international arena' (Vertzberger 1990: 68). The analysis presented here is based on a social constructivist perspective, in the sense that political ideas and perceptions are assumed to be part of cognitive structures that give meaning to the material world (cf. Adler 1997b).

At the core of the analytical framework presented below stand two key concepts: identity and role. The first is *identity*. Ideas about who 'we' are tend to serve as a guide to political action and basic worldviews. Collective identities express a sense of belonging to membership of a distinct group. As such, they tend to provide a system of orientation for self-reference and action (Ross 1997: 2). Thus, it is important to address the issue of how foreign policy is interconnected with national and/or European identity. Changes in self-conceptions, it is suggested, are intimately bound up with long-term foreign policy change. For its part, the concept of *role* facilitates a political–cultural approach to foreign policy analysis in two ways. The first is methodological. Role concepts provide us with an analytical and operational link between identity constructions and patterns of foreign policy behaviour. Role conceptions suggest how cultural norms and values are translated into verbal statements about expected foreign policy behaviour and action orientation. As Hudson and Vore (1995: 26) note, 'National role conception is one of the few conceptual tools we have for the study of how society and culture serve as a context for a nation's foreign policy. It allows one to bridge the conceptual gap between the general beliefs held in a society and the beliefs of foreign policy decision makers.'

Role conceptions could metaphorically be thought of as 'road maps' which facilitate the foreign policy-maker's navigation through a complex political reality. Human perception is theory-driven, as Jönsson, Tägil and Törnqvist (2000: 10) point out: 'Theories are like floodlights that illuminate one part of the stage but, by the same token, leave other parts in the shade or in the dark.' Given the emphasis on role conceptions, it should be apparent that the analytical framework presented in this chapter concerns the subjective dimension of foreign policy.

The second way in which the concept of role facilitates a political–cultural approach to foreign policy analysis is epistemological. Role concepts provide an essential link between agent and structure, as they incorporate the manner in which foreign policy is both purposeful and shaped by institutional contexts. Foreign policy, in other words, is not just a question of adaptation to structural forces (determinism), nor is it simply a function of political will (voluntarism). As Hollis and Smith (1990: 168) argue, 'Role involves judgement and skill, but at the same time it involves a notion of structure within which roles operate'. With an emphasis on the interplay between agency and structure, the European foreign policy-maker is considered to be both subject to norm-conforming social structures and involved as an agent in (re)constructing identities and interests – some of which may be imagined beyond the state.

From this line of thought it follows that the analysis of international institutions, such as the CFSP, should begin with an analysis of the self-understandings of the actors involved. This chapter contains a brief empirical section, which poses the question of whether national and European role conceptions are conflicting or converging. Examination of this question is based on a comparative study of British, French and German foreign policy in the context of the CFSP (Aggestam 2000a). The stability of the EU as a foreign policy actor, it is argued, is dependent on the member states modifying their behaviour according to each others' roles and expectations.

The politics of identity

In the international system, membership of a political community has traditionally been institutionalised spatially within territorial states (Krasner 1988). Foreign policy follows as a consequence of a political community being recognised as a sovereign state and is thus an essential confirmation of its identity by other sovereign actors. Wallace (1991: 65) has called this the 'grand strategy' definition of foreign policy – 'that foreign policy is about national identity itself: about the core elements of sovereignty it seeks to defend, the values it stands for and seeks to promote abroad'. With all the symbolic trappings of sovereignty and statehood, foreign policy plays a significant role in the sociopolitical imagination of a collective identity. Key foreign policy speeches frequently contain assertions referring to subjective we-feelings of a cultural group and its specific customs, institutions, territory, myths and rituals.[2] These expressions of a collective national identity reveal how foreign policy-makers view past history, the present and the future political choices they face. However, in contemporary Europe, many politicians are also increasingly emphasising a European identity:

> To be part of Europe is in the British national interest. So far from submerging our identity as a nation in some Eurosceptic parody of a Federal super-state, we believe that by being part of Europe we advance our own self-interest as the British nation. This is a patriotic cause. (British Prime Minister, Tony Blair 1999)

> We will always associate with Europe the absolute objective of finding common solutions to common problems and of acting with weight behind us in a rapidly changing world, not because we want to give up or level our national identities but rather precisely because we want to preserve these identities and to include them in a more comprehensive European identity. (German Chancellor, Gerhard Schröder 1999)

Does this emphasis on a European identity in foreign policy signify a shift away from a singular notion of political identity confined to the nation-state?

There is some evidence to suggest that the European integration process towards 'an ever closer union' has been accompanied by a decline in the political salience of national identity (Dogan 1994) along with the gradual evolution of multiple identities on regional, national and European levels (Aggestam and Hyde-Price 2000). This raises a number of intriguing questions about foreign policy in Europe: which social collectivities, interests and values do foreign policy-makers see themselves representing and advancing in foreign policy?

The politics of identity refer to a particular set of ideas about political community that policy-makers draw on to mobilise a sense of cohesion and solidarity in order to legitimate the general thrust of foreign policy. Since the early nineteenth century, nationalism has promoted the idea that the source of individual identity and loyalty lies with a 'people' constituted in the nation. The nation is seen as the source of sovereignty on which the state, in turn, is founded. In foreign policy, this political principle should lead the foreign policy-maker to promote the identity, independence and influence of the nation-state s/he officially represents.

The state is not, however, a natural, pre-given social construct. According to Giddens (1985: 221), the crucial function of nationalism is to 'naturalize the recency and contingency of the nation-state through supplying its myths of origin'. This political socialisation has an important security aspect. If the idea of the state fails to be supported in society, the state itself may lack a secure foundation (Buzan 1991: 78). Thus, a sense of belonging appears to be closely interrelated with membership of a political community that seems to offer protection from external threat (Garcia 1993: 13).

The 'institutionalisation' of national identity takes place through various forms of political socialisation and tends to make identity constructions relatively resistant to change. It reinforces certain practices and rules of behaviour which explain and legitimise particular identity constructions (March and Olsen 1998a: 7; see also Almond, Powell and Mundt 1993: 46). As a consequence of its articulation and institutionalisation in the political culture, national identity may become internalised in the cognitive framework – or prism – through which foreign policy-makers interpret political reality. If sufficiently internalised, these accounts of national identity may become part of the political culture and 'national style' of a state's foreign policy.

'Culture represents a unified set of ideas that are shared by the members of a society and that establish a set of shared premises, values, expectations and action predispositions among the members of the nation that as a whole constitute the national style' (Vertzberger 1990: 267). The conceptual lenses through which foreign policy-makers perceive international relations tend to set the norm for what is considered rational foreign policy-making.

Yet, despite the fact that self-conceptions tend to be relatively resistant to change, the processes by which they are perpetuated are certainly not static. Identity constructions are contextually dependent and develop and change over time: 'a continuing exercise in the fabrication of illusion and the elaboration of convenient fables about who "we" are' (Ignatieff 1998: 18). Just as they evolved in particular historical circumstances, definitions of identity and foreign policy interests may be redefined as a consequence of current transformations internal and external to the state.

In many states, the end of the Cold War and the deepening of European integration have sparked off soul-searching debates about the meaning of national and, for that matter, European identity (Aggestam 2000b: 54–63). For example, the unification of the eastern and western parts of Germany has provoked an intensive debate about German identity (the so-called *Berliner Republik* debate) and the meaning of 'normality' (*Normalisierung*) in German foreign policy (Baring 1994; Hellmann 1997; Aggestam 2000b; Hyde-Price 2000). In Britain, the very concept of Britishness has been called into question and resulted in constitutional change.[3] Similarly, in France the referendum on the Maastricht Treaty in the early 1990s and the growing unease at the impact of globalisation on French culture, have provoked a debate about the whole patriarchal conception of the French state and sovereignty (Hoffmann 1991; Flynn 1995; Moisi 1998).

In this context, the argument put forward is that profound changes in the predominant idea of the nation are likely to have significant foreign policy implications. Broader foreign policy approaches, particularly regarding European integration, are bound up with a sense of identity in foreign policy. This is why, for instance, there tends to be a competition of ideas at the EU intergovernmental conferences, as the position of each member state tends to reflect its own conception of political community (Aggestam 2000b: 75–83).[4]

Thus, it could be argued that the more the European Union is moving towards a part-formed polity, the greater the demand for a perceived harmonisation of a national and European identity. Reference to transnational practices and a European supranational identity will be accepted more easily among a broader public if these are in some way framed as compatible with a national identity. Yet, as public opinion surveys and debates on the European Union have indicated, foreign policy elites face a delicate balancing act in seeking to articulate views of European integration that are seen by the broader public not as a threat to national identity, but an enhancement of multiple identities.

The boundary position of the foreign policy-maker

Foreign policy-makers are understood in this chapter as agents collectively representing the state as a *social actor* in foreign policy (cf. Katzenstein 1996). This is because role conceptions are considered to have a social origin (a point which will be discussed further below). They are formed within a cultural context and their legitimacy and endurance are dependent on their being broadly shared at a particular time. In Europe, the agents of foreign policy are positioned at the intersection of transnational processes and domestic structures. Although they are primarily national agents of foreign policy, they find themselves in a boundary position from which they must mediate between two worlds of foreign policy-making: one in the national capital, the other centred in Brussels. While foreign policy role conceptions to a great extent are shaped primarily within the broader political culture of a state, one research problem that needs to be addressed is the extent to which the interaction and elite socialisation between EU members affect foreign policy perceptions. The role perspective developed below is based on the premise that actors _learn_ and are _socialised_ into playing roles through interaction within both domestic and international contexts.

The foreign policy-maker is guided by both rules and reasons in foreign policy. Foreign policy action is a mixture of political will and adjustment to structural factors. The analytical framework outlined here thus deviates from a strict interpretation of instrumental rationality that implies that action in foreign policy is simply based on the maximisation of power and security interests. Rational theory tends to ignore endogenous dynamics and focus on material utility maximisation. A reflective approach, on the other hand, emphasises the impact of cultural practices, norms and values on perceptions of interests (Keohane 1988). The two approaches reflect different logics of how human behaviour and intentionality are interpreted: rational instrumental action (logic of expected consequences) and rule-based action (logic of appropriateness) (Checkel 1998: 4).

Conceptualising the policy-maker as occupying a boundary position is similar in some aspects to the idea of 'two-level games', in that it highlights the interaction between the international and domestic context in negotiating international agreements (Putnam 1993). However, the analytical framework offered by role concepts places greater stress on how international interaction and socialisation between policy-makers may affect the way they conceptualise their interests during and after negotiations. It is not unreasonable to assume that a high degree of interaction between policy-makers within an international institution, such as the EU's CFSP, may encourage a process of social learning. However, the extent to which this process may lead to complex learning (a reassessment of fundamental beliefs and values) is an empirical question that needs to be explored further, but which is beyond the scope of this chapter.

Characteristic of international relations in Europe are the expanding networks of transnational and transgovernmental relations. These appear to be changing the context of foreign policy. One way to conceptualise this new context for policy-makers is to utilise the notion of a 'security community' developed by Deutsch and his associates (1957). They defined a security community as a transnational region in which the positive identification and interaction between the members would lead to a decline in military force and a rise in the expectancy of peaceful relations. In a similar vein, Wendt (1992: 400) has suggested that the process of European integration is leading towards 'a "cooperative" security system, in which states identify positively with one another so that the security of each is perceived as the responsibility of all'.

What makes the Deutschian perspective particularly useful is that it recognises that different social-communicative processes between actors may affect and shape their identities and interests. High levels of interaction between states can encourage the development of a growing 'we-feeling' and common 'role identity' (Deutsch 1957: 5–7). This mutual responsiveness and compatibility of interests may, according to a social constructivist understanding, make possible new repertoires of action and behaviour.

Many studies that focus on questions of identity emphasise that identity is a source of conflict due to the inherent process of defining a 'self' against an 'other'. This focus has tended to overshadow the equally interesting process in which identities may be reconstructed through cooperative and positive interaction with other actors, leading to intersubjective understandings and shared norms.

The concept of 'security community', which is currently experiencing a renaissance in the academic literature, emphasises the socio-cognitive imagination of a common destiny and identity that may take place within a transnational region. Adler and Barnett (1998: 30) distinguish between 'loosely' and 'tightly coupled' security communities according to (1) their depth of trust; (2) the institutionalisation of their governance system; and (3) the degree of anarchy in the system. '"Tightly coupled" pluralistic security communities . . . possess a system of rule that lies somewhere between a sovereign state and a centralised regional government. This is something of a post-sovereign system, comprised of common supranational, transnational and national institutions, and some form of a collective security system' (Adler 1997a: 255).

The relevance of this for our understanding of the EU's CFSP is that there are indications that foreign policy cooperation between EU member states has generated the first stages of a learning process through which the actors involved increasingly perceive themselves as a 'we'. The high density of multilateral interactions and the continuous communication and adjustment (coordination reflex) within CFSP point to certain qualitative new features of solidarity between EU members. Transparency, consultation and compromise are norms underpinning the CFSP framework. It is not unreasonable to suggest that there may be a degree of path dependency involved in this cognitive evolution: 'Trust, shared identities, and familiarity encourage further contact, further integration, an expansion of the number of topics viewed as appropriate for discussion, and the development of common definitions of problems and appropriate actions' (March and Olsen 1998a: 27). However, as we will see below, there are good reasons for questioning a linear view of European integration. This is because international norms agreed on the European level do not necessarily lead towards intersubjective understandings between states.

Role conception

The concept of role originates from studies in sociology and social psychology, where it has frequently signified an actor's characteristic patterns of behaviour given a certain position or situation (Goffman 1959; Biddle and Thomas 1966;

Jackson 1972). Role theory was introduced into foreign policy analysis by Holsti (1987a), when he sought to explore the link between social context and foreign policy.

A sociological understanding of role focuses on the nature of agency and its relationship to social structures. Given that role is conceived of in terms of a characteristic behavioural repertoire, it is a concept that captures elements of continuity in foreign policy. However, given a long enough time period, the role concept also captures processes of socialisation and thus provides insights into foreign policy change.

The concept of role can be used in different ways to explain or understand foreign policy. It is a broad concept that carries different connotations. Briefly, there are three different ways of defining 'role'. These are closely interlinked yet do not necessarily concur with one another. First, there is *role expectation*: this is a role that other actors (alter) prescribe and expect the role-beholder (ego) to enact. Second, there is *role conception*: normative expectations of a certain kind of foreign policy behaviour expressed by the role-beholders themselves. Third, there is *role performance*: this role refers to the actual foreign policy behaviour in terms of decisions and actions undertaken, and is particularly sensitive to the situational context in which it is enacted.

If we wish to understand how national and European identity influence foreign policy perceptions, the second distinction – role conception – offers a fruitful avenue for exploration. 'A *national role conception* includes the policy-makers' own definitions of the general kinds of decisions, commitments, rules, and actions suitable to their state, and of the functions, if any, their state should perform on a continuing basis in the international system or in subordinate regional systems' (Holsti 1987a: 12; original emphasis).

This definition by Holsti encourages an inductive empirical analysis to take place, in order to reveal how policy-makers themselves perceive and define roles. What Holsti (1987a: 28) found in his study was that the practitioners of foreign policy expressed a multitude of roles, in contrast to the more general and singular roles arrived at deductively by academics. Significantly, this conclusion seems to suggest that roles have multiple sources and are not exclusively generated by the international distribution of power. As Barnett (1993: 278) points out, 'The state's survival is rarely at stake but the government's domestic standing frequently is, so it is possible that domestic-generated roles will have greater force than roles dictated by power considerations.'

The aspect of role emphasised in this chapter is its function as a cognitive image; one that simplifies, provides guidance and predisposes an actor towards one intentional behaviour rather than towards another. As cognitive studies have revealed, most people tend to simplify complexities in the world (Gerner 1995: 25). The British diplomat, Robert Cooper (1996: 8) expresses this succinctly: 'Thinking about foreign affairs – like any other kind of thinking – requires a conceptual map which, as maps do, simplifies the landscape and focuses on the main features.'

A role conception embodies a mixture of norms, intentions and descriptions of reality, which vary in degree of specificity and manifestation. As noted above, it is important to underline that actors conceive of multiple roles. These vary in overall importance (centrality) and according to the situation and institutional context (salience). A role conception may become intersubjective and hence relatively stable over time, as policy-makers are socialised into and internalise these role conceptions. 'As these national role conceptions become a more pervasive part of the political culture of a nation, they are more likely to set limits on perceived or politically feasible policy alternatives, and less likely to allow idiosyncratic variables to play a crucial part in decision-making' (Holsti 1987a: 38–9).

However, it is important not to 'over-socialise' the agency in foreign policy. Roles have multiple sources and in order not to over- or underestimate the significance of institutions in the formulation of foreign policy, it is important to consider how roles are generated from a combination of structure, interaction and intention.

Structure refers to patterns of social relationships, practices and shared perceptions of reality (Lundquist 1987: 40). A structural approach, in other words, brings to our attention how institutions, not actors, determine norms and roles. It is important, however, to emphasise that national and international structures consist not only of normative, but also material elements. In international relations theory, the sources of roles have frequently been considered to be predominately systemic (anarchy) and based on material factors (Walker 1987: 271; Rosenau 1990: 213). To be sure, material attributes, such as economic strength, geographic location and system of government, play a crucial part in how states view themselves and their relationships with other states. However, if we discard the utilitarian assumption that foreign policy is primarily driven by power maximisation within an anarchic structure, then the concept of role can facilitate an understanding of obligations and commitments which are not derived simply from basic national interests.

The interactional approach stresses role-playing; that is, the processes by which actors learn and are socialised into playing roles.[5] This is a crucial component in the analytical framework presented in this chapter and captures the processes of foreign policy integration between EU member states. A structural approach runs the risk of making role analysis static and deterministic, thereby failing to apprehend change in foreign policy perceptions. In contrast, the interactional approach is dynamic and illuminates the actors involved in the process. The actors play a crucial part in defining their own roles in a process of negotiation. Given that roles are generated in the interaction, it follows that roles tend to fluctuate and change over time (Searing 1991: 1246).

Finally, it is argued that the longevity and centrality of role conceptions can only be fully understood if we take into account the goals and intentions that drive them. As noted above, the policy-maker is guided by both rules and reason in foreign policy. Purposive roles are a result of a dynamic interaction between institutional constraints and the actor's preferences (Searing 1991: 1248). The idea of role rests on an analogy of the theatre, in which an actor is expected to behave in predictable ways according to a script (rule-based action). In the past, sociological theorising of role has tended to underestimate the actor's objectives and intentions contained in the contents of a role conception. However, actors do not simply act passively according to a script, but are actively involved in categorising themselves with an action orientation.

The emphasis here on identity and the socio-cultural context of foreign policy does not contradict strategic action and subjective rationality in foreign policy. Indeed, we will not be able to understand the dynamics of how policy-makers reason if we do not acknowledge that human behaviour and intentionality are grounded in both a logic of expected consequences and a logic of appropriateness (Aggestam 1999: 11–12). The concept of role can provide us with a vital link between the two logics. As March and Olsen (1998a: 12) point out, 'the two logics are not mutually exclusive'. 'Political actors are constituted both by their interests, by which they evaluate their anticipations of consequences, and by the rules embedded in their identities and political institutions. They calculate consequences and follow rules, and the relation between the two is often subtle.'

Hence, the approach outlined here falls in the middle ground between rational and reflectivist understandings of how the actors in foreign policy are reasoning. The culture-bound prism through which foreign policy-makers view the world and consider their interests does not preclude strategically motivated action in a bounded rational sense. Yet, it tends to demarcate the limits for what are perceived and defined in the first place as acceptable and viable goals and interests in foreign policy. 'Culture does not impose a cognitive map upon persons but provides them with a set of principles for map-making and navigation' (Ehrenhaus, quoted in Vertzberger 1990: 270).

Role conceptions are broad categories that allow a certain flexibility of interpretation, depending on the extent to which they have become formally institutionalised with a specific guide to action. Furthermore, the centrality of a role conception does vary depending on situational context and time. Barnett (1993: 275) makes a useful distinction between *position* and *preference* roles. The former provide an actor with well-defined and detailed guides to action. The latter contain greater flexibility of interpretation as to the meaning of a role.

A certain amount of discretion in interpreting roles appears indispensable to policy-makers in order to accommodate the potentially conflicting roles that different institutional contexts and interactional processes generate. A role conflict may arise when role conceptions in an overarching role-set are incompatible with one another. Changes in role conceptions may be induced by role conflicts or when the centrality and salience of a role conception are called into question. The literature on belief systems suggests that the impact of new information is largely determined by whether the structure of a belief system is 'open' or 'closed'. New information tends to be interpreted and adopted in view of pre-existing beliefs.

Yet, their centrality may alter in the light of new information, which can bring prior beliefs into 'cognitive dissonance'. This can be seen as a process of learning, giving rise to new definitions and understandings of a role conception (Hermann 1990: 10–11).

However, there is an inherent resistance to change in role conceptions for two reasons. First, if role conceptions are constantly fluctuating, they fail to provide policy-makers with the consistency they seek as intentional actors in foreign policy. Second, there is a dialectic relationship between national identity and foreign policy role conceptions. The more central a role conception becomes, the more likely it is to be surrounded by myths and institutions, thus becoming part of a nation's political culture.[6] These impeding factors help explain why, for example, the end of the Cold War did not lead to drastic re-orientations of foreign policy for the majority of European states (see Niblett and Wallace 2001). The question to be addressed below is whether three decades of foreign policy cooperation between EU member states have resulted in a convergence of national and European role conceptions.

National and European role conceptions: conflict or convergence?

That the European Union may be characterised as a security community is hardly a controversial statement to make. It is, however, an open question as to how deep 'a sense of community' is felt within the EU and how this feeling may be affecting foreign policy perceptions. The attempt to harmonise different foreign policy traditions goes back to the early 1970s. In 1983, EU members made a pledge in a so-called 'Solemn Declaration' that they would henceforth endeavour to seek common positions in international affairs, which should constitute the central reference point for national foreign policy. Has the interaction and institutionalisation of foreign policy cooperation over the years resulted in a growth of common values and a Europeanisation of role conceptions?

The stability of the EU as a foreign policy actor is dependent on the member states consistently adopting common role conceptions and modifying their behaviour according to each others' roles and expectations. If a Europeanisation of foreign policy is taking place, we would anticipate that member states would be adopting *position roles* that increase the predictability of foreign policy and stable expectations.

The aim of this section is to provide a brief discussion of national and European role conceptions, based on a comparative study of British, French and German foreign policy in the context of the CFSP (Aggestam 2000a, 2000c, 2000d). The purpose is to illustrate European developments in foreign policy, though within the limited scope here, no attempt can be made to give a detailed account of the extent to which foreign policy has become Europeanised.

Three role conceptions will be discussed. These roles indicate how policy-makers conceive of political influence; their depth of feeling for the EU as a security community; and the independence of the state as an actor in foreign policy.

1   *Leader:* This role reflects how policy-makers perceive influence and how they relate to power. In a security community, power can be understood in terms of having a significant influence on the norms that specify common action (cf. Adler and Barnett 1998: 52).

2   *Partner:* Commitments to support and cooperate closely with another state indicate perceptions of a 'special relationship' and strategic partnership. This role is interesting, as it communicates the depth of trust essential to collective identity formation.

3   *Independent:* This role conception involves commitments to retain independence of action in foreign policy and an emphasis on the primacy of national interests. It should, however, be pointed out that this role could also be conceived of in a European discourse with an emphasis on the EU as an independent actor in world politics.

In terms of preference and position roles discussed above, the role conception of 'independent' belongs in the former category; 'partner' in the latter; and 'leader' somewhere in between the two.

A comparison between British, French and German foreign policies indicates that policy-makers in these three countries see themselves as members of a collective security community. Few, if any, politicians are directly hostile to the development of the CFSP. Quite the opposite – most policy-makers are generally enthusiastic about the added weight and influence that the CFSP brings in international affairs. Thus, European interests tend to be seen as largely compatible and complementary to national interests.

As three of the largest member states of the European Union, it is not surprising that foreign policy speeches in Britain, France and Germany make reference to 'leadership'. However, the meanings they attach to this role conception differ and reflect the different ways in which they perceive political influence.

References to leadership in the British political discourse fulfil a function in justifying and legitimating participation in the process of European integration. The British self-image as a political and military medium power reinforces this role conception. Both the Conservative and Labour governments have regarded British leadership of the CFSP as enhancing Britain's influence in world politics. As a leading EU member, it is recognised that British foreign policy has gained a distinctive European dimension, which is perceived as an important complement to, but not a replacement of, national foreign policy. Yet, at the same time, it is not precisely clear what this leadership entails, given that British foreign policy-makers, particularly in the past, have been very reluctant to express the kind of visionary thinking that is required to exert a leadership role within a security community. British proposals for strengthening a common European foreign policy have primarily been confined to pragmatic suggestions focused on improving operational procedures. Nonetheless, a significant change has taken place following the Labour election landslide of 1997. The Blair government continues to emphasise Britain's global role as a nation with worldwide interests, but is also much more concerned to provide some substance to its leadership aspirations. This is evident above all in the area of defence. Since the Anglo-French summit of Saint-Malo in December 1998, the British government has made a vigorous attempt to influence the evolving principles of what should constitute common EU action in security and defence.

The French conception of their leadership role has deep historical roots and constitutes, as in Britain, an important legitimating function for French participation in the European integration process.[7] French presidents have repeatedly proclaimed the idea of France playing a leading role at the core of a Europe of concentric circles (*le cercle des solidarités renforcées*) – an idea that enjoys considerable domestic support. It is perceived to be a political and historical responsibility of France to take a lead towards a European political union. The European Union is thus ultimately conceived of as a political project aimed at making the EU a powerful actor in world politics: *Europe puissance.* As part of this power projection, Europe needs to develop an independent defence component. It is therefore not surprising to note the unease with which the French reluctantly recognise American leadership in European security through NATO.

In Germany, the idea of exerting leadership is formulated very cautiously to avoid any association with historical analogies. Nonetheless, the role of leader is conceived of as emancipation from the past, in the sense that Germany has a historical responsibility – even a duty (*Verpflichtung*) – to promote European integration to secure peace and stability on the continent. A long-standing belief during the post-war period was that German unification must take place hand in hand with European unification. Germany is to be the 'engine', exercising leadership in terms of ideas and initiatives. In other words, exerting power over the normative contents and meaning of a deepening process of European integration in foreign policy.

However, German policy-makers are reluctant to exercise leadership unilaterally, particularly in foreign policy. Instead, they attempt to provide directional leadership with France. The role conception of leader is thus closely linked to the idea of a partnership between Germany and France. This partnership is perceived in both countries as the bedrock on which the whole process of European integration rests. It is a strongly held belief in both countries that if France and Germany fail to act in concert, there is a considerable risk that European developments may become seriously derailed. Thus, a distinguishing feature of this relationship is its institutional embeddedness, which is aimed at encouraging proximity of interests between them. Symbolism is an important ingredient and political leaders from the two countries frequently seek to launch joint policy initiatives to demonstrate their common resolve. This was illustrated on a number of occasions during the negotiations of the 1996 IGC, when the German and French governments launched a number of initiatives to improve the effectiveness of the CFSP and to provide the EU with a 'strategic capacity'.

However, a key problem faced by Germany and France in their attempt to provide directional leadership in the field of foreign policy is that they have had, at least until recently, different conceptions of political union and Europe as a global power. First of all, they appear to differ in their emphasis on the extent to which the CFSP should remain an essentially intergovernmental framework. While Germany is a keen advocate of majority voting and wishes a greater involvement of the European Parliament in the CFSP, France wants second pillar issues to be primarily developed within the European Council (where the presence of the French president is safeguarded). Second, the French vision of a European foreign policy is concerned with the projection of power and independence as a global actor. For Germany, with its post-war tradition as a civilian power, the deepening of foreign policy integration has been less about exerting European power and more about diffusing it internally, thereby preventing a re-nationalisation of foreign policy that could lead to national rivalry and instability between EU members. As a rule, German foreign policy-makers tend to be more reluctant than their French counterparts to use military means of foreign policy and to think in global power political terms.

Furthermore, German policy-makers are always much more keenly aware of the implications that a deepening process of foreign policy integration may have on transatlantic relations. The German government favours a more cohesive European actor capacity to shoulder a greater burden of security, thereby becoming a more equal partner to the US. Nonetheless, this must not jeopardise the continued presence of American involvement in European security, which is considered a fundamental security interest.

Interestingly, despite the high degree of institutionalisation and interaction between French and German policy-makers, there is still considerable friction in the relationship. Both parties tend to admit they are not an obvious 'couple'. The German Foreign Minister, Joschka Fischer (1999), captures this dynamic well when he asserts that,

> Together Germany and France are the driving-force behind European integration and in its European dimension their special relationship is indispensable. As neighbours with a shared history, they are nonetheless very different, yet herein and in the resulting tensions lies a source of productivity, a creative potential that is the secret of this motor for integration.

The Franco-German relationship has certainly changed from the days of the symbolic holding of hands between Mitterrand and Kohl. In France, questions are raised about the *banalisation* of the Franco-German relationship: a fear about a declining attachment to the partnership which could result in new tensions. Though officially welcomed, the debate in Germany on *Normalisierung*, the Berlin Republic, and assertions of German national interests in foreign policy, are closely monitored in France in case it indicates a decline in Germany's European identity and a rise in German particularism.

Where does Britain figure as a partner? Officially, policy-makers in Germany and France tend to say that their relationship is not an exclusive one. Initiatives originating from this bilateral relationship have always been made open for other countries to join. French policy-makers, in particular, tend to emphasise that without full British participation, the CFSP will be less effective. As the French President Chirac (1998) stated after the 1998 Saint-Malo meeting: 'Europe taking new foreign and security policy initiatives, requires a very high degree of entente between Britain and France, two countries with great and strong diplomatic and military traditions.' As two medium powers and permanent members of the UN Security Council, they do in fact share a number of common interests. Yet, in the past, the Anglo-French relationship has frequently been characterised more by rivalry than partnership.

The main stumbling block between them has for a long time been their different conceptions of Europe. While the British wax lyrical about a transatlantic Europe, the French dream of a cohesive and independent Europe. German policy-makers, on the other hand, refuse to see a contradiction between the two visions of Europe.[8] Britain's close relationship with the United States has in the past fuelled deep-seated French suspicions that Britain is primarily a faithful US ally supporting American hegemony in Europe.

The Saint-Malo agreement of 1998 is thus significant in that it set in motion a genuine attempt to address the question of how to develop a common security and defence policy of the European Union. There are two reasons for the warming of Anglo-French relations. First, both Britain and France have become increasingly pragmatic and less dogmatic in their competing visions of a transatlantic vs European Europe. France supports the idea of a European pillar in NATO, while Britain endorses the development of an autonomous defence capability in the EU. Second, the experience of recent peacekeeping operations, particularly in the former Yugoslavia, has demonstrated common grounds of interest.

The role of 'independent' is significant only because it does not appear as a major preoccupation in the minds of foreign policy-makers. The realist assumption that national independence is a major concern in foreign policy does not, therefore, find support in this study. Not unexpectedly, German policy-makers are the most outspoken about denouncing a policy based on *Realpolitik* and balance of power. There are no indications that Germany's considerable political, military and economic resources impel German policy-makers to conclude that they should seek independent action.

The insignificance of an independent role does not, however, correspond to an endorsement of a supranational European foreign policy along the lines of the old idea of a European Defence Community. As recent decisions have indicated, the institutional and decision-making structures on security and defence questions (the so-called European Security and Defence Policy), has been firmly placed outside the orbit of the first supranational pillar of the European Union. For states, such as Britain and France, the primacy of national interests remains fundamental. However, if the CFSP were to assume a more supranational character, the inherent dilemma between a deepening process of integration and the continued emphasis on the nation-state as the basis of collective foreign policy action would become more exposed.

French policy-makers, in particular, reveal how the idea of *independence* has been replaced by a major preoccupation about enhancing French influence in multilateral structures. French *rapprochement* towards NATO and its confederal approach to EU foreign policy cooperation are indicative of this change in foreign policy perception. Yet the role concept of independent has not been entirely discarded. During the Cold War, the Gaullist interpretation of national independence contained a strong identitative dimension in French foreign policy.[9] In the post-Cold War context, this idea of French independence is being transposed to the European level to counteract a perceived American hegemony in a unipolar world.

British and German policy-makers do not share this French view of the United States. However, they seem increasingly to share the idea that national independence has to give way to a pooling of resources to safeguard a greater measure of collective European independence and power in world politics. This convergence towards a common European role conception approaches the French idea of *Europe puissance*. The German Chancellor, Gerhard Schröder, openly endorsed this concept in the French Assembly in the autumn of 1999. The British Prime Minister, Tony Blair, previously reluctant to employ the French concept, formally echoed it in his speech of 7 October 2000 in Warsaw where he looked forward to 'an EU whose vision of peace is matched by its vision of prosperity; a civilised continent united in defeating brutality and violence; a continent joined in its belief in social justice. A superpower but not a superstate.'

The convergence of views is in fact taking place because the traditional French meaning of the concept is also changing. The development of Europe as a strategic actor concerns the capability (*pouvoir*) to carry out the so-called 'Petersberg tasks', rather than power projection (*puissance*) in its own right. Thus, less emphasis is made of the realist notion of *Europe puissance* as an attribute of hard power in a balance-of-power system. Instead, this meaning has given way to an emphasis on Europe as an ethical and restrained power. As a senior French policy-maker puts it, 'the ambition to make Europe into a power in its own right is unwise . . . it should regard power as a means to be used rarely and deliberately rather than as an objective of its foreign policy, and it should discard traditional power politics as the measure of its success' (Andréani 1999: 26). On a deeper level, it could be argued that this evolving European role conception is indicative of how the process of integration indeed has begun to cement a 'cooperative security system', where the security of each is perceived as the responsibility of all.

Concluding remarks

The central theme of this chapter has been the analytical utility of a political–cultural approach to explore perceptions of long-term foreign policy change and stability in contemporary Europe. The picture that emerges from this type of analysis is that the process of European integration in foreign and security policy is marked by some ambivalent, if not contradictory, trends. In the early years of the twenty-first century, EU member states are, on the one hand, endowing the Union – through CFSP – with the means to act militarily. This integrative move has been made possible by the evolving role conception of the EU as an ethical and restrained power, in combination with the decline of the role of 'independent'. Yet, on the other hand, the CFSP itself remains overwhelmingly intergovernmental in form. This indicates that the actors involved still regard their interaction in a strategic and self-interested manner. Legitimisation of foreign policy action still takes place primarily at the level of the nation-state. As the analysis above has highlighted, the roles that policy-makers in Britain, France and Germany conceive of for their countries are a mixture of preference and position roles. These three states, perhaps with the partial exception of Germany, conceptualise foreign policy objectives first and foremost in a national mind-set. Despite years of intensive interaction, the perceived partnerships between Britain, France and Germany illustrate the uneven processes of socialisation and collective identity formation. What has become notably Europeanised in foreign policy is the means to fulfil foreign policy goals. It would thus be premature to predict yet again the 'withering away of the state' as a key foreign policy actor, even though the process of European integration is increasingly compromising its pre-eminence.

Notes

I would like to thank Adrian Hyde-Price for valuable comments on this chapter.

1 Interview with Pauline Neville-Jones (former European Correspondent and Political Director of the British Foreign and Commonwealth Office), London, 16 January 1996.
2 The combination depends on the extent to which civic or ethnic elements predominate in the identity construction.
3 Since taking office in 1997, the British Prime Minister, Tony Blair, has given a number of speeches where he has attempted to articulate a vision of what a British identity stands for. See also the speech by Linda Colley ('Britishness in the 21st Century', Millennium Lecture, 1999) and a recent commission on multi-cultural Britain chaired by Lord Parekh.
4 Cf. for example the centralised French model of the state with a strong executive; the German federal model dispersing authority on different political levels; and the British informal model based on the common-law approach.
5 Biddle and Thomas (1966: 7) distinguish between 'role-playing' and 'role-taking': role-taking is an attitude already frozen in the behaviour of the person. Role-playing is an act, a spontaneous playing; role-taking is a finished product, a role conserve.
6 On the other hand, if national identity is contested, the stability of role conceptions is more likely to be challenged.
7 Charles de Gaulle formulated a distinct vision of France's uniqueness and role as a guiding light – *une certaine idée de la France* – drawing on France's historical legacy of the 1789 revolution and the Enlightenment.

8   German foreign policy-makers are known to avoid acknowledging potential role conflicts in case that would involve privileging a particular institution or set of relationships
to the detriment of another. According to Garton Ash (1996: 92), this *Sowohl-als-auch*
(as-well-as) approach to foreign policy means that German foreign policy-makers
'choose not to choose'.

9   French *exceptionalisme* between the two superpower blocs.

ADRIAN HYDE-PRICE

7

Interests, institutions and identities in the study of European foreign policy

The uneven but manifest emergence of a more coherent EU Common Foreign and Security Policy, which now includes significant elements of defence and military cooperation, makes it even more imperative to refine a theory and a set of analytical tools for studying the role of the EU as an international actor. As has often been noted, however, CFSP and its predecessor, European Political Cooperation, have not been well served by theory. 'Like the debate over a common Community foreign policy itself, there is no agreement among academics on the most useful theoretical approach for comprehending this activity' (Holland 1994: 129). Consequently, much of the literature on European foreign policy defines itself as 'pre-theoretical' (Hill 1993a), while limited importance is attached to the EU as an actor vis-à-vis its member states. In part, this reflects the dominance of the realist paradigm in international relations and traditional foreign policy analysis, which accords analytical primacy to states. In addition, it is a consequence of the multi-level and institutionally polyphonous character of EU decision-making in the second pillar (CFSP), and the continuing impact of national rather than communitarian approaches to foreign policy and conflict management – as the experience of the wars of Yugoslav succession amply demonstrates.

Nonetheless, as other contributors to this volume have argued, there are a number of non-realist approaches to international relations and foreign policy analysis that provide useful insights relevant to the study of the EU as an international actor. This chapter provides an overview and analysis of some of these approaches, and proposes an analytical framework with which to explore the complex interplay of factors affecting European foreign policy. This framework is based on a synthesis of elements of social constructivism, the new institutionalism and neo-classical realism. Foreign policy, it has been argued, 'is the result of a complex interplay of stimuli from the external environment and domestic-level cognitive, institutional and political variables' (Checkel 1993: 297). The analytical framework outlined below is based on three main concepts – interests, institutions and identities – and departs in two crucial respects from neo-realist and rationalist models of foreign policy analysis. First, it stresses that 'institutions matter' and, second, it views interests not as a given but as contingent on norms, beliefs and values (Schaber and Ulbert 1994). It also draws attention to the importance of foreign policy culture as 'a set of attitudes, beliefs, and sentiments which give order to the foreign policy process and which provide the underlying assumptions and rules that govern behaviour in the international system' (Kirste and Maull 1996: 284). Only by taking cognisance of the reflexivity inherent in the relationship between interests, institutions and identity, this chapter suggests, is it possible to understand the nature and dynamics of the European Union as an international actor.

Foreign policy analysis and the end of the Cold War

The pealing back of Cold War bipolarity has revealed the extent to which underlying processes of societal transformation have changed the structural dynamics of international society in late modern Europe. These transformations have been concentrated in Western Europe but their impact has also been felt across Central and Eastern Europe. Of particular significance has been the emergence of a zone of stable peace (Singer and Wildavsky 1996), with the transatlantic security community at its core. This has helped erode some of the main pillars of the Westphalian state system, and reduced the prevalence of balance-of-power and *Realpolitik* considerations in European order (Hyde-Price 2000: 70–101). Given that much traditional analysis of foreign policy has been grounded on realist assumptions about international anarchy and the state as 'coherent units' (Keohane and Nye 1977: 24), there is a pressing need for conceptual and theoretical innovation in this field.

New conceptual tools are particularly needed for analysing the external relations of the European Union, given its *sui generis* nature. Neo-realism offers little of value in this endeavour. For neo-realists like Kenneth Waltz (1979) and John Mearsheimer (1990), the behaviour of an international actor – in their case, states – is determined, first and foremost, by its relative power capabilities and its structural position in the anarchical states' system.[1] This dictates an endless struggle for power and survival, in which states seek to cope with an intractable security dilemma through a balance of power. The decisions of states 'are shaped by the very presence of other states as well as by interactions with them'. It is the 'situation in which they act and interact' which 'constrains them from some actions, disposes them towards others, and affects the outcomes of their interactions' (Waltz 1979: 65).

The problems with neo-realist explanations of state behaviour in late modern Europe are threefold. First, neo-realism's paradigmatic assumptions are no longer appropriate to twenty-first-century Europe. The pursuit of parsimonious theory leads neo-realists to ignore the impact of historical, political and societal change on the structural dynamics of European order. Key neo-realist concepts such as 'anarchy' and 'multipolarity' are too ahistorical to offer much insight into contemporary European international politics. Neo-realist theory is unable to account for change or the enormous variation in behaviour between states with comparable power capabilities within 'anarchic' and 'multipolar' systems,[2] and overlooks the socially textured nature of European international society in the late modern era.

Second, 'the refusal to consider what goes on within states is perhaps the most serious flaw of neorealism' (Hoffmann 1995: 283). Because of the overarching explanatory weight neo-realists attach to structural factors such as 'anarchy', they overlook the importance of domestic factors on foreign policy behaviour. Finally, neo-realism underestimates the effects of economic interdependence and the impact of international organisations on state behaviour.[3] In addition to its more general weaknesses, Thomas Pedersen notes (1998: 30), 'structural realism has some particularly weak spots, the case of European integration being one'. Neo-realism's pessimistic assumptions about the possibilities of cooperation means that it is hard-pressed to account for the extent to which multilateral integration has developed in Europe. Neo-realism's crucial weakness is thus 'its inability to provide an explanation of the high degree of institutionalisation and notably its durability in the European region' (ibid.).

In contrast to neo-realism's privileging of the structural determinants of state behaviour (which is shared by some versions of social constructivism[4]), the analytical framework outlined below considers both actor-level and structural determinants of foreign policy behaviour. The analysis itself draws on a number of sources. First: some of the more innovative approaches within the field of foreign policy analysis, particularly those associated with so-called 'second generation' theorists (Neak, Hey and Haney 1995). Work in this field has focused, *inter alia*, on the institutional processes involved in foreign policy decision-making, and on the cultural and societal context within which policy options are considered.

Second: the insights of social constructivists such as Emmanuel Adler (1997b) and Jeff Checkel (1997, 1998a), who have sought to carve out an analytically robust 'middle ground' between rationalists and reflectivists. Constructivism's most important insight is that 'the manner in which the material world shapes and is shaped by human action and interaction depends on dynamic normative and epistemic interpretations of the material world' (Adler 1997b: 322).

Third: what has been termed 'neo-classical realism' (Schweller 1996; Snyder 1996; Rose 1998). Scholars working in the classical realist tradition continue to place emphasis on the importance of material power capabilities of a state in relation to the wider international system as a dominant factor shaping broad patterns of foreign policy over time. However, they also recognise that there is no direct transition belt linking material capabilities to foreign policy behaviour, and acknowledge the importance of both elite concepts of national role and identity, and the institutional policy-making process. In this way, neo-classical realists 'open spaces for conversations, perhaps even mutually profitable sharing of insights', involving 'constructivists of various stripes (including the English School)' (Donnelly 1998: 403; see also Dunne 1995; Williams 1997: 300).

Interests

Defining the 'national interest'

Understanding the behaviour of actors in international society is impossible without some notion of their interests; that is, their preferences and concerns. The concept of 'interests' has long been central to political analysis, yet substantial methodological and epistemological difficulties remain in defining collective 'interests'. This is particularly the case with the concept of 'national interests'.[5] However, if 'society as a whole is granted a reality other than that of the sum of its contending parts, then it becomes difficult to deny that the group defined by the society has its "interests" just as the smaller, more particular groups have theirs' (Clinton 1991: 49). Similarly, if states have their national interests, the EU as an international actor must also have its own interests, however diffuse and amorphous they may be at times.

The central problem in defining the 'European interests' of the EU is how to distinguish between the interests of the EU as a whole and those of the specific interests of its individual member states and other influential non-state actors within it (such as the agricultural lobby). Once one discards neo-realist assumptions about states and international actors as rational utility maximisers in favour of a conception of international actors as complex institutional ensembles, then 'European' interests can only be seen as the outcome of a discrete political process. The main actors involved in this political process are the member states, the Commission, powerful lobby groups and public opinion articulated partly through the medium of the European Parliament. The analysis of the EU's interests thus involves consideration of both the political discourse surrounding its external role conceptions and of the institutional policy-making process within the EU.

The limits of materialism

How a political community defines its interests depends on objective, material factors (such as geography, size and wealth), but also on a range of subjective, normative considerations. These include the identity of a community, its political culture, dominant moral and ethical values, sense of justice and conception of the common good, and its belief in what makes it distinctive as a political community.

Stanley Hoffmann has argued that the foreign policy of a state can only be understood by considering its 'national situation'. This refers to both the domestic characteristics of a state and its people, and to its position in international society.

'It is a composite of objective data (social structure and political system, geography, formal commitments to other nations) and subjective factors (values, prejudices, opinions, reflexes, traditions toward and assessments of others, and others' attitudes and approaches).' This national situation is not a 'given' that dictates policy, but it does 'set up complicated limits that affect freedom of choice' (1995: 75–6).

Although Hoffmann's concept of the 'national situation' was developed with a view to analysing the foreign policy behaviour of individual nation-states, it can be utilised to understand the EU's role as an international actor. It certainly provides a much richer approach to the study of international politics than that of neo-realism, which focuses almost exclusively on material power capabilities. John Mearsheimer, for example, emphasises that state behaviour 'is largely shaped by the *material* structure of the international system', and it is the 'distribution of material capabilities among states' that provides 'the key factor for understanding world politics' (1995: 91; original emphasis). This assumption of the 'objectivity' of interests is shared by structural Marxists, who emphasise the centrality of economically determined class interests, and by neo-liberal institutionalists, who 'continue to treat actor identities and interests themselves as pre-existing and fixed' (Kowert and Legro 1996: 458).

However, the problem with rationalist approaches is that '[m]aterial capabilities *as such* explain nothing; their effects presuppose structures of shared knowledge, which vary and are not reducible to capabilities' (Wendt 1995: 73; original emphasis). 'The inescapable fact seems to be that this type of analysis stressing strategic and geopolitical factors is badly flawed' (Hilsman 1990: 30). The importance of normative and epistemic interpretations of the material world was evident to an earlier generation of classical realists. Hans Morgenthau, for example (1948: 11), quoted Weber to the effect that 'Interests (material and ideal), not ideas, dominate directly the actions of men.' However, he went on to observe that 'the "images of the world" created by these ideas have very often served as switches determining the tracks on which the dynamism of interests kept actions moving'. Morgenthau thus concluded that 'the kind of interest determining political action in a particular period of history depends on the political and cultural context within which foreign policy is formulated'. Consequently, '[t]he goals that might be pursued by nations in their foreign policy can run the whole gamut of objectives any nation has ever pursued or might possibly pursue' (1948: 11).

A central concern of contemporary foreign policy analysis is thus to explore the 'national situation' within which international actors are located. Material factors are important in setting the broad parameters within which the EU operates. However, the study of these material factors is not sufficient to indicate the course and objectives of the EU's Common Foreign and Security Policy. Understanding this involves considering two other factors: institutions and identities.

Institutions

Institutional analysis provides the second leg of the foreign policy analysis model presented here. As we have seen, while the systemic distribution of material capabilities establishes the broad parameters of foreign policy behaviour over time, specific foreign policy decisions result from a complex process of institutional policy-making. Institutional structures are therefore a decisive factor in determining what has been called 'the capacity for collective action'; in other words, the ability of a state to extract and utilise resources for foreign policy goals (Hoffmann 1995: 268).

The assumption underpinning this leg of the conceptual model is 'that institutions sometimes matter, and that it is a worthy task of social science to discover how, and under what conditions, this is the case' (Keohane and Martin 1995: 40). Institutions 'do not merely reflect the preferences and power of the units constituting them; the institutions themselves shape those preferences and that power' (Keohane 1988: 382). They can do this by altering 'the calculations of interest by assigning property rights, providing information, and altering patterns of transaction costs' (Keohane 1993a: 29). Over time, commonly agreed and jointly observed principles and norms become internationalised by the actors involved, thereby reshaping the perception of interests (Rittberger 1993: 19).

The important point to note about institutions is that they do not simply facilitate the bargaining process between political actors by reducing transaction costs and reducing uncertainty, as liberal institutionalists suggest. More importantly, institutions play a key role in the process of interest and identity formation. This has been one of the most important insights of both social constructivism and the 'new institutionalism'. Institutions 'offer a normative context that constitutes actors and provides a set of norms in which the reputation of actors acquires meaning and value' (Katzenstein 1997: 12–13). International institutions and multilateral structures thus facilitate the emergence of a sense of *Gemeinschaft* (community) based on shared interests, trust and a common identity.

The constitutive and transformationalist impact of institutions on the process of interest and identity formation is clearly evident from the operation of EPC/CFSP over the last two decades. The institutionalisation of regular consultation, negotiation and cooperation between diplomats involved in shaping the EU's external relations has transformed the working practices of foreign ministers and ministries, and generated new styles of operating and communicating. As Hill and Wallace (1996: 6) note,

> The COREU telex network, foreign policy working groups, joint declarations, joint reporting, even the beginnings of staff exchanges among foreign ministries and shared embassies: all these have moved the conduct of national foreign policy away from the old nation-state national sovereignty model towards a collective endeavour, a form of high-level networking with transformationalist effects and even more potential.

Organisational process and bureaucratic politics

The seminal text for understanding the role of institutional actors in the foreign policy-making process is Graham Allison's classic work, *Essence of Decision* – 'one of the few genuine classics of modern International Relations' (Brown 1997: 75). Allison outlined three models of foreign policy decision-making: the *rational actor model* (RAM), the *organisational process* model and the *bureaucratic politics* model. The rational actor model assumes that foreign policy decisions are rational responses to a particular situation, formulated by a single unitary state actor operating on the basis of perceived national interests. The problem with the RAM approach is that states are not unitary actors and that interests are not endogenously given.

Allison's other two models are of more use in understanding the institutional dimension of EU foreign and security policy. His second model (organisational process) takes as its point of departure the institutional pluralism of modern states and focuses on intra-organisational factors. It posits that policy outcomes result from the interaction of multiple organisations, each of which has distinctive ways of making policy decisions – *organisational routines* and *standard operating procedures*. These organisations are highly resistant to attempts at centralised control and coordination. While Allison's model was based on the US experience, it is also relevant to the EU, given the institutional polyphony that characterises its complex, multi-level decision-making processes.

Allison's third model (bureaucratic politics) focuses on inter-organisational factors. While the two previous models suggest that foreign policy decisions will be taken on foreign policy grounds, the bureaucratic politics model suggests that this is not necessarily so. Political, economic and other factors external to the specific foreign policy issue being considered may affect decision-making. In particular, bureaucracies have their own specific interests and concerns to defend (budgets, resources, influence), and may therefore propose policy options that enhance their position within the overall policy-making process. Allison's third model thus stresses that bureaucracies make decisions on the basis of their own specific organisational interests – in a nut-shell, 'where you sit determines where you stand'.

As Allison argued, the three different models each have a certain explanatory power and need to be integrated rather than segregated. Allison's analytical framework is certainly of relevance when it comes to investigating the role and impact of the key institutional actors involved in policy-making in pillar two. These include the European Council, which determines the CFSP's principles and general guidelines, and its common strategies; the foreign affairs ministers in the General Affairs Council, who can recommend common strategies to the European Council and who are responsible for implementing them, notably through the adoption of common positions and joint actions; COREPER (the Permanent Representatives Committee), which prepares the proceedings of the General Affairs Council; the Political Committee, which monitors the international situation, provides opinions for the Council and oversees the implementation of policy; the Presidency of the European Council, which represents the Union in CFSP matters and is responsible for the implementation of CFSP decisions; the High Representative of the CFSP, who assists the Presidency and the Council by contributing to the formulation, drawing up and implementation of political decisions; and the European Commission, which, according to the Maastricht Treaty on European Union, is to be 'fully associated' with the work carried out in the CFSP field. In addition, a 'policy planning and early warning unit' has been established in the General Secretariat of the Council under the responsibility of the High Representative.

With the launch of the Union's European Security and Defence Policy at the Cologne Council of June 1999 and the adoption of the ambitious 'Headline Goal' by the Helsinki Council of December 1999, the second pillar has acquired a number of new institutional decision-making structures. In addition to ad hoc meetings of defence ministers within the framework of the General Affairs Council, a Political and Security Committee, a Military Committee and a Military Staff (including a Situation Centre) have been established. With the exception of its Article V mutual security guarantee, all of the WEU's key functions and responsibilities have been folded into the EU. The rapid development of the ESDP means that the institutional structures and decision-making procedures in the second pillar are still very much in flux, and substantial study and analysis is required before their effectiveness can be assessed. Indeed, the development of the institutional complexity of the second pillar underlines the necessity for detailed institutional analysis in order to understand the behaviour of the EU as a foreign and security policy actor. For such an analytical undertaking, Allison's work remains an essential reference point.

However, the biggest lacuna in Allison's work, and in the literature on 'institutional pluralism' more generally, is an insufficient account of the cognitive and ideational dimension of decision-making. This has been an area of considerable theoretical innovation over recent years, although many questions remain to be addressed. The ideational or socio-cognitive dimension thus constitutes the third leg of the analytical framework developed in this chapter.

Identities

The 'cognitive revolution'

While an analysis of institutional policy-making processes can provide valuable insights into the making and execution of European foreign policy, it can only reveal part of the picture. One of the important developments in the field of foreign policy analysis since Allison's path-breaking study has been the increased awareness accorded to cognitive and psychological influences on policy-making. This has been part and parcel of what has come to be known as the 'cognitive revolution'. The central insight of the cognitive revolution is that 'structural factors – such as institutions, bureaucracies, international regimes, the state of the economy, geopolitical emplacement, etc. – are *cognitively* mediated by the actors in question rather than affecting policy actions directly' (Carlsnaes 1994: 284; original emphasis). 'Thinking about foreign affairs', one British diplomat has written, ' – like any other kind of thinking – requires a conceptual map which, as maps do, simplifies the landscape and focuses on the main features' (Cooper 1996: 8).

The cognitive revolution has further eroded rationalist assumptions about the pre-given and objectively determined character of interests. The central argument of the cognitive revolution has been that rationality is *bounded*. Actors 'satisfice' rather than optimise. They do not have access to all relevant information, nor do they seek it. They process information differently in times of stress than under routine conditions. They act on the basis of hidden agendas, such as their specific institutional or bureaucratic concerns. Above all, historical precedents, cultural values, normative beliefs and other socio-psychological factors influence the perception of interests. Consequently, 'images of other states are difficult to alter. Perceptions are not responsive to new information about the other side; small changes are not likely to be detected. Once a statesman thinks he knows whether the other needs to be deterred and what kind of strategy is appropriate, only the most dramatic events will shake him' (Jervis 1983: 25–6).

In an important study of the impact of ideas on foreign policy, Judith Goldstein and Robert Keohane (1993) have proposed a threefold categorisation of ideas or beliefs. First, 'world views': these are embedded in the symbolism of a culture and entwined with identity conceptions. Second, 'principled beliefs': these are normative ideas for distinguishing between right and wrong. Third, 'causal beliefs': these are beliefs about cause–effect relationships which provide guides as to how to achieve a given policy objective.

They go on to suggest that ideas can influence foreign policy behaviour in three ways. First, they can serve as 'road maps', guiding actors' preferences and indicating ways of achieving them. Second, they can act as a 'focal point' for actors in the absence of compromise or cooperation. Third, they can become 'institutionalised'; that is, embedded in the operation of institutions and social practices. Their argument is that 'ideas influence policy when the principled or casual beliefs they embody provide road maps that increase actors' clarity about goals or end–means relationships, when they affect outcomes of strategic situations in which there is no unique equilibrium, and when they become embedded in political institutions'. In contrast to many social constructivists, however, they do not argue that it is ideas rather than interests that 'move the world'. Rather, they follow a Weberian approach in arguing that 'ideas *as well as* interests have causal weight in explanations of human action' (Goldstein and Keohane 1993: 3–4; original emphasis).

Goldstein and Keohane's Weberian assumptions that both ideas and material interests shape foreign policy behaviour are of considerable utility in understanding European foreign policy, even if one does not accept their rationalist approach to empirical research. Understanding and explaining the behaviour of the EU as an international actor necessitates a research strategy that examines different national discourses on Europe (see for example Carlsnaes and Smith 1994). The purpose of this should be to uncover the ideas and cultural assumptions that influence policy debates (particularly in the larger and most influential member states) and to explore the impact on EU foreign policy of an underlying set of cultural norms and values, understood as 'social knowledge structures that define collective expectations of appropriate action' (K. Aggestam 1999: 36). This approach assumes that international actors behave according to the 'logic of appropriateness' rather than the 'logic of expected consequences' (March and Olsen 1998b: 8–11).[6] The EU's role as a foreign and security policy actor can thus only be fully understood by considering the cultural determinants which shape it, and which provide 'a framework for organizing the world, for locating the self and others in it, for making sense of the actions and interpreting the motives of others, for grounding an analysis of interests, for linking collective identities to political action, and for motivating people and groups toward some actions and away from others' (Ross 1997: 42).

Identity and foreign policy

One of the most important areas of theoretical innovation in foreign policy analysis over recent years has been the growing awareness that identities matter in international relations. Identities shape the definition of national and European interests and thereby constitute an important influence on foreign policy behaviour. National identity 'serves not only as the primary link between the individual and society, but between a society and the world' (Pritzel 1998: 19). In the case of the EU, its foreign and security policy rests on a shared European 'identity' which has evolved gradually and, at times, fitfully, over the last few decades. This emerging sense of European identity is important in defining Europe's role in international society, its friends and enemies, and its common interests and preferences. This sense of an emerging European identity has been, and is, continually contested and redefined, in response to the shifting domestic elite and mass attitudes to the European integration process. Nonetheless, however indistinct and contested Europe's identity may at times seem, it does have some core elements which have evolved since the early 1970s, if not before. These core elements are associated with the values of liberal-democracy, social market economies and the peaceful resolution of disputes, and have been further defined and reinforced by the experience of 1989 and the post-communist democracies' 'return to Europe'.

Europe's evolving political identity helps shape the broad directions of its Common Foreign and Security Policy by providing cognitive lenses for policy-makers, based on political judgements about the 'national interest'. Analyses of official discourses on European identity can only explain the grand schemes of European diplomacy. They cannot provide explanations of discrete foreign policy behaviour or the nuances of negotiating positions on specific policy issues. They cannot, for example, shed significant light on the EU's negotiations on bananas, or on specific policies with the framework of the Northern Dimension Initiative. These are determined by a political process involving relevant officials within the Commission in association with national ministries and governments, other political actors and private sector interests. Conceptions of the European interest only affect this political process indirectly, by establishing the broad ideational parameters within which competing policy options are considered. European identity thus provides the cognitive framework within which the EU's foreign and security policy is formulated.

Role theory

As a result of the cognitive revolution, it was increasingly recognised in foreign policy analysis circles that perceptions were vital in the policy-making process. Perceptions provided a means of intercepting, classifying and interpreting information in terms of pre-established beliefs. These beliefs, it was suggested, were organised into structured systems that set cognitive limits to rational decision-making. However, 'most of the studies which focus on decision-makers' perceptions include only perceptions of the external environment, especially enemy characteristics and actions, and very few investigate decision-makers' perceptions of their own nations' (Wish quoted in Jönsson 1984: 3). One notable exception to this was the research tradition on national role conceptions.

Role theory was first introduced to foreign policy analysis by Kalevi Holsti in a seminal article originally published in 1970. He drew on sociological interpretations of role in order to suggest how perceptions may structure and guide foreign policy-making. He argued that a state's foreign policy is influenced by its 'national role conception'. This is a product of a nation's socialisation process and is influenced by its history, culture and societal characteristics. 'A *national role conception*', he argued, 'includes the policymakers' own definitions of the general kinds of decisions, commitments, rules, and actions suitable to their state, and of the functions, if any, their state should perform on a continuing basis in the international system or in subordinate regional systems' (Holsti 1987b: 12; original emphasis). His methodology involved analysing elite perceptions of national role, and initiated a research tradition focused on role conceptions (see for example Walker 1979; Wish 1980; Jönsson and Westerlund 1982). This approach has been relatively neglected for many years, although more recently it has received growing academic interest (see for example. Aggestam 1999; Kirste and Maull 1996; Tewes 1998).

'Why the new interest in role conceptions?', Hudson and Vore ask (1995: 226). The answer, they suggest, is that national role conceptions provide 'one of the few conceptual tools we have for the study of how society and culture serve as a context for a nation's foreign policy'. Role theory thus 'allows one to bridge the conceptual gap between the general beliefs held in a society and the beliefs of foreign policy decision makers'. Defining a foreign policy role and having it accepted by others is one of the basic objectives of a state. As Le Prestre (1997: 5–6) notes, a role concept 'reflects a claim on the international system, a recognition by international actors, and a conception of national identity'. Consequently, foreign policy change 'must rest on a redefinition of a role and on the role's congruence with politics'. Moreover, 'contrary to what structural realists would assert, capacities alone do not define a role'. Thus he argues that role theory 'can help explain the general direction of foreign policy choices'.

The articulation of national role betrays preferences, operationalises an image of the world, triggers expectations, and influences the definition of the situation and the available options. It imposes obligations and affects the definition of risks. Focusing on this concept, therefore, allows one to go beyond the traditional explanation of foreign policy, which is based on security or on the national interest defined as the prudent search for power. Roles help define national interests and divorce them from power (Le Prestre 1997: 5–6).

THE EU'S EVOLVING ROLE-SET

The importance and analytical utility of role theory for an understanding of European foreign policy are discussed at greater length elsewhere in this volume (see chapter 6 by Lisbeth Aggestam). In terms of the discussion here, therefore, only three points will be made.

First, the EU's evolving role-set in the 1990s has been defined primarily by the end of the Cold War and the desire of the new democracies of East Central Europe to 'return to Europe'. This role-set involves both the *role perceptions* ascribed to the EU by outsiders and *role conceptions* expressed by the role-holders themselves (see chapter 6). In the early 1990s, these role perceptions and conceptions coalesced around a view of the EU as the institutional embodiment of the 'European ideal'. The EU was seen as performing the roles of an anchor of stability in the new Europe; a magnet for the new democracies of Central and Eastern Europe; and a focus for European cooperation and integration. Above all, the EU was seen as a bastion of liberal democratic values and practices, involving a respect for human rights and the rule of law, and the peaceful resolution of disputes.

Second, the EU's foreign and security policy role-set has been steadily evolving over the last decade or so, but is likely to undergo a more profound redefinition in the coming years. The catalyst for this will be the development of the European Security and Defence Policy (Missiroli 2000: 2–3). The EU has traditionally regarded itself, and has been seen by others, as a 'civilian power' (see Duchêne 1973; Bull 1982). This self-image as a 'civilian power' will, however, be hard to sustain as the EU moves to acquire what the Cologne Council defined as 'the capability for autonomous action, backed up by credible military forces, the means to decide to use them, and a readiness to do so, in order to respond to international crises without prejudice to actions by NATO' (for details see Van Ham 2000; Heisbourg 2000; Howorth 2001). The policy implications of this shift in role perceptions of the EU by Russia or countries in the Middle East and the Maghreb may be quite profound, especially as regards attitudes towards EU enlargement or the role of the Union in the Arab–Israeli peace process.

Third, the EU's political identity and its role conceptions are highly contested, given the different national foreign and security policy traditions of its member states, and the EU's relatively short history as a foreign policy actor. As suggested above, the experience of working closely together in common institutions within the framework of the second pillar may in time lead to a process of *engrenage*, in which habits of working together gradually generate shared perceptions of common interests. However, as Lisbeth Aggestam concludes, foreign policy objectives are still conceptualised by the three largest EU member states 'first and foremost in a national mind-set' (see p. 97 of this volume). This illustrates all too clearly the problems facing the EU as an international actor. The success of its CFSP – especially in the area of preventive diplomacy and crisis management in regions such as the Eastern Europe, the Middle East and the Balkans – will depend above all on the willingness of member states to reach a broadly acceptable consensus on the aspirations, goals and means of EU foreign policy. This will be a long-term task, and one that is likely to be complicated by the enlargement process (Sjursen 1999).

Conclusion

The aim of this chapter has been to outline a conceptual framework for understanding the role of the EU as an international actor. This analytical model rests on three 'legs' – interests, institutions and identities. A constant theme throughout has been the limitations of the dominant neo-realist approach to foreign policy analysis, and the need to consider both the material and ideational factors defining Europe's Common Foreign and Security Policy. Attention has been drawn both to the role of institutional politics in shaping policy outcomes, and to the importance of culture and identity to foreign policy behaviour. In terms of this last point, the utility of role theory as a conceptual tool for operationalising the study of identity and socio-cognitive factors on foreign policy has been underlined.

As was noted in the introduction to this chapter, the study of EPC/CFSP has been under-theorised. It is hoped that the ideas presented above will contribute to the growing debate within international relations and European studies on the need to think more conceptually and theoretically about the EU as an international actor. It does so in the spirit of theoretical pluralism. Although much of the analytical framework presented above draws primarily on social constructivism and the new institutionalism, it also incorporates some insights from classical realism, which has been enjoying something of a revival in recent years. This is because exclusivist and partisan claims to knowledge, either from neo-realists or post-positivists, should be viewed with a high degree of scepticism. As Michael Clarke has argued, if we wish to 'understand the working of political power in our contemporary world' we need to draw on a wide range of disciplinary and theoretical perspectives. 'The world into which we are moving offers prima facie evidence that nothing less than such an ambitious attempt at eclecticism will do' (Clarke 1993: xvi). Understanding and explaining the foreign and security policy of an actor as complex and multi-faceted as the EU thus involves utilising an eclectic analytical framework that draws from a plurality of different traditions and approaches. Only in this way can we open up spaces for theoretical debate and discussion on the EU as an international actor.

Notes

1   State behaviour, Mearsheimer has asserted, 'is largely shaped by the *material* structure of the international system. The distribution of material capabilities among states is the key factor for understanding world politics. For realists, some level of security competition among great powers is inevitable because of the material structure of the international system' (1995: 91; original emphasis).

2   One important attempt to redress the obvious limitations of mainstream realism's obsession with material structures and relative power capabilities is Stephen Walt's influential work, *The Origins of Alliances* (1987). Walt seeks to modify Kenneth Waltz's structural realist approach by suggesting that states balance not against power *per se* but rather against *threats*. Anarchy and the distribution of power alone are unable to predict which states will be identified as threats. Walt argues that threats derive from a combination of geostrategic and military factors and 'aggressive intentions'; in other words, of capabilities and intentions (1987: 22–6). He therefore offers a 'balance of threats' approach in place of the traditional realist 'balance of power' approach. Walt's approach is clearly a major advance on mainstream structural realism. The problem, however, is that his key concept of 'intentions' is left under-specified and under-theorised. While he provides ample evidence that it is ideational rather than material forces which drive alliance formation (at least in the Middle East, his chosen empirical focus), he fails to establish a casual relationship between anarchy and the balance of power on the one hand, and intentions on the other. His theory is also unable to account for the divergent behaviour of France and the United Kingdom towards NATO in the 1960s. Both perceived the same threat (the USSR) and disposed of roughly equally relative power capabilities, and yet their policies towards the Atlantic Alliance diverged sharply after 1966 (see Spirtas 1996: 393–4). Walt's attempt to address the limitations and inconsistencies of neo-realist structural theory are thus ultimately unconvincing, reflecting the weakness of its underlying paradigmatic assumptions. In his critique of Walt, Michael Barnett suggests that '[i]t is the politics of identity rather than the logic of anarchy that often provides a better understanding of which states are viewed as a potential or immediate threat to the state's security' (Barnett 1996: 401).

3   Neo-realism has signally failed to develop an adequate model of the origins and effectiveness of institutions. John Mearsheimer (1994: 7, 24, 47) simply dismisses institutions as having 'no independent effect on states 'behaviour'. Institutions, he asserts, 'matter only on the margins'. They 'have minimal influence on state behaviour, and thus hold little promise for promoting stability in the post-Cold War world'. 'What is impressive about institutions', he insists, 'is how little independent effect they seem to have had on state behaviour'. Such dogmatic assertions effectively close off investigation of a key feature of late twentieth-century European international politics and underline the limitations of neo-realism. Joseph Grieco has made a valiant attempt to develop a neo-realist theory of institutional cooperation (1996), but his efforts are ultimately unconvincing (Spirtas 1996: 402–4). Neo-realism's analytical blind-spot when it comes to institutions has been an important catalyst in the current intellectual movement away from the

barren parsimony of neo-realism to the 'richer analytical framework of traditional realism' (Schweller and Priess 1997: 23).

4   'Constructivism', according to Alexander Wendt, 'is a structural theory of the international system which makes the following core claims (1) states are the principal units of analysis for international political theory; (2) the key structures in the states' system are intersubjective, rather than material; and (3) state identities and interests are in important part constructed by these social structures, rather than given exogenously to the system by human nature or domestic politics' (Wendt 1994: 385). This structural definition of constructivism is problematic in a number of respects. A better definition of constructivism as the 'middle ground' is provided by Emmanual Adler (1997b).

5   Positing the 'state' as an actor is clearly problematical, given that it can be disaggregated down into different departments and even individuals. However, to disaggregate everything into individuals is not very helpful, because 'much of social life is understandable only when collectivities are seen as more than the sum of their "members" and are treated as social realities (methodological collectivism)' (Buzan, Wæver and de Wilde 1998: 40).

6   The 'logic of expected consequences' assumes that states act as rational utility maximisers on the basis of stable consistent and exogenously determined preferences. One example would be the work of Andrew Moravcsik on European integration (1998). The problem with the 'logic of expected consequences', however, is that 'it seems to ignore the substantial role of identities, rules, and institutions in shaping human behaviour' (March and Olsen 1998b: 11). The 'logic of appropriateness', on the other hand, underlines norms and identities as the basis for action. 'Within the tradition of a logic of appropriateness', March and Olsen argue, 'actions are seen as rule-based. Human actors are imagined to follow rules that associate identities to particular situations, approaching individual opportunities for action by assessing similarities between current identities and choice dilemmas and more general concepts of self and situations. Action involves evoking an identity or role and matching the obligations of that identity or role to a specific situation. The pursuit of purpose is associated with identities more than with interests; and with the selection of rules more than with individual rational expectations' (ibid.).

SIBYLLE BAUER AND
ERIC REMACLE

8

Theory and practice of multi-level foreign policy: the European Union's policy in the field of arms export controls

Theories of integration usually provide monocausal explanations of integrative processes. They cannot therefore be considered as general theories but rather as ideological models which reflect the state of the European construction, state the preferences and values of the actors in EU policy-making, and contribute to the inevitable compromises between them (Caporaso and Keeler 1995). From a constructivist perspective (Adler 1997b), one could say that integration theories are social and ideological constructs that contribute to shaping the reality of integration rather than to explaining it.

European foreign policy is a case in point. Each area of foreign policy decision-making in the EU seems to be inspired by different ideological approaches to integration favoured by the different foreign policy actors. Accordingly, European foreign policy functions as a 'system' (Monar 1997) of multi-level policies structured in four levels, each of which refers indirectly to one of the main integration theories (Remacle 1997). This approach will be applied in this chapter to the field of arms export policies.

Conflicting intergovernmentalism results from a perception of national policies as being the core of, and key to, explaining European policy-making. It is mainly inspired by the realist paradigm. Fundamental to this approach are the traditional application of the concept of sovereignty and the inter-state balance of power (Hill 1983; Pijpers 1991). The management of the Yugoslav crisis by EU countries best illustrates this aspect of EU foreign policy, as do national arms exports policies.

Cooperative intergovernmentalism corresponds to theories of functionalism (Mitrany 1966), of adaptation (Rosenau 1970; Petersen 1998) and of maximisation of the national interest and/or convergence of preferences (Milward 1992; Moravcsik 1993; Pfetsch 1994). Illustrations of this type of European foreign policy are reflected in various forms of ad hoc bi- and multilateral cooperation between EU member states in the field of foreign policy. These include: reference to common interests in Article 11 of the TEU, the policy process of European political cooperation 1970–93, EU consultations in the United Nations,[1] and participation in export control regimes such as the 'Wassenaar arrangement'.

Institutionalised regime-type intergovernmentalism is based on assumptions of regime and interdependence theories (Keohane and Nye 1977; Krasner 1981). Their application to the institutional system of the EU leads to the development of a security community among EU states (Deutsch 1954) and to a new type of polity called a 'confederal system' (Wallace 1994), a 'consociational confederation' (Taylor 1993; Chryssochoou 1996), an 'intergovernmental federation' (Quermonne 1998) or a 'federation of states' (Telò and Magnette 1996). The institutionalisation of the Common Foreign and Security Policy (CFSP) and its associated instruments established by the Maastricht and Amsterdam Treaties is an illustration of this regime-building approach. Examples of these instruments include the EU Code of Conduct on Arms Exports of 1998 and the EU Joint Action on Small Arms of 1998, both of which were agreed within the framework of the CFSP.

Supranationalism requires the existence of a foreign policy dimension based on first pillar instruments, which has also been called an integrated structural foreign policy (Keukeleire 1998). It relates to theories developed by federalists (Sidjanski 1992), neo-functionalists (Haas 1958; Lindberg 1963; Schmitter 1992) or neo-institutionalists (Regelsberger and Wessels 1996; Wessels 1997), all of whom predict the transformation of the Community into an international and global player which influences its partners both by its existence and its actions (Ginsberg 1999). With regard to the field of arms exports, while there is no first pillar EU competence, a grey zone of dual-use items[2] exists to which Community legislation applies (European Council 1994a, b and 2000a).

The development of the EU's foreign policy can be interpreted either as a combination or as a chronological/teleological succession of these four levels. Whichever interpretation is chosen, the following three concepts are key to understanding the mechanisms of European foreign policy: first, convergence (or vertical coherence) between national policies and EU policy; second, consistency (or horizontal coherence) between policies carried out in the different pillars of the EU institutional system; and third, variable geometry in policy-making and institutions. These three dimensions of European foreign policy-making will be discussed hereafter with reference to the case of arms export controls.

Convergence

EPC in the 1970s and 1980s had already allowed the EC member states to build channels of communication and methods of socialisation among their diplomats in order to define common objectives and coordinate the first joint diplomatic actions (de Schoutheete de Tervarent 1986; Pijpers 1991; Nuttall 1997). The CFSP continued this process (Willaert and Marques-Ruiz 1995; Maury 1996;

Holland 1997) and has given rise to parallel tendencies towards a Europeanisation of national policies as well as towards a maximisation of national positions through European channels (Hill 1983; Peterson and Sjursen 1998). Studies on the Spanish and Portuguese cases (Algieri and Regelsberger 1996), on the Nordic dimension (Jopp and Warjovaara 1998) and on the Europeanisation of national structures and policies (Hanf and Soetendorp 1998; Tonra 2000) provide solid empirical evidence of this double trend. The question of arms export policies can be added to these case studies.

Arms export policy falls simultaneously into the fields of economic, competition, foreign, security and defence policy with their different degrees of community and member state competence. At the same time, this policy area has traditionally been considered as inextricably linked to national sovereignty. This led to the inclusion of an 'opt-out clause' in the Treaty of Rome (Article 296 of the Treaty establishing the European Community, former Article 223), which gives EU member states the right to exclude arms exports from EU competence.[3] Member states have been reluctant to open up a sector that has traditionally been protected from outside competition, highly subsidised, and subject to a high degree of state intervention and control. Article 133 (former Article 113) of the EC Treaty states that the 'common commercial policy shall be based on ... the achievements of uniformity in measures of trade liberalisation, export policy and measures to protect trade such as those to be taken in the event of dumping or subsidies'. Article 296 (Bauer and Küchenmeister 1996; Emiliou 1996) allows member states to invoke their security interests to exempt armaments from these provisions.

According to EU member states' interpretation of Article 296, matters related to the production of and trade in armaments have therefore been dealt with within the framework of national jurisdiction of the individual member states (Anthony 1991; Costa and Pereira 1999). The current process of Europeanisation of the defence industry, however, has made it imperative for member states increasingly to coordinate export policies. The tradition of national decision-making with regard to arms exports was linked to the existence of national defence industries, which have gradually ceased to exist due to fundamental structural changes in the industry, such as mergers, joint ventures and increased dependence on components from abroad (De Vestel 1993, 1995; Gummet and Walker 1993; Schmitt 2000).

This process of defence industry Europeanisation has been determined to a large extent by the post-Cold War reduction in military expenditure; the fast pace of technological change and spiralling costs of modern weapons systems; shrinking domestic and export markets; and increased availability of surplus weapons. Other factors contributing to an increased co-ordination of export policies are the creation of a common market for civilian and, with some restrictions, also for dual-use goods, and the fear of 'undercutting'[4] in the face of shrinking markets. These developments have also led to a push towards harmonisation at EU level from the defence industry itself, to create a 'level playing field' (European Defence Industries Group 1995). Furthermore, the need for more restrictive regulations across the EU as a tool of conflict prevention has become increasingly apparent, particularly considering the boomerang effect illustrated by the Gulf War and in peacekeeping missions where European soldiers fight troops equipped with weapons and equipment exported by their own governments. Linked to this, the need for a coherent EU foreign policy has become all too obvious given cases where past EU arms deliveries have been counterproductive for the EU's humanitarian efforts and have contributed to the very development of these humanitarian disasters.

Cooperation has therefore been increasing in this field, but arms export policies have nevertheless remained national preserves. Those aspects of policy have so far remained within the intergovernmental second pillar. At the European Councils of Luxembourg and Lisbon in 1991 and 1992, the Council agreed eight criteria for arms exports. On the basis of these, a more comprehensive EU Code of Conduct for Arms Exports was elaborated by COARM, the Council Working Party on Conventional Armaments, and adopted by the Council of Ministers on 8 June 1998 as a Council Declaration. The Code document consists of three parts: a preamble, which outlines aims and underlying principles of the Code; export guidelines in the form of an elaboration of the eight criteria of 1991/92; and a number of operative provisions, which set out mechanisms for EU member states to cooperate on certain clearly defined matters. Primarily, member states are required to provide each other with annual reports on implementation of the Code, to review implementation of the agreement[5] and to exchange information on the denial of export licences. This consultation mechanism, unprecedented in this field, aims to prevent undercutting. Before undercutting can take place, the two governments involved are required to enter into consultations.

As a Council Declaration, the Code agreement is only politically, not legally binding. And since it was agreed within CFSP, on the basis of Title V of the TEU, its implementation cannot be enforced by the European Court of Justice (Article 46 TEU). Thus no Community legislation on arms exports exists to date. And while the Code includes an elaboration of the original eight criteria, it leaves ample room for subjective interpretation by national governments (Amnesty International et al. 1998; Bauer 1998), even with regard to the operative provisions, for example regarding the contents of annual reports. Implementation is up to individual member states and can only be verified if information is provided by governments through other transparency mechanisms (such as national reports on arms exports, the UN Register for Conventional Arms, etc.) or by non-governmental sources (such as the defence industry).

The review and further development of the Code since its adoption reflect an increased Europeanisation of export policies. For example, a number of clarifications and agreements for practical implementation were made during the first two years (European Council 1999b; 2000b). While a clear European dimension of national export policies has developed, national governments have also tried to maximise their national positions through European channels.

During negotiations for the Code of Conduct, for example, it was primarily the French government that blocked the agreement of more transparent mechanisms. On the other hand, under the Finnish Presidency, with its tradition of public and parliamentary transparency, the first annual report on implementation of the Code was published, although this had not been provided for in the original document. The document is a compromise agreement which reflects national traditions and negotiating positions. The Code is therefore a result of a Europeanisation dynamic as well as of member states' attempts to maximise their national positions.

Inter-pillar consistency and the tension between supranationalism and intergovernmentalism

Foreign policy remains a competence of member states, who are not ready to cede it to the supranational level. Therefore attempts to build a European foreign policy since the Fouchet Plan in the 1960s have centred on the distribution of competencies between intergovernmental cooperation and control by supranational institutions. The Maastricht and Amsterdam Treaties illustrate this tension (Petite 1997; Remacle 1997; Dehousse 1998; Franck 1998). In the preparation of the Maastricht Treaty, the supranationalists, especially the Commission and the Benelux states, insisted vehemently on the need to give to the Community the coordinating role of an integrated external policy (Remacle 1992). The question of consistency between the three pillars thus became the sacred cow of supranationalists (Krenzler and Schneider 1997; Tietje 1997).

The emphasis on the need for a legal personality of the Union and its capability to sign agreements with third parties in the field of CFSP represented another example of the same debate (Bribosia and Weyembergh 1999). In Amsterdam, the approach appeared to be less ambitious and more pragmatic. Instead of reviving the old tensions between supranationalists and intergovernmentalists, negotiators adopted institutional working procedures designed to overcome some of the deep-rooted tensions (Gourlay and Remacle 1998). First, no legal personality is given to the Union as a whole, but Article 24 of the TEU allows the Union to sign agreements with third countries or organisations in the second and third pillars. Second, Article 3 of the TEU emphasises the need for consistency between all external policies and joint responsibility of the Council and the Commission in their implementation. Co-management of CFSP and other external policies by the Council and the Commission remains effectively the only way for the Union to proceed in shaping its political international profile. The appointment of Javier Solana as Secretary-General of the Council/High Representative for CFSP according to Article 26 of the TEU (and as Secretary-General of the WEU) as well as the designation of Chris Patten as 'Super-Commissioner' for External Relations[6] are structural measures towards this objective. Despite some criticisms of federalists against the creation of the post of 'Mr CFSP' (Dehousse 1998), this solution of a

Council–Commission tandem seems to be the only one able to reflect the consociational/confederal nature of the second pillar which makes it necessary to base it jointly on states and supranational institutions.

The question of consistency confirms therefore our theoretical assumption that EU foreign policy has to be conceived of as a 'system' of multi-level foreign policies rather than a unified set of external relations. This has led scholars to study how policy-making in this field addresses the consistency question and how institutions cooperate or compete in the clarification of their respective roles in the three pillars. Again, the case of arms exports is informative. We have already mentioned, for example, that the Code of Conduct is based on a Council Declaration, not on Community law. The regulation on dual-use goods of 1994 is also often quoted as an interesting case because it was a mix of a Community regulation and a CFSP joint action (European Council 1994a, b; Holland 1997), while in 2000 competence for dual-use goods was transferred to the European Commission (European Council 2000a). These cases concern primarily the question of the relationship between the Council and the Commission. Since 1998, the issue of arms exports has also been addressed by the Court of Justice, thereby creating a new dynamic in the field.

According to the Treaties, the jurisdiction of the ECJ does not extend to the second pillar, the field of CFSP. Title V of the Treaty on European Union is expressly excluded from the Court's jurisdiction (Article 46 TEU). Nevertheless, decisions on access to second pillar documents agreed under Title V can be subject to European jurisdiction. A precedent for this has been set by a transparency case against the Council on access to second pillar documents, which was brought before the Court of First Instance in 1998 (Case T-14/98).

Heidi Hautala, a Finnish Green Member of the European Parliament, put a written question to the Council on the implementation of the eight EU criteria for arms exports of 1991 and 1992 (Hautala 1996). Subsequently, she requested access to a report on this matter, which had been agreed at the Political Committee level in 1993 (Hautala 1997a, b, 1999). Having been refused access to the document, Ms Hautala sued the Council, asking the Court of First Instance to annul the Council decision made at the ministerial level and to order the Council to bear the costs of the case (European Court of Justice 1999, para. 32). The Court ruled positively regarding both aspects and requested the Council to consider partial access to the document (para. 87). The Council, supported by Spain, appealed against this ruling, while Heidi Hautala was supported by Denmark, France, Finland, Sweden and the United Kingdom. The following aspects of the case are particularly relevant with regard to inter-pillar consistency:

Parties before Court

The General Affairs Council's contested decision to refuse access to the document was not made unanimously: four states voted in favour of granting access to the document (European Court of Justice 1999, para. 20). Two governments, those of Sweden and Finland, even intervened in the written and oral procedures in support of the plaintiff's request to annul the contested decision and her position on the Court's competence (paras 25–6). The French government intervened in favour of the Council and dismissed the option of partial access (para. 63). Member states defending different positions before the ECJ can clearly be qualified as a first pillar practice, since the second pillar is formally excluded from ECJ competence.

Competence of the ECJ

Access to the contested document is governed by Council Decision 93/731 on public access to documents (European Council 1993). Therefore the applicant, supported by the two Scandinavian governments, maintained that it fell under Article 173 of the EC Treaty (now Article 230), regarding 'review by the Court of Justice of the legality of Council acts'. Thus, according to Hautala, access to the document was within the Court's jurisdiction, even if the document fell within Title V (European Court of Justice 1999, paras 21–2).

In the written procedure, the Council, supported by the French government, challenged the Court's competence in this matter on the grounds of the relevant Treaty provisions (Vesterdorf, Judge-Rapporteur 1999, paras 21–2). It did not, however, argue in favour of inadmissibility and 'left it to the Court of First Instance to consider the question of its jurisdiction' (European Court of Justice 1999, para. 36). During the oral hearing, it acknowledged the Court's competence in this specific case, while it outlined certain limits.[7]

The Court argued, as in a similar third pillar case,[8] that the decision on rules governing access to Council documents, as an act based on Article 151(3) of the EC Treaty (now Article 207(3)) applied to all Council documents (European Court of Justice 1999, para. 41). It further held that the Court not having 'jurisdiction to assess the lawfulness of acts falling within Title V did not exclude its jurisdiction to rule on public access to those documents' (ibid., para. 42). The Court, however, limited its own jurisdiction using a distinction between political and legal assessments. It stated that ruling on the question of whether partial access had to be considered fell within its competence, since it was a legal question (ibid., para. 76). However, it did not consider a ruling on the Council's assessment of potential threats to the public interest and the EU's external relations as falling within its jurisdiction (ibid., para. 71). It defined its own competence as 'limited to verifying whether the procedural rules have been complied with, the contested decision is properly reasoned, and the facts have been accurately stated, and whether there has been a manifest error of assessment of the facts or a misuse of power' (ibid., para. 72).

Interpretation of the principle of widest possible access to documents

A key document on the principles of transparency and citizens' right of access to information is a Code of Conduct agreed by Council and Commission on public access to these institutions' documents (European Commission and European Council 1993), which establishes a principle of 'widest possible access to documents held by the Commission and the Council' (p. 41). Public access to a document can be refused under specifically named circumstances,which are also confirmed in Council Decision 93/731 on public access to documents (European Commission and European Council 1993: Article 4).⁹ This adds to interpillar consistency, although the lack of an enforcement mechanism is a clear difference with regard to the Council. To some extent (taking into consideration the limited competence of the Court) this consistency gap is narrowed through the Court case in question.

In the case discussed here, the Council evoked public security as one of the limitations to widest public access provided for in Article 4(1) of Decision 93/731 (European Council 1997a) and potential harm to the EU's relations with third countries (European Council 1997b). It further maintained that the type of document requested automatically led to a refusal of access.¹⁰

This court case was the first one at EU level in which the Court explicitly ruled that partial access had to be considered by one of the EU institutions (Hautala 1999). The Council interpreted the rules governing access to documents as only providing for access to complete documents and stated that fragmentary information could be misleading. It emphasised that a case where partial access was granted by the Council had been an exception (European Court of Justice 1999, paras 55–9). The Court interpreted access to documents as access to the information contained in them (para. 75). It further based its position on the principle of proportionality, maintaining that the aim of protecting 'the public interest with regard to international relations' could be achieved even when parts of a document are published (para. 85). While the Court emphasised that its competence did not extend to an assessment of the Council's decision based on the contents of the report, it ruled that partial access had to be considered. The Court therefore assumed a role in the interpretation of the Council Decision and thus participated in its further legal development through the creation of case-law.

One can conclude that first pillar practices and principles were applied to a second pillar issue, thereby providing an example of a spillover effect from the first to the second pillar with regard to access to documents, and therefore transparency and accountability, through the admission of ECJ jurisdiction. European Court of Justice jurisdiction regarding public access to a second pillar document thus illustrates at the same time an aspect of Europeanisation of arms export policies (in the sense of a new dimension to national policies) as well as the problem of inter-pillar consistency.

Variable geometry

The trends towards convergence and consistency in EU foreign policy indicate that decision-making processes have been integrated to some extent. But they also show that this integration process is not similar to first pillar policy-making, but is rather more complex and multi-level. Our hypothesis about the peculiarity of foreign policy integration is again verified when we take into account a third dimension of the Europeanisation process; that is, variable geometry. The shaping of concentric circles, differentiated security dilemmas and interlocking regional security subsystems and organisations (Remacle and Seidelmann 1998) as aspects of variable geometry characterise the evolving nature of the European security system since the end of bipolarity. In addition, variable geometry has been gradually introduced into the institutional framework of the European Union with the development of the second pillar (Edwards and Philippart 1997; Missiroli 1998).

The Amsterdam Treaty does not formally include a provision for enhanced cooperation in the second pillar, as it does for the first and third ones. No agreement was possible on this point because of the reluctance of large member states which were interested in maintaining the option of establishing contact groups or '*directoires*' for managing international questions or crises. Nevertheless, Article 23 introduces the option of constructive abstention of countries, if they represent at most one-third of votes in the Council, when adopting guidelines or common strategies. In addition, qualified majority voting was introduced for decisions on common positions and joint actions, although a country can still evoke national interests to veto such a majority decision. As far as the outside representation of the Union is concerned, foreign policy will generate a system of variable 'troikas': besides the traditional troika (preceding, present and succeeding Presidencies plus the Commission), a special troika is created for CFSP (present and next Presidencies plus the High Representative for CFSP plus the Commission). Yet another troika has been set up for the external representation of the euro (the Presidency of euro-,[11] the President of the European Central Bank, and one of the three EMU participants in G-7 assisted technically by the Commission). This means the introduction of a kind of variable geometry in foreign policy. Furthermore, security policy is most affected by variable geometry, and again the field of armaments policy provides a clear example of this trend.

In the past, member states have interpreted Article 296 of the EC Treaty such that all matters relating to the production and trade in arms have been considered as falling within national jurisdiction. While attempts were made within the first and second pillar (Agstner 1998; European Commission 1996, 1997) to achieve some progress along the lines of coordination and harmonisation of armaments policies, few substantial results have been produced. This is due to dramatically diverging interests as a result of the different sizes of national defence industries, different defence doctrines, and membership in different defence alliances or even the status of neutrality. To date, there has been no integration of defence procurement and defence markets in the EU, although Article 17 of the TEU mentions the importance of coordination on armaments issues.

Since the beginning of the 1990s, economic, technological, strategic, political and industrial developments have pushed governments to seek progress in the field of armaments cooperation (Bauer and Winks 2001). Economic imperatives of cost reduction and the increased integration of the defence industry have arguably been the most important factors driving this process. This has led to a revitalisation of established bodies and to the creation of new mechanisms outside the existing institutions.

Armaments cooperation within NATO involves a complex structure of initiatives and bodies, including the Conference of National Directors of Armaments. The thirteen European member states of NATO (except Iceland) also meet in the West European Armaments Group, and can use the WEU's continuing treaty-based legal personality through the West European Armament Organisation to commission studies and sign contracts. Third, the four main arms producers in the EU – that is, Britain, France, Germany and Italy – have founded a multilateral structure of co-ordination in the field of arms procurement called the Joint Armaments Cooperation Structure (JACS, mostly known by its French acronym OCCAR), which gained legal status in January 2001 (Agence Europe 2001).

In addition to cooperation within these bodies, there has been a recent trend to deal with armaments policy outside the established institutionalised framework. This is due to the failure of previous multilateral attempts to agree a common political and legal framework for the European defence industry. In July 2000, the defence ministers of the EU's six biggest arms producers and exporters (Germany, France, Sweden, Spain, Italy and the UK) signed a Framework Agreement, 'Concerning Measures to Facilitate the Restructuring and Operation of the European Defence Industry'[11] (Schmitt 2000; Bauer and Winks 2001; House of Commons 2001). This initiative goes back to a 'Letter of Intent' signed by the aforementioned six countries in July 1998, in which the six defence ministers stated their desire to 'establish a co-operative framework to facilitate the restructuring of the European Defence Industry'.[12] Working groups consequently negotiated agreements within the following areas: security of supply; transfer and export procedures; security of classified information; defence-related research and technology; treatment of technical information; harmonisation of military requirements; and protection of commercially sensitive information. The document will be fleshed out through subsequent agreements in these specific areas. The Treaty has been ratified by all signatory states except Italy, and is in principle open for other states to join, provided there is consensus among the original signatories.

In the field of export policies, the Agreement established a mechanism to negotiate common 'white lists' of countries eligible to receive certain defence goods. Those countries involved in the joint production will negotiate these product-specific lists in advance. The mechanism contains a provision for adding or deleting potential recipients at the request of a contributing country. A rule of consensus through each participating state's right to veto an export destination was thus integrated into the treaty. The current provision is a departure from the previous principle applied in Europe, which placed the responsibility for an export on the country in which the final assembly takes place.

Export decisions will be based on the principles laid out in the EU Code of Conduct. The Agreement also facilitates transfers of equipment between the participating countries. This could be a first step towards a common market for defence goods within the EU.

Despite the impression of dispersion generated by variable geometry, previous experience has shown that variable geometry and enhanced cooperation are the best solutions for maintaining the momentum of integration and leading to an integration of most EU countries in new circles of cooperation (Telò and Remacle 1998). EMU and Schengen are two good examples of this. The transfer of the WEU 'acquis' into the EU, decided in 1999 and legalised by the Nice Treaty, seems to support this trend. Therefore, variable geometry is not only an indication of fragmentation of the Union but also an element of the continuing process of integration.

Conclusions

The delicate balance between integration and fragmentation is shaping a very peculiar model of foreign policy-making which cannot simply be described as a traditional international organisation nor as a state-like polity, but rather as a multi-level system. Evidence of all four analytical levels (conflicting, cooperative and institutionalised intergovernmentalism, and supranationalism) can be seen. There is clear evidence of spillover from the first to the second pillar. It has, however, been shown that functionalism, while an important driver for integration, is not the sole driving force behind the Europeanisation process. Institutional factors also play an important role. Various forms of ad-hoc cooperation between EU member states outside the established institutionalised system are driven by a convergence of preferences and attempts to maximise national interests. At the same time, political resistance to joint decision-making remains, arising from the traditional culture in this domain which is centred around an insistence of sovereignty, as traditionally defined, and nation-state competence for security and defence matters.

In looking at the aforementioned four levels of EU foreign policy through the aspects of consistency, convergence and variable geometry, this contribution shows parallel processes of integration and fragmentation. The field of arms export policies illustrates these tendencies. On the one hand there is a clear Europeanisation dynamic towards a harmonisation of national policies at the EU level. On the other hand, member states resist legal changes that would cede competence regarding arms exports to the supranational level. Therefore, decision-making on armaments and dual-use goods takes place at all four levels. The various levels of foreign policy-making inside the EU allow for different speeds and degrees of integration in different policy areas of the three pillars as well as within the pillars, and also in various aspects of the same policy area.

Notes

1 For example, in the framework of the UN Conference on the Illicit Trade in Small Arms and Light Weapons in All Its Aspects, held in July 2001.
2 Items with both military and civil applications.
3 Article 296(1) states: '(a) No Member State shall be obliged to supply information the disclosure of which it considers contrary to the essential interests of its security; (b) any Member State may take such measures as it considers necessary for the protection of the essential interests of its security which are connected with the production of or trade in arms, munitions and war material; such measures shall not adversely affect the conditions of competition in the common market regarding products which are not intended for specifically military purposes.'
4 'Undercutting' refers to the delivery of weapons by a government after the export of essentially the same category of weapons was denied by a different government.
5 The first annual review took place on 21 September 1999, during the Finnish Presidency.
6 The Amsterdam negotiators had proposed to appoint a Vice-President of the Commission for External Relations. President Prodi was not able to fulfil this request but gave to Commissioner Patten a wide portfolio in external affairs which is almost equivalent to the power of a vice-president.
7 It stated that 'assessment of the harm which might be caused to the public interest by the disclosure of one of its documents is within its sole discretion' (European Court of Justice 1999, para. 57).
8 In case T-174/95 (Svenska Journalistförbundet v Council of the European Union), the Swedish Journalists' Association challenged denial of access to a document and won the case, even though third pillar matters are also expressly excluded from the Court's competence (European Court of Justice 1998). Thus, parallel to the case discussed here, the Court's competence was also not evident from the Treaties. That case therefore established a precedent which is relevant for second pillar matters.
9 'Access to a Council document shall not be granted where its disclosure could undermine:
   – the protection of the public interest (public security, international relations, monetary stability, court proceedings, inspections and investigations),
   – the protection of the individual and of privacy,
   – the protection of commercial and industrial secrecy,
   – the protection of the Community's financial interests,
   – the protection of confidentiality as requested by the natural or legal person who supplied any of the information contained in the document or as required by the legislation of the Member State which supplied any of that information.'
   Also, '[a]ccess to a Council document may be refused in order to protect the confidentiality of the Council's proceedings'.
10 The Council argued that publication of an internal working document could impact the functioning of CFSP mechanisms and thereby harm public interest (European Court of Justice 1999: para. 60).
11 Available via www.sipri.org.
12 Also available via www.sipri.org.

Helene Sjursen and
Karen E. Smith

9

Justifying EU foreign policy: the logics underpinning EU enlargement

The foreign policy of the European Union is in many ways a puzzle to students of international relations. Doubts about whether there is in reality a European foreign policy contrast with empirical observations of the considerable influence exerted by the EU, if not always in the international system at large, then at least in Europe. Such observations imply that the EU has a 'foreign policy' of sorts. To better capture the EU's foreign policy, we need to ask different questions, beyond those of whether or not we are moving 'towards a common foreign and security policy' (Hoffmann 2000). Hence, in this chapter, we ask what the EU's foreign policy (such as it is) is *for*; in other words, what is its *raison d'être*? Taking the existence of an EU foreign policy as a given, we examine how this policy is justified.

Justifications of the EU's foreign policy have two addressees: the first is internal to the EU and consists of the member states and their citizens; the second is external and consists of non-member states and their citizens. The principal focus here will be on the EU's attempts to validate its foreign policy externally. At the same time, we assume that there is a connection between these attempts at external and internal justification in the sense that the former both shapes and reflects the latter. [1]

Before entering into a discussion about the *raison d'être* of the EU's foreign policy, it is important to clarify what we mean by foreign policy. We consider the EU's policy on enlargement as foreign policy. Defining enlargement as a form of foreign policy is not entirely uncontroversial, although it is hardly novel. In 1989, Roy Ginsberg classified enlargement as a type of foreign policy action, which resulted specifically from the process of 'externalisation': a foreign policy option that could be executed in response to outside pressure from eligible non-members who want to join the club. We would go further, and argue that enlargement is not merely reactive. In fact, the current enlargement process is influenced by explicitly political objectives that aim to reshape political order in

Europe.[2] Several observers have, however, argued that enlargement must be seen more broadly, not just as external policy. Lykke Friis and Anna Murphy (1999) have argued that enlargement has significant internal consequences, particularly for the internal development of the Union, and thus affects decision-making. This does not contradict the fact that the EU's enlargement policy addresses itself to, and has consequences for, actors outside the EU. As such, it is an example of the form of foreign policy that develops in a world where the domestic and international spheres have become increasingly intertwined. It should be stressed that enlargement is not a policy defined in the CFSP pillar, but is an EU policy spanning the pillars. Thus, we do not consider the CFSP to be the exclusive foreign policy production 'centre' of the EU.

In the next section, we present three analytically distinct approaches for examining the basis of legitimacy for foreign policy in general. We then examine how the EU seeks to justify its foreign policy towards the applicant states in Central, Eastern and Southern Europe.

Three approaches to legitimisation

There are three analytically distinct ways in which a foreign policy can achieve legitimacy. They are grounded in different logics of action or justification for an individual actor: a logic of consequences, a logic of appropriateness and a logic of moral justification (March and Olsen 1998 and Eriksen 1999). Different criteria identify these logics: utility, values and rights, respectively. *Utility* refers to an effort to find efficient solutions to concrete problems or dilemmas. Policy-makers seek legitimisation by achieving an output that could be seen as an efficient solution to given interests and preferences. *Values* refer to a particular idea of the 'good life' that is grounded in the identity of a specific community. Policy would be legitimised through reference to what is considered appropriate given a particular group's conception of itself and of what it represents. *Rights* refer to a set of principles that are mutually recognised as morally acceptable. In other words, policy would be legitimised with reference to principles that can be recognised as 'just' by all parties, irrespective of their particular interests, perceptions of the 'good life' or cultural identity (Fossum 2000).

According to a logic of expected consequences, actors in the international system are rational, in the sense that they seek to develop policies that allow them to maximise their own interest. Policy-makers try to ensure the policy outcome that is the most efficient translation of a given set of interests or preferences. The assumption is that policy-makers do this by assessing the costs and benefits of various possible policy choices and their possible outcomes in light of their preferences and interests (March and Olsen 1998).

This approach has, explicitly or implicitly, dominated studies of foreign and security policy. The classical realists, as well as their inheritors the neo-realists and neo-liberal institutionalists, ground their analysis in assumptions drawn from a logic of consequences (Baldwin 1993; Moravcsik 1998; Krasner 1999). It is often argued that this approach is particularly suited to studies of foreign policy issues (as opposed to domestic political issues) because of the assumption of international anarchy. There is no superior authority that can 'lay down the law' from a more independent or objective position than the individual states. The international system is, in other words, seen to be in a 'state of nature'. In such a system, politics is a struggle for power and the best that one can hope for is a form of compromise between various and conflicting interests and preferences. Questions of values or of morality have little or no place in such a system: they belong to domestic politics. The interest to be defended is given: ultimately the aim is guaranteeing the survival of the state. Often this slides into the position that it is the 'moral duty' of governments to defend the interests of their states against outsiders (Morgenthau 1948).

Much of the literature on the CFSP also seems to draw on such assumptions. Thus a central concern in many analyses of the CFSP is whether or not it is efficient, in the sense that it achieves the goals that it actually sets for itself. The conclusion is often that because the CFSP is inefficient it is also virtually non-existent (Bull 1982; Hill 1998b; Jørgensen 1998).

As long as foreign policy is conceived of as a policy that seeks to protect the territorial integrity of a unitary state, it might be possible to argue that we do not need more than the logic of consequences to understand it. In other words, in the Westphalian system, the principal and ultimate *raison d'être* of foreign policy could easily be seen as given.[3] But this might not be the case any longer. 'Foreign policy' is changing. Domestic and foreign policies are intertwined in ways that they have not previously been. As actors other than the state exercise a form of foreign policy, the ability of the state to control the international activity of its citizens is reduced. Furthermore, states must, to a much larger extent than previously, refer to international norms and rules and to the interests and perspectives of actors outside their own territory when they formulate their own foreign policy. This intertwining of internal and external policy also leads to international calls for a justification of national policy choices – on issues that previously were considered part of the national domain. In parallel one might expect that the requests for legitimisation emerging from the domestic community become more diverse. Utility arguments would rely on a shared idea of the 'national interest', but in an increasingly interdependent world a blanket reference to the national interest seems untenable. The whole conception of the national interest is founded on the idea of a state facing the outside world as one. As the state today controls movements across national borders to a much lesser extent, transnational bonds can develop more freely. Furthermore, as domestic audiences become more diverse, their understanding of the 'national interest' may vary considerably. Hence it is by no means certain that all actors will agree on what the national interest should be. Furthermore, it is not certain that all actors will feel the reflex of national loyalty and rally against 'foreign' interests.

If it is increasingly difficult for nation-states to refer to the 'national interest', it is even more so for a collectivity such as the European Union. In a situation where the member states share the same threat perception from the outset, it might only be necessary to make instrumental calculations about how to respond to such threats. Hence, for a traditional alliance operating in a bipolar system, a logic of consequence might be sufficient. However, in a situation such as post-1989 Europe, where there is no obvious common threat or threat perception, the answers to the questions of why a common foreign and security policy is needed and what issues it should deal with are not self-evident. Thus other types of arguments in favour of a common foreign and security policy are needed. Security and foreign policy for whom and against whom becomes a logical enquiry. Thus in the case of the EU a central concern emerges: 'what is EU foreign policy for?' The common interest is not self-evident, nor is common identity, the second 'leg' on which the foreign policies of states seem to stand.

The changing nature of foreign policy, and the emergence of foreign policy-making on a collective EU level, raise the question of the basis on which we should act also at the international level – which interests, values, norms should be promoted and protected. The challenge is increasingly to establish a collective understanding between different states of not only what needs to be done, but also the very issues to be dealt with. Furthermore, action needs to be recognised as legitimate and necessary by a collection of states – and their citizens – and not by the citizens of a single state. Such dilemmas of justification have traditionally been seen as the privilege of the domestic political sphere. So, for example, when discussing environmental policy in the domestic political arena the question has not only been how one should go about ensuring the best possible protection of the environment, but why we should protect nature in the first place. What is ultimately at stake, then, is the kind of society we want to live in – which values we should defend. These are questions of qualities and standards that are difficult to resolve through a logic of consequences (Eriksen 1999). What we observe is that such questions also emerge at the European level.

A further factor contributing to foreign policy-making in the EU may also be the need to legitimise the policy in the eyes of its intended addressees. This would seem particularly necessary in the case of states seeking to join the EU. If applicant states do not feel that the EU's enlargement policy is legitimate, not only could the EU find it difficult to exercise influence over those states (e.g. by convincing them to fulfil the membership conditions), but doubts about the legitimacy of the EU's decisions to include or exclude states could damage the credibility of the borders of the EU. Finally, the doubts of new member states about EU legitimacy could be carried with them into the EU. The perceived lack of external legitimacy could thus feed into perceptions of a lack of internal legitimacy.

Legitimisation of foreign policy may be provided through a second logic of action – a logic of appropriateness. Policy would develop on the basis of a particular idea of the values represented by a specific community. The question of security for whom and against whom would be answered with reference to the values considered central to the community's self-understanding and identity.[4] However, such culturally bound conceptions may be difficult to defend at the international (including European) level. It could be too optimistic to assume that there is a collective identity at the European level that could underpin the development of a common foreign policy. Values could collide at that level. In this case, there is a third way that might provide the basis for cooperation other than one based on values.

To assess the validity of different perspectives, and to resolve collisions between different norms and different ideas of the good life, it would be necessary to find out whether or not a particular position could be universalised. The 'test' for the various positions then would be to what extent the particular solution would be considered fair by all parties, if they switched places. This is the logic of moral justification (see Eriksen 1999). A decision would have to be considered fair by all participants regardless of their particular cultural identity, interests and preferences. The analysis is not based on a 'means–ends' conception of rationality where actors are rational when they choose the most efficient means to achieve exogenously defined ends. Rather, actors are seen as rational when they are able to justify and explain their actions. They are not just seen as self-interested, but also as having the ability to be reasonable. The political process is conceptualised as a process of reason-giving where actors aim to come to a shared understanding. The outcome would be determined by the better argument – the argument that would be considered just by all parties – rather than a process of bargaining where the outcome is determined by the balance of power between the actors.

In wielding enlargement and specifically the conditional offer of membership, what kind of logic underpins the EU's foreign policy? What can be considered to be the *raison d'être* of the EU's foreign policy?

Setting conditions for enlargement

First of all, what are the EU's membership conditions? In this section, the evolution of the conditions is traced, and we use the three logics of action to analyse them. To what extent are the conditions the outcome of calculations of utility? Are they based on a particular idea of the EU or are they legitimised with reference to universal principles that can be viewed to be of equal validity to all actors regardless of their cultural identity? In the section that follows, we use the logics of action to analyse how the EU has actually applied membership conditionality and how it has justified its actions.

The conditions for membership have clearly been evolving since the Community's beginnings. The basic condition – European identity – was set out in the 1958 Rome Treaty (Article 237): 'Any European state may apply to become a member of the Community.' During the Cold War eligibility was not such a troublesome issue, as membership for states outside the Western half of the continent was unthinkable. Other Western European countries were either not interested and/or were not democratic. The first enlargement of the Community, to Britain, Ireland and Denmark, did not take place on the basis of explicit membership criteria.

It was not until the mid-1970s that membership conditions became a matter of concern, because of the unfolding events in Southern Europe. In April 1978, the European Council declared that respect for and maintenance of representative democracy and human rights in each Member State are essential elements of membership in the European Community. This was a clear signal to Greece, Portugal and Spain that they could become Community members if they proceeded with democratisation. Specific membership conditions for the three countries were not spelt out, but certainly included genuine free elections, the right balance of party strength (pro-democracy parties in the ascendance) and a reasonably stable government (Pridham 1994: 24). The Commission's opinions on the three applications, however, only mention briefly the transition to democracy. Much more attention was given to consideration of the applicants' economic and administrative capacities, and implications for the Community of enlargement (see European Commission 1976, 1978a, b). Nonetheless, the importance of democracy as a basis for membership at this stage of the Community's history was an important signal that it was not just an economic integration project: deeper values linked the member states. This interpretation is reinforced if we bear in mind that Portugal and Spain asked to open membership negotiations in the early 1960s and that their candidatures were not taken seriously because they did not have democratic governments.

This remained the situation on membership eligibility until the end of the Cold War, which had the effect of dramatically increasing the number of states wanting to join the Community. The ever-growing queue of membership applicants, including the members of the European Free Trade Association (EFTA) as well as the Central and Eastern European countries, made it imperative for the Community to set out additional membership requirements. This was a way to impose order on a clamour of demands that threatened to engulf the Community and, more significantly, endanger the process of deepening begun with the 1987 Single European Act and the 1989 Delors Report on Economic and Monetary Union (Sjursen 1997).

In a report to the June 1992 Lisbon European Council, the Commission restated its view that there were three basic conditions for membership: European identity, democratic status and respect for human rights. But it suggested several additional criteria. The trend towards 'variable geometry' or 'multi-speed Europe' – codified in the Maastricht Treaty opt-outs for Britain and Denmark – was to stop with the current member states. Applicants had to accept the entire Community system, the *acquis communautaire*, and be able to implement it. This included the single European market and the Maastricht provisions on Economic and Monetary Union. An applicant state had to have a functioning and competitive market economy; if not, 'membership would be more likely to harm than to benefit the economy of such a country, and would disrupt the working of the Community' (European Commission 1992: 11). Applicant states also had to accept and be able to implement the Common Foreign and Security Policy. This was implicitly aimed at the neutral applicants (Austria, Finland, Sweden), which might impede development of a common defence policy, which was now an objective following the Maastricht Treaty: 'An applicant country whose constitutional status, or stance in international affairs, renders it unable to pursue the project on which the other members are embarked could not be satisfactorily integrated into the Union' (European Commission 1992: 11). What the Commission set out clearly, therefore, was that 'widening must not be at the expense of deepening. Enlargement must not be a dilution of the Community's achievements' (European Commission 1992: 10). The Community thus seems to be applying a logic of consequences here: enlargement could not be permitted to damage the progress made in implementing a single European market, a single currency or a Common Foreign and Security Policy. But the logic of appropriateness seems to fit even better: enlargement could be justified only if it contributed to, or at least did not threaten, the ongoing process of integration agreed at Maastricht. And the assumption clearly is that the applicants would not be seeking to join if they did not consider this a legitimate policy basis. Finally, the logic of moral justification becomes important if we view these conditions as an attempt to protect and promote certain key principles – those of democracy and human rights.

The 1992 report was just the first step of the 1990s to explicate membership conditions. The next step arose as a result of the widening versus deepening debate within the Community, specifically with respect to the Central and Eastern European countries. Soon after the end of the Cold War, the CEEC declared that their number one foreign policy objective was to 'rejoin Europe', which entailed joining the entire panoply of European institutions including the EU and NATO. Many within the EU and Eastern Europe argued that the Union would have to promise that the CEEC could eventually become member states, because this would provide them with a 'reward' for continuing with reforms even as those reforms caused hardship. Furthermore, the sense of duty and responsibility of Western Europe towards 'the other half' of Europe was underlined. For some time, these voices were weaker than those urging a more cautious approach, who cited the considerable upheaval widening would cause within the EU. The widening versus deepening debate within the EU eventually resulted in the Copenhagen Summit Declaration in June 1993. The European Council agreed to enlarge as part of its pledge to support the reform process in the CEEC, on which peace and security in Europe depended (European Council 1993). But it also set specific conditions that the CEEC applicants would have to meet.

The Copenhagen European Council declared that those CEEC that had concluded a Europe Agreement were eligible for EU membership, provided they could meet three conditions: they must have a functioning market economy with the capacity to cope with competitive pressures and market forces within the EU; they must have achieved stability of institutions guaranteeing democracy, the rule of law, human rights and respect for and protection of minorities; and they must be able to take on the obligations of EU membership, including adherence to the aims of economic and political union. An additional condition specifies that the EU must be able to absorb new members and maintain the momentum of integration. The Copenhagen conditions are by and large similar to the conditions set out in the Commission's 1992 report, with an important addition: respect for and protection of minorities. This reflects the 'lessons learned' from conflicts in the former Yugoslavia.[5] Again, the conditions can be interpreted as utility-enhancing: the more the applicants did for themselves in terms of implementing political and market economic reforms, the fewer the difficulties to be faced by the Union and its member states.

But the logic of appropriateness also fits here: the values that the CEEC must accept are quite specific to the EU (implementation of the *acquis*, adherence to EU objectives). In addition, the logic of moral justification is also present in the form of the political conditions (democracy, rule of law, human rights and protection of minorities). Incidentally, the first three political conditions (excluding the protection of minorities) are also the basis for the EU's relations with other 'third countries'. Since 1995, agreements with third countries have contained a human rights clause, which allows for measures to be taken if human rights and democratic principles are violated by the parties to the agreement.[6] The Union justifies this stance by explicit reference to universal instruments, in particular the United Nations Declaration on Human Rights (Commission of the European Communities 1995). The 'universality' of these conditions suggests that these are not just EU-specific values but reflect widely accepted principles.

The Copenhagen conditions applied only to Europe (association) Agreement signatories: Bulgaria, Czech Republic, Estonia, Hungary, Latvia, Lithuania, Poland, Romania, Slovakia and Slovenia. They were not specifically intended for Cyprus, Malta or Turkey, which had applied for membership in 1990, 1990 and 1987, respectively. But since then, they have been understood to form the basic conditions even for these three applicants.

Since Copenhagen, more general statements of the membership conditions have been made. The Amsterdam Treaty formalised the political conditions of membership, declaring that 'the Union is founded on the principles of liberty, democracy, respect for human rights and fundamental freedoms, and the rule of law, principles which are common to the Member States' (Article 6). Any European state that respects these principles may apply to become a member of the Union (Article 49).

The Amsterdam Treaty conditions are explicitly stated to be the common values of the member states. But one important omission, as compared with the Copenhagen conditions, should be noted: protection of minorities. Minority rights are controversial within the EU, as the member states are divided over the concept. France, for example, is more inclined to emphasise individual rights and has neither signed nor ratified the Council of Europe's Framework Convention on National Minorities, whereas Belgium, Greece, Luxembourg and the Netherlands have signed the Convention but not yet ratified it.[7] Yet the protection of minorities has formed an important condition in relations with Central and Eastern European countries (most notably, in the Copenhagen conditions) – a case of the EU setting conditions for outsiders which it could not set internally. The insistence on minority rights can be attributed, at least in part, to the logic of consequences: the danger of 'importing' ethnic conflict into the Union had to be countered by the efficient solution of guaranteeing minority rights. That minority rights are not an explicit part of the Union's 'political *acquis*' reinforces the interpretation. However, it could also be argued that the minority rights condition reflects a logic of moral justification, or reference to more universal principles motivating individuals. Since 1990, state conduct towards minorities has increasingly been the subject of standard-setting at both European (OSCE) and international (United Nations) levels (Jackson Preece 1997). While some member states have not fully accepted these standards, there is certainly pressure on them to do so, precisely because of the public exposure of a 'double standard' in the EU's conditionality.

Another condition has also since been set: that of 'good neighbourliness'. Good neighbourliness implies a willingness to cooperate with neighbours but also – more concretely – to agree on borders. It first cropped up in the EU's Pact for Stability, the conference held in 1994–95 to encourage the Central and Eastern European applicants to reach bilateral and multilateral agreements guaranteeing minority rights and borders. In its *Agenda 2000* report on enlargement, published in July 1997, the European Commission stated that it 'considers that, before accession, applicants should make every effort to resolve any outstanding border dispute among themselves or involving third countries. Failing this they should agree that the dispute be referred to the International Court of Justice' (European Commission 1997: 51). The Helsinki European Council reiterated this condition in December 1999: it

> stresses the principle of peaceful settlement of disputes in accordance with the United Nations Charter and urges candidate States to make every effort to resolve any outstanding border disputes and other related issues. Failing this they should within a reasonable time bring the dispute to the International Court of Justice. The European Council will review the situation relating to any outstanding disputes, in particular concerning the repercussions on the accession process and in order to promote their settlement through the International Court of Justice, at the latest by the end of 2004. (European Council, Presidency Conclusions 1999: para. 4)

This condition can be said to reflect the common values of the EU. The way in which the EU approaches dispute resolution is via cooperation and, preferably, integration. As Lily Gardner Feldman (1999: 66) has argued, one of the EU's core legitimating values is 'the development of a "peace community" entailing reconciliation between former enemies'. The encouragement of regional cooperation is a long-standing objective of the Union. And good-neighbourliness is one of the conditions for closer ties with the EU that the Southeast European countries (Albania, Bosnia-Herzegovina, Croatia, Macedonia and Serbia/Montenegro) must meet. Still, there is a universal principle in favour of peaceful resolution of disputes over the use of force, so that it is difficult to see this as a value that is distinctive of the identity of the EU. Furthermore, it must be pointed out that considerations of utility also underpin the Union's insistence on good-neighbourliness: there is clearly no desire to 'import' disputes into the Union. This becomes even more important bearing in mind that the condition regarding peaceful resolution of disputes could also be seen as the result of Greek pressure to use the Union to compel Turkey to resolve the Cyprus dispute according to Greek preferences. Justifying this, not only within the Union but also outside of it (not least in Turkey itself), is however proving controversial, and not all of the member states are willing to place so much pressure on Turkey (*European Voice*, 23–29 November 2000).

All three logics thus seem to be at work in the formulation of the EU's membership conditions. The conditions reflect not only considerations of utility and efficiency (only countries with market economies, capable of abiding by the obligations of membership and implementing the *acquis* can join; they must also protect minority rights so as to prevent conflict), but EU-specific values (only European states can apply; acceptance of the *acquis* and commitment to continue integration are necessary) and universal principles (minority rights, human rights, democracy) also play an important part. Problems may arise in the process of implementing the enlargement policy if these considerations collide or turn out to be incompatible, and priorities must be set. This is discussed in the next section.

As long as utility considerations give way to respect for universal principles it is possible to conclude that the overarching logic for the EU's policy is that of moral justification. In other words, for the EU's policy to be based on a logic of justification this logic must be applied consistently.

The EU's use of conditionality: following the logic of moral justification?

In applying membership conditionality, the EU has not been entirely consistent. Candidates have been treated differently – and the EU's reasons for so doing have not always been clear. The use of conditionality with respect to the CEEC has been most consistent, although even here the conditions have been ignored in favour of other considerations. But still the CEEC strongly desire to join the EU – and thus accept its values – and are willing to try to meet the conditions; furthermore they consider the prospect of membership highly likely. The contradictions among the logics guiding EU membership conditionality are not causing serious problems – the EU's policy is accepted as legitimate in that the applicants continue to fulfil the conditions.

All membership applications must be judged by the Commission in terms of the extent to which the applicant state meets the Copenhagen conditions. The emphasis on the criteria of respect for human rights and democratic principles has been important. A couple of examples of this can be cited here.

In 1994 and 1995, Romania appeared to be heading towards more nationalistic and racist politics, as extremist parties gained power. The EU indicated that these developments would not help Romania's application for membership, and from mid-1995 the Romanian government – prompted by President Ion Ilescu – changed its course: over the next year, the ruling Social Democrats broke with extremist parties and an agreement with Hungary was negotiated. A new reformist government took office in November 1996 and relations with the EU improved significantly (Smith 1999: 142–3). This was not enough, however, for the Commission and European Council to include Romania in the first round of membership negotiations, because Romania did not meet the conditions regarding economic readiness and acceptance of the *acquis*.

Even more pressure was put on Slovakia during the period of the Meciar government – the EU delivered demarches and issued numerous warnings that Slovakia must meet democratic norms before it could join the EU. In 1997, the Commission and European Council agreed that Slovakia should not be included in the first round of membership negotiations, primarily on the basis of political criteria (Smith 1999: 142–3). Yet the Meciar government remained in power and did not alter its behaviour in response to the EU's pressure. In October 1998, however, Slovak voters chose a new coalition government, which was united by a desire to join the EU and NATO.

The European Commission in the first instance (*Agenda 2000*, July 1997) considered that only five CEEC were eligible to open negotiations with the EU because they came the closest to meeting the Copenhagen conditions. The Luxembourg European Council in December 1997 agreed with this assessment and the Czech Republic, Estonia, Hungary, Poland and Slovenia began negotiations in March 1998. This in and of itself increased the pressure on the remaining five CEEC to make faster progress towards meeting the conditions. But there were concerns that differentiating among the CEEC would alienate those that were further behind. In particular, two applicant countries, Bulgaria and Romania, were already suffering as a result of instability and war in Southeastern Europe, and were in danger of being even further isolated.

The Helsinki European Council in December 1999 agreed to open negotiations with the remaining five applicant countries. The justification for opening negotiations was that all five of these countries met the Copenhagen political conditions (as opposed to Turkey, which did not – see below), and some came closer than others to meeting the remaining conditions. Although negotiations were opened with all ten CEEC candidates, the European Council made it clear that 'in the negotiations, each candidate state will be judged on its own merits. This principle will apply both to opening of the various negotiating chapters and to the conduct of the negotiations' (European Council 1999: para. 11). This kept up the pressure on all the applicant states to meet the Copenhagen conditions, while still reassuring them that they would join as soon as they were ready. In December 2002, the European Council then concluded negotiations with eight CEEC, and promised to conclude talks with the remaining two, Bulgaria and Romania, in 2007. With this policy, the EU glossed over some of the difficulties the CEEC were having in meeting the 'non-political' conditions. But, by and large, conditionality was applied consistently and the applicant states were clear about what was required of them, and considered the process legitimate enough to continue to strive for membership by fulfilling the conditions.

The case of the eastern Mediterranean, and specifically the Republic of Cyprus and Turkey, is quite different. In both, the same formal conditions were an issue, even though, technically speaking, neither application was subject to the Copenhagen conditions (which were formulated for those CEEC that had concluded Europe Agreements). The EU evaluated the economic situation, ability to implement the *acquis*, human rights and democracy. The Republic of Cyprus applied for membership in 1990. In June 1993, the Commission's opinion on the application was largely positive – not only did the Republic of Cyprus meet the necessary political and economic criteria, but the Commission was also convinced that Cyprus' accession would 'increase security and prosperity' and help 'bring the two communities closer together'. It stated that 'Cyprus' integration with the Community implies a peaceful, balanced and lasting settlement of the Cyprus question'. The Commission felt that a positive signal should be sent that Cyprus is eligible 'and that as soon as the prospect of a settlement is surer, the Community is ready to start the process with Cyprus that should eventually lead to its accession' (Avery and Cameron 1998: 95–6). In June 1994, the Corfu European Council agreed that Cyprus should be involved in the next enlargement. A year later, the Cannes European Council declared that negotiations with Cyprus should be opened six months after the conclusion of the 1996 intergovernmental conference. Formal membership talks with Cyprus opened in March 1998. The prospect of a settlement, however, seemed no surer than it had been in 1993.

The Union has repeatedly stated that it supports a just and lasting settlement of the Cyprus question, and that the prospect of accession will provide an incentive for this. But it did not state that accession would be blocked should no settlement be reached, and it continued to negotiate with the Republic of Cyprus although no representatives of the Turkish Cypriot community were included in the delegation (the Republic of Cyprus effectively negotiated the entry of the entire island). The Helsinki European Council stated that 'a political settlement will facilitate the accession of Cyprus to the European Union'. But 'if no settlement has been reached by the completion of accession negotiations, the Council's decision on accession will be made without [this] being a precondition' (European Council 1999: para. 96). Conditionality was not applied consistently here, as good-neighbourliness was ignored. And so it was: negotiations were concluded with Cyprus in December 2002, and the accession treaty signed in

April 2003, even though no settlement had been reached. The Greek position seems by and large to have prevented the Union from stressing the criteria of good-neighbourliness, although other member states also appear to be reluctant (see Nugent 2000). At the same time, the EU's policy does not seem to be inspired by utility, because the cost of including Cyprus before the conflict is solved would be high, perhaps higher than the internal difficulties that might follow from refusing to give way to Greece. One of the reasons why the EU is reluctant to insist too strongly on 'good-neighbourliness' could instead be linked to a logic of appropriateness: there could be agreement that all EU member states must take into consideration the particular problems of one of their fellow member states, or there may be a sense in which the Greek community in Cyprus is 'one of us' to an extent that the Turkish community is not. Further investigation of this possibility is still needed.

The case of Turkey is equally complicated. In 1987, it applied for membership; in 1989, the Commission's opinion concluded that it would not be appropriate or useful to open accession negotiations with Turkey. The Commission, Council and European Parliament have persistently raised problems regarding Turkey's human rights and democracy situation, and the European Parliament has blocked aid and the customs union because of Turkey's human rights record. However, Turkey had reasons to suspect that it would never become a member of the club even if it had a fully functioning democracy and exemplary human rights record. It has watched the EFTA member states and the CEEC jump the queue while, in different contexts, various European politicians cited cultural and religious factors for its exclusion,[8] and Greece placed obstacles in the way of closer relations. This doubt seemed to be confirmed when the December 1997 European Council placed Turkey in its own separate category of applicant states, although it confirmed its eligibility for membership. Turkey then suspended its relations with the EU.

More recently, of course, relations have improved. The Helsinki European Council in December 1999 classified Turkey as an official candidate (entailing inclusion in the pre-accession strategy and conclusion of an Accession Partnership), although it made it clear that membership negotiations would only be opened once the political conditions have been met. The good-neighbourliness condition can also be interpreted to imply that Turkey's disputes with Greece over territory as well as Cyprus must be resolved first: the extent to which Turkey is to contribute to resolving the Cyprus dispute before it can start negotiations has been the source of some tension in its relations with the EU (*European Voice*, 23–29 November 2000).[9] As a result of the inclusion of Turkey in the accession process, the EU's credibility seems to have increased. Yet it is still not clear how willing Turkey is to undertake the necessary reforms (such as outlawing the death penalty). Turkish elites, as Lauren McLaren notes, do not put as much emphasis on key political and foreign policy reforms as does the EU (McLaren 2000).

In the process of implementation of the enlargement conditions some inconsistencies become evident. This is particularly so in the case of the EU's policy towards Cyprus and Turkey. Here this inconsistency leads to doubts about the suggestion that the overarching logic of enlargement is that of moral justification.

Conclusion

This chapter took as its starting point the empirical observation that the EU has an impact on the world and that we can thus assume that it has a foreign policy of sorts. Following from this intuitive starting point we sought to enquire what the *raison d'être* of this policy might be. Whereas most of the literature on the CFSP seems to assume implicitly that the EU's foreign policy can only be justified if it produces concrete results that correspond to the collective or individual interests of the EU member states, we suggested that two additional approaches to justifying the EU's foreign policy might be employed: the first of these would refer to common values, the second to universal principles. These approaches should be seen as analytically distinct, which means that all three could be present in the EU's foreign policy. They rely on an assumption of rationality that extends beyond that of 'rational choice' theory. An actor is considered to be rational if he/she is capable of explaining and justifying his or her reasons for making a particular policy choice. These reasons could be material gain, but they could also be a sense of what is appropriate given an actor's role or duties or what is right given universal standards of justice. This expansion of the possible *raisons d'être* of the EU's foreign policy seems all the more reasonable bearing in mind that national foreign policies do not seem to suffer from the same 'existentialist dilemmas' when they fail to obtain their objectives. For example, if US foreign policy is ineffective, we do not conclude that it is non-existent. This suggests that also here there are other elements that help to justify the existence of national foreign policies.

As an illustration of the EU's foreign policy, we used the policy on enlargement, and in particular the use of membership conditionality. Thus, the aim here has not been to produce an exhaustive study of the EU's enlargement policy in all its dimensions, but to suggest an alternative approach of studying the EU's foreign policy.

Looking at the conditions that the EU sets out for membership we found that all three logics seem to be present. The important question then becomes the extent to which one logic can be seen either as overarching, or if not overarching then at least as having more 'weight' than the others. Here, we discussed whether or not the logic of moral justification is overarching. Our preliminary discussion found that in the case of the EU's policy towards the CEEC, there seemed to be consistency in favour of this logic. However, in the case of the Mediterranean applicants such a conclusion at this point seems more difficult. Two preliminary conclusions can be drawn from this, both of which need further investigation. One would be to say that the EU is a primarily self-interested actor in the enlargement process: in other words, when push comes to shove, when it will cost something either in terms of concrete funds or in terms of having to confront specific national interests, universal principles have to give way. Alternatively, one could stress the importance of values. This would suggest that in addition to the considerable cost of confronting Greece over Turkey, there are value-based assumptions involved in the decisions made on enlargement, about who is European and who is not. Some indication of this is found in a comparative study of the EU's financial aid to democratic reform in Turkey and Poland. It is clear that Poland has received much more support towards democratic transition than has Turkey since the end of the Cold War, thus suggesting a clear prioritisation (Lundgren 1998).

Such a conclusion would be particularly interesting given that we often take it for granted that 'there is no such thing as a European identity' and that this is a drawback for the EU's foreign policy. Such a conclusion would suggest that, despite the looseness of this identity, a sense of a common cultural sphere is assumed and might – for good and for bad – be the source of further foreign policies.

Notes

The authors would like to thank the members of the ARENA group on Legitimate Governance, and in particular Erik Oddvar Eriksen, for comments on a previous draft of this chapter.

1 It is of course possible that the approach to legitimation will be different in these two cases. But in this context we assume that foreign policy can be seen as a part of a larger whole in the sense that the external image of a community also reflects inwards and contributes to shaping its internal distinctiveness.

2 In late 2000 Guiliano Amato (the Italian Prime Minister) and Gerhard Schröder (the German Chancellor) wrote that 'enlargement to Central and South-Eastern Europe, by creating stability, will contribute to reinforcing decisively our security' (author's translation), La Repubblica, 21 September 2000.

3 According to Held (1993), the model of the Westphalian system holds the following characteristic features:

1 The world consists of, and is divided by, sovereign states which recognise no superior authority.

2 The processes of law-making, the settlement of disputes and law enforcement are largely in the hands of individual states subject to the logic of 'the competitive struggle for power'.

3 Differences among states are often settled by force: the principle of effective power holds sway. Virtually no legal fetters exist to curb the resort to force; international legal standards afford minimal protection.

4 Responsibility for cross-border wrongful acts is a 'private matter' concerning only those affected; no collective interest in compliance with international law is recognised.

5 All states are regarded as equal before the law: legal rules do not take account of asymmetries of power.

6 International law is oriented to the establishment of minimal rules of coexistence; the creation of enduring relationships among states and peoples is an aim, but only to the extent that it allows national political objectives to be met.

7 The minimisation of impediments on state freedom is the 'collective' priority.

4   The concept of 'appropriateness' is ambiguous in the sense that it suggests rule-bound behaviour. Behaviour could thus be seen as guided by either habit or duty. Whereas 'habit' does not require much conscious reflection on the part of the actors, 'duty' – defined as related to the actor's particular role – does. This ambiguity is not the main point here because we assume that actors are rational in the sense that they are able to explain and justify their actions. Thus a logic of appropriateness is seen to grow out of duty rather than of habit.

5   These lessons also inspired agreement on a French plan for a Stability Pact in Europe. The Pact was a forum in which the Central and Eastern European applicants were strongly encouraged to settle problems over borders and minorities, which could threaten European security – and much more importantly, any eventual enlargement process (European Council 1993). See the Joint Action convening the Pact (European Council 1993); the 'Concluding Document from the Inaugural Conference for a Pact on Stability in Europe', *EU Bulletin*, no. 5, 1994; and the 'Political Declaration adopted at the Conclusion of the Final Conference on the Pact on Stability in Europe and List of Good-Neighbourliness and Cooperation Agreements and Arrangements', *EU Bulletin*, no. 3, 1995.

6   The human rights clause is really two clauses: the first states that respect for human rights and democratic principles are 'essential elements' of the agreement; the second permits appropriate measures to be taken in case a party to the agreement has failed to fulfil an essential element.

7   So the Council of the European Union's *Annual Report on Human Rights 1999/2000* does not list the Council of Europe Framework Convention for National Minorities as one of those human rights instruments signed by EU member states. But the European Commission's *Enlargement Strategy Paper 2000* makes a point of listing (in Annex 3) which applicant states have signed the Framework Convention (Poland and Latvia have signed the Convention but have not ratified it, and Turkey has neither signed nor ratified it).

8   Most notoriously, in 1997 EU Christian Democratic leaders rejected the idea of Turkish membership largely on cultural grounds (Buzan and Diez 1997: 45). As Buzan and Diez also note (p. 43), fears of large-scale waves of migration from Turkey into the EU (most particularly, into Germany) have also been high on the list of concerns of the effects of Turkish membership.

9   This is particularly contentious because membership negotiations with Cyprus have not been made conditional on precisely the same issue.

BIBLIOGRAPHY

Adler, E. (1997a), 'Imagined (Security) Communities: Cognitive Regions in International Relations', *Millennium: Journal of International Studies*, 26:2.

Adler, E. (1997b), 'Seizing the Middle Ground: Constructivism in World Politics', *European Journal of International Relations*, 3:3.

Adler, E. and B. Crawford (eds) (1991), *Progress in Post-war International Relations*, New York: Columbia University Press.

Adler, E. and M. Barnett (1998), *Security Communities*, Cambridge: Cambridge University Press.

Agence Europe (2001), 'OCCAR Secures Legal Status – Expected Enlargements to the Netherlands and Spain', *Atlantic News*, Brussels, 31 January.

Aggestam, K. (1999), *Reframing and Resolving Conflict: Israeli-Palestinian Negotiations 1988–1998*, Lund: Lund University Press.

Aggestam, L. (1999), *Role Conceptions and the Politics of Identity in Foreign Policy*, Oslo: ARENA Working Paper No. 8.

Aggestam, L. (2000a), '*A Common Foreign and Security Policy: Role Conceptions and the Politics of Identity in the EU*', in L. Aggestam and A. Hyde-Price (eds), *Security and Identity in Europe: Exploring the New Agenda*, Basingstoke: Macmillan Press.

Aggestam, L. (2000b), '*En gemensam utrikes- och* säkerhetspolitik? *En jämförelse av brittiska, franska och* tyska *rolluppfattninga*', in L. Aggestam et al. *Europeisk Säkerhetspolitik*, Lund: Studentlitteratur.

Aggestam, L. (2000c), 'Germany', in I. Manners and R. Whitman (eds), *The Foreign Policies of European Union Member States*, Manchester: Manchester University Press.

Aggestam, L. (2000d), '*Europe Puissance*: French Influence and European Independence', in *Redefining Security? The Role of the European Union in European Security Structures*, Oslo: ARENA Report No. 7.

Aggestam, L. and A. Hyde-Price (eds) (2000), *Security and Identity in Europe: Exploring the New Agenda*, Basingstoke: Macmillan Press.

Agstner, R. (1998), 'Europäische Rüstungspolitik Drei Jahre Ad Hoc-Gruppe des EU-Rates, Europäische Rüstungspolitik (POLARM) – Eine Bestandaufnahme', *Österreichische Militärzeitung*, 5: 98.

Algieri, F. and E. Regelsberger (eds) (1996), *Synergy at Work. Spain and Portugal in European Foreign Policy*, Bonn: Institut für Europäische Politik.

Alker, H. (1999), 'On Learning from Wendt', *Review of International Studies*, 26:1.

Allen, D. (1996), *The European Rescue of the National Foreign Policy*, London: Routledge.

Allen, D. (1998), 'Who Speaks for Europe? The Search for an Effective and Coherent External Policy', in J. Peterson and H. Sjursen (eds), *A Common Foreign Policy for Europe? Competive Visions of the CFSP*, London: Routledge.

Allen, D. and A. Pijpers (1984), *European Foreign Policy Making and the Arab–Israeli Conflict*, The Hague: Martinus Nijhoff.

Allen, D. and M. Smith (1990), 'Western Europe's Presence in the Contemporary International Arena', *Review of International Studies*, 16:3.

Allen, D., R. Rummel and W. Wessels (eds) (1982), *European Political Cooperation: Towards a Foreign Policy for Western Europe*, London: Butterworth Scientific.

Allison, G. (1971), *Essence of Decision: Explaining the Cuban Misssile Crisis*, Boston: Little & Brown.

Allison, G. and P. Zelikow (1999), *Essence of Decision: Explaining the Cuban Missile Crisis*, New York: Addison Wesley Longman.

Almond, G., G. B. Powell and R. Mundt (1993), *Comparative Politics. A Theoretical Framework*, New York: Harper Collins College Publishers.

Amato, G. and G. Schroeder (2000), 'La Porta Stretta della Grande Europa', *La Repubblica*, 21 September.

Amnesty International, BASIC, Christian Aid, Saferworld and the World Development Movement (1998), *The EU Code of Conduct on Arms Exports: Final Analysis*, London: Amnesty International.

Anderson, B. (1983), *Imagined Communities – Reflections on the Origin and Spread of Nationalism*, London: Verso.

Andersen, K. G. (1998), *The (Re)Construction of a Common Foreign and Security Policy for the European Union*, Aarhus: Department of Political Science.

Andréani, Gilles (1999), *Europe's Uncertain Identity*, London: Centre for European Reform.

Anthony, I. (ed.) (1991), *Arms Export Regulations, SIPRI*, Oxford: Oxford University Press.

Avery, G. and F. Cameron (1998), *The Enlargement of the European Union*, Sheffield: Sheffield Academic Press.

Bacot-Decriaud, M. (1998), *L'Union européenne: la PESC, une dynamique en panne*, Paris: La Documentation française.

Baldwin, D. A. (ed.) (1993), *Neorealism and Neoliberalism. The Contemporary Debate*, New York: Columbia University Press.

Ball, T. (1995), *Reappraising Political Theory. Revisionist Studies in the History of Political Thought*, Oxford: Clarendon Press.

Baring, A. (ed.) (1994), *Germany's New Position in Europe: Problems and Perspectives*, Oxford: Berg.

Barnett, M. (1993), 'Institutions, Roles, and Disorder: The Case of the Arab States System', *International Studies Quarterly*, 37:3.

Barnett, M. (1996), 'Identity and Alliances in the Middle East', in P. Katzenstein (ed.), *The Culture of National Security: Norms and Identity in World Politics*, New York: Columbia University Press.

Bauer, H. and T. Küchenmeister (1996), 'Exportkontrollpolitik bei Rüstung und dual-use Gütern', *Arbeitspapier des Instituts für europäische Politik*, 31:3.

Bauer, S. (1998a), 'Der EU-Verhaltenskodex für Rüstungsexporte', *Antimilitarismus Information*, 28:7.

Bauer, S. (1998b), 'EU-Verhaltenskodex für Rüstungsexporte – (k)eine Antwort auf die Kleinwaffenproblematik?', *Wissenschaft und Frieden*, 16:3.

Bauer, S. and R. Winks (2001), 'The Institutional Framework for European Arms Policy Co-operation', in Claude Serfati et al. (eds), *The Restructuring of the European Defence Industry. Dynamics of Change*, European Commission, Directorate-General for Research, COST Action A10. Luxembourg: Office for Official Publications of the European Communities.

Berger, P. (1986), 'Epilogue', in James D. Hunter and Stephen C. Ainley (eds.), *Making Sense of Modern Times. Peter L. Berger and the Vision of Interpretive Sociology*, London and New York: Routledge and Kegan Paul.

Bertilsson, M. and M. Järvinen (eds) (1998), *Socialkonstruktivisme: bidrag til en kritisk discussion*, Copenhagen: Hans Reitzels Forlag.

Biddle, B. J. and E. J. Thomas (1966), *Role Theory: Concepts and Research*, New York: Wiley.

Blair, T. (1999), 'The Case for Britain', speech, London, 14 October.

Bonvicini, G. (1983), *Italy: An Integrationist Perspective*, London: George Allen & Unwin.

Bonvicini, G. (1996), *Regional Reassertion: The Dilemmas of Italy*, London: Routledge.

Bonvicini, G. (1998), *Making European Foreign Policy Work*, London: Routledge.

Brenner, M. (1993), 'The Politics of NATO', *Survival*, 35:2.

Bretherton, C. and J. Vogler (1999), *The European Union as a Global Actor*, London: Routledge.

Bribosia, E. and A. Weyembergh (1999), *La personnalité juridique de l'Union européenne*, Brussells: Editions de l'Université de Bruxelles.

Brown, C. (1997), *Understanding International Relations*, Basingstoke: Macmillan.

Brückner, P. (1990), 'The European Community and the United Nations', *European Journal of International Law*, 1:2.

Buchan, David (1993), *Europe: The Strange Superpower*, Brookfield, VT: Dartmouth Publishing Co.

Bull, H. (1982), 'Civilian Power Europe, a contradiction in terms?', *Journal of Common Market Studies* Nos 1–2, September/October.

Bull, H. and A. Watson (1984), *The Expansion of International Society*, Oxford: Clarendon.

Bulmer, S. (1983), 'Domestic Politics and European Community Policy-Making', *Journal of Common Market Studies*, 21 (4).

Bulmer, S. (1991), *Analysing European Political Cooperation: The Case for Two-Tier Analysis*, London: Macmillan.

Burghardt, G. (1997), 'The Potential and Limits of CFSP: What Comes Next?', in E. Regelsberger P. de Schoutheete de Tervarent and W. Wessels (eds.), *Foreign Policy of the European Union: From EPC to CFSP and Beyond*, Boulder: Lynne Rienner.

Burr, V. (1995), *An Introduction to Social Constructivism*, London: Sage.

Burrows, B., G. Denton and G. Edwards (eds) (1978), *Federal Solutions to European Issues*, London: Macmillan.

Buzan, B. (1983), *People, States and Fear*. Brighton: Wheatsheaf.

Buzan, B. (1991), *People, States & Fear: An Agenda for International Security Studies in the Post-Cold War Era*, Hemel Hempstead: Harvester Wheatsheaf.

Buzan, B. (1995), *Security, the State, the "New World Order," and Beyond*, New York: Columbia University Press.

Buzan, B. and T. Diez (1997), 'The European Union and Turkey', *Survival*, 41:1.

Buzan, B., C. Jones and R. Little (1993), *The Logic of Anarchy: Neorealism to Structural Realism*, New York: Columbia University Press.

Buzan, B., O. Wæver and J. de Wilde (1998), *Security: A New Framework for Analysis*, Boulder: Lynne Rienner Publishers.

Cameron, F. (1999), *The Foreign and Security Policy of the European Union. Past, Present and Future*, Sheffield: Sheffield Academic Press.

Campbell, D. (1992), *Writing Security: United States Foreign Policy and Politics of Identity*, Manchester: Manchester University Press.

Caporaso, J. A. and J. T. S. Keeler (1995), *The European Union and Regional Integration Theory*, Boulder, Lynne Rienner, and London, Longman.

Carlsnaes, Walter (1992), 'The Agency-Structure Problem in Foreign Policy Analysis', *International Studies Quarterly*, 36:3.

Carlsnaes, W. (1994), 'In Lieu of a Conslusion: Compatibility and the Agency–Structure Issue', in W. Carlsnaes and S. Smith (eds), *European Foreign Policy: The EC and Changing Perspectives in Europe*, London: Sage.

Carlsnaes, W. and S. Smith (eds) (1994), *European Foreign Policy. The EC and Changing Perspectives in Europe*, London: Sage.

Chabod, F. (1996), *Italian Foreign Policy*, Princeton: Princeton University Press.

Checkel, J. (1998a), 'The Constructivist Turn in International Relations Theory', *World Politics*, 50:2.

Checkel, J. (1998b), 'Social Construction and Integration', *ARENA Working Paper No. 14*.

Checkel, J. (1993), 'Ideas, Institutions, and the Gorbachev Foreign Policy Revolution', *World Politics*, 45: January.

Checkel, J. (1997), 'International Norms and Domestic Politics: Bridging the Rationalist–Constructivist Divide', *European Journal of International relations*, 3:4.

Chirac, J. (1998), Press conference statement, Saint-Malo, 4 December.

Chouliaraki, L. and L. Phillips (eds) (2001), *Diskursanalyse på tværs af discipliner*, Copenhagen: Samfundslitteratur.

Christiansen, T. K., E. Jørgensen and A. Wiener (2002), *The Social Construction of Europe*, London: Sage.

Chryssochoou, D. N. (1996), 'European Union and the Dynamics of Confederal Consociation: Problems and Prospects for a Democratic Future', *Journal of European Integration*, 18:2–3.

Chryssochoou, D. N., M. J. Tsinisizelis, S. Stavridis and K. Ifantis (1999), *Theory and Reform in the European Union*, Manchester: Manchester University Press.

Clarke, M. (ed.) (1993), *On Security*, London: Brassey's.

Clarke, M. and B. White (eds) (1989), *Understanding Foreign Policy: The Foreign Policy Systems Approach*, Aldershot: Edward Elgar.

Clinton, D. (1991), 'The National Interest: Normative Formations', in R. Little and S. Smith (eds), *Perspectives on World Politics*, London: Routledge, 2nd edition.

Clinton, D. (1993), 'International Obligations: To Whom Are They Owed?', *Review of Politics*, 55:2

Collin, F. (1997), *Social Reality*, London and New York: Routledge.

Collini, S. (ed.) (1992), *Interpretation and Overinterpretation*, Cambridge: Cambridge University Press.

Commission of the European Communities (1995), 'On The Inclusion of Respect for Democratic Principles and Human Rights in Agreements between the Community and Third Countries', *COM* (95) 216 final, 23 May.

Commission of the European Communities (1996), Les defis auxquels sont confrontés les industries européennes lieés à la defense – Contribution en vue d'actions au niveau européenne', Bruxelles: Communication de la Commission au Conseil, au Parlement européen, au Comité economique et social et au Comité des regions, février.

Commission of the European Communities (1997), Mettre en ouvre la stratégie de l'Union en matière d'industries lieés à la défense', Bruxelles: Communication de la

Commission au Conseil, au Parlement européen, au Comité economique et social et au Comité des regions, 12 novembre.

Commission of the European Communities (1999), 'Annual report in conformity with operative provision 8 of the European Union Code of Conduct on Arms Exports' (OJ C 315 of 3 November)

Cooper, R. (1996), *The Post-modern State and the World Order*, London: Demos.

Cosgrove-Sacks, C. (1999), *The European Union and Developing Countries: The Challenge of Globalisation*, London/New York: Macmillan/St. Martin's.

Costa, J. P. and P. Pereira (1999), *The Policy of the Member States of the European Union in the Fields of Arms Exports*, Luxembourg: Working paper, Political Series POLI 112 EN 8-1999, Directorate General for Research, European Parliament.

Council Regulation (EEC) No. 428/89 of 20 Feb. 1989 concerning the export of certain chemical products, OJ L50 of 22 Feb. 1989

Da Costa Pereira, P. S. (1998), *The Use of a Secretariat*, Dordrecht: Martinus Nijhoff.

De la Serre, F. (1988), *The Scope of National Adaptation to EPC*, Dordrecht: Martinus Nijhoff.

De la Serre, F. (1996), *France: The Impact of François Mitterrand*, London: Routledge.

De Schoutheete de Tervarent, P. (1986), *La coopération politique européenne* Brussels : Nathan-Labor (2nd edn.).

De Schoutheete, de Tervarent P. (1988), *The Presidency and the Management of Political Cooperation*, Dordrecht: Martinus Nijhoff.

De Vestel, P. (1993), *L'industrie européenne de l'armement: recherche, développement, technologique, reconversion, rapport réalisé pour le Scientific and Technological Options Assessment Unit (STOA) du Parlement Européenne*, Luxembourg: STOA.

De Vestel, P. (1995), 'Defence Markets and Industries in Europe: Time for Political Decisions?' *WEU Institute for Security Studies, Paris, Chaillot Papers*, No. 21.

Dehousse, F. (1998), 'After Amsterdam: A Report on the Common Foreign and Security Policy of the European Union', *European Journal of International Law*, 9:3.

Dehousse, R. and J. H. H. Weiler (1991), *EPC and the Single Act: From Soft Law to Hard Law?*, London: Macmillan.

Denzin, Norman K. and Yvonna S. Lincoln (1994), 'Major Paradigms and Perspectives', *Handbook of Qualitative Research*, London: Sage.

Deutsch, K. W. (1954), *Political Community at the International Level: Problems of Measurement and Definition*, Garden City: Doubleday.

Deutsch, K. et al. (1957), *Political Community in the Northern Atlantic Area*, Princeton: Princeton University Press.

Dogan, M. (1994), 'The Decline of Nationalisms within Western Europe', *Comparative Politics*, 25:3.

Donnelly, J. (1998), 'Realism: Roots and Renewal', *Review of International Studies*, 24:3 (July).

Dony, M. (1999), *L'Union européenne et le monde après Amsterdam*, Brussels: Editions de l'Université de Bruxelles.

Doty, Roxanne (1993), 'Foreign-Policy As Social Construction – A Post-Positivist Analysis Of United-States Counterinsurgency Policy In The Philippines', *International Studies Quarterly*, 37(3).

Doty, Roxanne (1997), 'Aporia: A Critical Exploration of the Agent–Structure Problematique in International Relations Theory', *European Journal of International Relations*, 3:3.

Duchêne, F. (1972), *Europe's Role in World Peace*, London: Fontana.

Duchêne, F. (1973), *The European Community and the Uncertainties of Interdependence*, London: Macmillan.

Duff, A. (ed.) (1997), *The Treaty of Amsterdam. Text and Commentary*, London: Federal Trust.

Dunne, T. (1995), 'The Social Construction of International Society', *European Journal of International Relations*, 1:3.

Edwards, G. (1992a), 'The Potential and Limits of the CFSP: The Yugoslav Example', in Elfriede Regelsberger, Philippe de Schautheete de Tenavent and Wolfgang Wessels (eds), *Foreign Policy of the European Union. From EFC to CFSP and Beyond*, London: Lynne Rienner Publishers.

Edwards, G. (1992b), *European Political Cooperation Put to the Test*, Dordrecht: Martinus Nijhoff

Edwards, G. (1996), 'National Sovereignty v. Integration? The Council of Ministers', in J. Richardson (ed.), *European Union, Power and Policy-making*, London: Routledge.

Edwards, G. and E. Philippart (1997), *Flexibility and the Treaty of Amsterdam: Europe's New Byzantium?*, Cambridge: Centre for Legal Studies (CELS Occasional Paper No. 3)

Edwards, G. and E. Regelsberger (eds) (1990), *Europe's Global Links. The European Community and Inter-regional Cooperation*, London: Pinter Publishers.

Ekengren, M. (1997), *The Temporality of European Governance*, Houndsmills: Macmillan.

Eliassen, K. (1998), *Foreign and Security Policy in the European Union*, London: Sage Publications.

Emiliou, N. (1996), 'Strategic Export Controls, National Security and the Common Commercial Policy', *European Foreign Affairs Review*, 1:1.

Eriksen, E. O. (1999), 'Towards a Logic of Justification. On the Possibility of Postnational Solidarity', in M. Egeberg and P. Legreid (eds), *Organizing Political Institutions. Essays for Johan P. Olsen*, Oslo: Scandinavian University Press.

Eriksen, E. O. and J Weigård (2000), *Kommunikativ handling og deliberativt demokrati: Jurgen Habermas teori om politikk og samfunn*, Oslo: Fagbokforlaget.

European Commission (1976), 'Opinion on Greek Application for Membership', *EC Bulletin* 2/76

European Commission (1978a), 'Opinion on Portuguese Application for Membership', *EC Bulletin* 5/78

European Commission (1978b), 'Opinion on Spain's Application for Membership', *EC Bulletin* 9/78

European Commission (1997), 'Agenda 2000: For a Stronger and Wider Union', *EU Bulletin Supplement 5/97.*

European Commission (1992), 'Europe and the Challenge of Enlargement', *EC Bulletin Supplement 3/92.*

European Commission (1996), *The Challenges Facing the European Defence-Related Industry: A Contribution for Action at the European Level*, Communication COM (96) 10 final, Brussels, 25 January.

European Commission and European Council (1993), *Code of Conduct concerning Public Access to Council and Commission documents*, 93/730/EC, OJ L 340 of 31 December 1993.

European Council (1993), 'Council Decision on Public Access to Documents of 20 December 1993 93/731/EC', OJ L 340 of 31 December.

European Council (1993a), Council Decision no. 93/728/CFSP on a Pact on Stability in Europe, in OJ L339, 31 December.

European Council (1993b), Conclusions of the Presidency, *SN/180/93*

European Council (1994a), 'Council Regulation (EC) No. 3381/94 of 19 December 1994 Setting Up a Community Regime for the Control of Exports of Dual-Use Goods', OJL 367 of 31 Dec.

European Council (1994b), 'Council Decision of 19 December 1994 on the Joint Action Adopted by the Council of the Basis of Article J.3 of the Treaty on European Union Concerning the Control of Exports of Dual-Use Goods', 94/942/CFS, OJL 367 of 31 December.

European Council (1997a), Letter to Heidi Hautala of 25 July.

European Council (1997b), Letter to Heidi Hautala of 4 November.

European Council (1999b), 'Second Annual Report According to Operative Proviion 8 of the European Union Code of Conduct on Arms Exports', OJC 315 of 3 November.

European Council (2000a), 'Council Regulation (EC) No. 1334/3000 of 22 June 2000 Setting Up a Community Regime for the Control of Exports of Dual Use Goods and Technologies, OJL 159 of 30 June

European Council, Presidency Conclusions (1997) European Council, Luxembourg, 12–13 December.

European Council, Presidency Conclusions (1999) European Council, Helsinki, 11–12 December, http://europa.eu.int/council/off/conclu/dec99/dec99_en.htm.

European Council, Presidency Conclusions (2000) European Council, Santa Maria da Feira, 20 June,http://ue.eu.int/Nowsroom/Loadoc.asp?BID+76BDID+62050&from =&LANG=1.

European Court of Justice (1998), 'Judgement of the Court of First Instance (Fourth chamber), extended composition) of 17 June 1998, Svenska Journalistförbundet v. Council of the European Union, Case T-174/95', *European Court Reports, 1998*, Luxembourg, pp. II-2289ff.

European Court of Justice (1999), 'Judgement of the Court of First Instance (First chamber) of 19 July 1999, Hautala v. Council of the European Union, Case T-14/98', *European Court Reports*, 1999, Luxembourg, pp. II-2389ff.

European Defence Industries Group (1995), *The European Defence Industry. An Agenda Item for the 1996 Intergovernmental Conference.* Memorandum of the European Defence Industries Group.

European Foreign Policy Bulletin online www.iue.it/EFPB/Welcome.html.

European Voice, 23–29 November 2000.

Evans, P., H. Jacobson and R. Putnam (eds) (1993), *Double-Edged Diplomacy: International Bargaining and Domestic Politics*, Berkeley and Los Angeles: University of California Press.

Fairclough, N. (1992), *Discourse and Social Change*, Cambridge: Polity Press.

Featherstone, K. and R. H. Ginsberg (1996), *The United States and the European Union in the 1990s*, Basingstoke: Macmillan.

Feld, W. J. (ed.) (1980), *Western Europe's Global Reach. Regional Cooperation and Worldwide Aspirations*, New York: Pergamon Press.

Fierke, K. and K. E. Jørgensen (eds) (2001), *Constructing International Relations: The Next Generation*, New York: M. E. Sharpe.

Fischer, Joschka (1999), Speech at the General Meeting of the German Society for Foreign Affairs, Berlin, 24 November.

Flockhart, T. (1998), *From Vision to Reality: Implementing Europe's New Security Order*, Boulder: Westview.

Florini, A. (1996), 'The Evolution of International Norms', *International Studies Quarterly*, 40:3.

Flynn, G. (ed.) (1995), *Remaking the Hexagon: The New France in the New Europe*, Boulder, CO: Westview Press.

Forster, A. and W. Wallace (1996), *Common Foreign and Security Policy*, Oxford: Oxford University Press.

Fossum, J. E. (2000), 'Constitution-Making in the European Union', in E. O. Eriksen and J. E. Fossum (eds), *Democracy in the European Union: Integration through Deliberation?*, London: Routledge.

Foucault, M. (1989), *The Archaeology of Knowledge*, London: Routledge.

Franck, C. (1998), *La CIG 1996 et l'Union politique*, Brussels: Bruylant.

Frankel, B. (ed.) (1996), *Realism: Restatements and Renewal*, London: Frank Cass.

Friis, Lykke and Anna Murphy (1999), 'The European Union and central and Eastern Europe'. *journal of Common Market studies*, 37:2.

Garcia, S. (ed.) (1993), *European Identity and the Search for Legitimacy*, London: Pinter Publishers.

Gardner Feldman, L. (1999), *Reconciliation and Legitimacy: Foreign Relations and Enlargement of the European Union*, London: Routledge.

Garton Ash, T. (1996), *Germany's Choice*, New Brunswick: Transaction Publishers.

George, S. (1991), *European Political Cooperation: A World Systems Perspective*, London: Macmillan.

Gerner, D. (1995), *The Evolution of the Study of Foreign Policy*, Englewoods Cliffs: Prentice-Hall.

Giddens, A. (1985), *The Nation-State and Violence*, Cambridge: Polity Press.

Ginsberg, R. (1989), *Foreign Policy Actions of the European Community: The Politics of Scale*, Boulder: Lynne Rienner.

Ginsberg, R. H. (1999). 'Conceptualising the European Union as an International Actor: Narrowing the Theoretical Capability–Expectations Gap', *Journal of Common Market Studies*, 37:3.

Glarbo, K. (1999), 'Wide-Awake Diplomacy: Reconstructing the Common Foreign and Security Policy of the European Union', *Journal of European Public Policy*, 6:4.

Goffman, E. (1959), *The Presentation of Self in Everyday Life*, Harmondsworth: Penguin.

Goldstein, Judith (1989), 'The Impact of Ideas on Trade Policy: The Origins of U.S. Agricultural and Manufacturing Policies', *International Organization*, 43:1.

Goldstein, J. and R. Keohane (1993), *Ideas and Foreign Policy: Beliefs, Institutions and Political Change*, New York: Cornell University Press.

Gomez, Ricardo (1998), 'The EU's Mediterranean Policy: Common Foreign Policy by the Back Door?', in J. Peterson and H. Sjursen (eds.), *A Common Foreign Policy for Europe?* London: Routledge.

Gordon, P. (1997), 'Europe's Uncommon Foreign Policy´, *International Security*, 22:2.

Gourlay, C. and E Remacle (1998), *The 1996 IGC: The Actors and their Interaction*, London: Sage.

Graubard, S. R. (ed.) (1964), *A New Europe?*, Boston: Houghton Mifflin Company.

Greenstein, F. and N. Polsby (eds) (1975), *Handbook of Political Science*, Reading, MA: Addison-Wesley.

Grieco, J. M. (1988), 'Anarchy and the Limits of Cooperation: A Realist Critique of the Newest Liberal Institutionalism', *International Organization*, 42:3.

Grieco, J. M. (1990), *Cooperation among Nations. Europe, America, and Non-tariff Barriers to Trade*, Ithaca: Cornell University Press.

Grieco, J. M. (1993), *Understanding the Problem of International Cooperation*, New York: Columbia University Press.

Grieco, J. M. (1995), 'The Maastricht Treaty, Economic and Monetary Union and the Neorealist Research Programme', *Review of International Studies*, 21.

Grieco, J. M. (1996), *State Interests and Institutional Rule Trajectories: A Neorealist Interpretation of the Maastricht Treaty and European Economic and Monetary Union*, London: Frank Cass.

Grilli, E. R. (1993), *The European Community and the Developing Countries*, Cambridge: Cambridge University Press.

Grønbach-Jensen, C. (1998), "The Scandinavian Tradition of Open Government and the European Union: Problems of Compatibility?", *Journal of European Public Policy*, 5:1.

Guénno, J. M. (1998), *A Foreign Policy in Search of a Polity*, The Hague/London/Boston: Kluwer Law International.

Guénno, J. M. (2000), *Le Modèle européen*, Dunod: IFRI.

Gummet, P. and W. Walker (1993), Nationalism, Internationalism and the European Defence Market, *WEU Institute for Security Studies, Paris, Chaillot Papers, No. 21.*

Haagerup, N. J. and C. Thune (1983), *Denmark: The European Pragmatist*, London: George Allen & Unwin.

Haas, E. B. (1958) *The Uniting of Europe: Political, Social and Economic Forces, 1950–57*, Stanford :Stanford University Press.

Haas, E. B. (1961), 'International Integration: The European and the Universal Process', *International Organization*, 15:3.

Haas, E. B. (1964), *Technocracy, Pluralism and the New Europe*, Boston: Houghton Mifflin Company.

Haas, E. B. (1967), 'The Uniting of Europe and the Uniting of Latin America', *Journal of Common Market Studies*, 5:4.

Haas, E. B. (1970), 'The Study of Regional Integration: Reflections on the Joy and Anguish of Pretheorizing', *International Organization*, 24:4

Haas, E. B. (1975), *The Obsolescence of Regional Integration Theory*, University of California, Berkeley: Institute of International Studies.

Haas, E. and P. Haas (1995), 'Learning to Learn: Improving International Governance', *Global Governance*, 1:3.

Haftendorn, H. and C. Tuschhoff (eds) (1993), *America and Europe in an Era of Change*, Boulder: Westview Press.

Halliday, F. (1994), *Rethinking International Relations*, London: Macmillan.

Hanf, K. and B. Soetendorp (eds) (1998), *Adapting to European Integration. Small States and the European Union*, London and New York: Longman.

Hansen, B. (ed.) (1995), *European Security towards the Year 2000*, Copenhagen: Forlaget Politiske Studier.

Hansen, B. and B. Heurlin (eds) (2000), *The New World Order: Contrasting Theories*, London: Macmillan.

Hansen, L. (1995), 'NATO's New Discourse', in B. Hansen (ed.), *European Security towards the Year 2000*, Copenhagen: Forlaget Politiske Studier.

Hansen, L. (1998), *Western Villains or Balkan Barbarism: Representations and Responsibility in the Debate over Bosnia*, PhD dissertation, Institute of Political Science, University of Copenhagen.

Hassner, Pierre (1987), 'The View From Paris', in Lincoln Gordon (ed.), *The Eroding Empire. Western Relations With Eastern Europe*, Washington, DC: Brookings Institution.

Hautala, H. (1996), *Written Question to the Council*, 14 November, P-3219/96, OJ C 186 of 18 June.

Hautala, H. (1997a), Letter to the Council of 17 June.

Hautala, H. (1997b), Letter to the Council of 1 September.

Hautala, H. (1999), *Hautala Wins the Case for More Transparency*, Press Release, 19 July, Brussels.

Heisbourg, F. (2000), *European Defence: Making It Work*, Paris: WEU Institute for Security Studies, Chaillot Paper No. 42.

Held, D. (1993), 'Democracy: From City-States to a Cosmopolitan Order?', in D. Held (ed.), *Prospects for Democracy: North, South, East, West,*Cambridge: Polity.

Hellmann, G. (1997), 'The Sirens of Power and German Foreign Policy: Who is Listening?' *German Politics*, 6:2.

Helsinki European Council (1999), Presidency Conclusions, 10–11 December.

Hermann, C. (1990), 'Changing Course: When Governments Choose to Redirect Foreign Policy', *International Studies Quarterly*, 34:1.

Hill, C. (1974), 'The Credentials of Foreign Policy Analysis', *Millennium*, 3:2.

Hill, C. (ed.) (1983), 'National Interests – the Insuperable Obstacles?' in Christopher Hill (ed.), *National Foreign Policies and European Political Cooperation*, London: George Allen & Unwin.

Hill, C. (1988), *Research into EPC: Tasks for the Future*, Dordrecht: Martinus Nijhoff.

Hill, C. (1990), *European Foreign Policy: Power Bloc, Civilian Model – or Flop?*, Boulder, San Francisco and Oxford: Westview Press.

Hill, C. (1992), *The Foreign Policy of the European Community: Dream or Reality?*, Englewood Cliffs, NJ: Prentice-Hall.

Hill, C. (1993a), 'The Capability–Expectations Gap, or Conceptualizing Europe's International Role', *Journal of Common Market Studies*, 31:3.

Hill, C. (1993b), 'Shaping a Federal Foreign Policy for Europe', in Brian Hocking (ed.), *Managing Foreign Relations in Federal States*, (Leicester: Leicester University Press.

Hill, C. (ed.) (1996a), *The Actors in Europe's Foreign Policy*, London: Routledge

Hill, C. (1996b), 'United Kingdom: Sharpening Contradictions', in Christopher Hill (ed.), *The Actors in Europe's Foreign Policy*, London: Routledge.

Hill, C. (1997), *Paradoxes of European Foreign Policy. Convergence, Divergence and Dialectics: National Foreign Policies and the CFSP*, EUI Working Paper 97/66, Florence: European University Institute.

Hill, C. (1998a), *Convergence, Divergence and Dialectics: National Foreign Policies and the CFSP*, The Hague: Kluwer Law International.

Hill, C. (1998b), 'Closing the Capabilities–Expectations Gap?', in J. Peterson and H. Sjursen (eds), *A Common Foreign Policy for Europe? Competing Visions of the CFSP*, London: Routledge.

Hill, Christopher and William Wallace (1996), 'Introduction: Actors and Actions', in Christopher Hill (ed.), *The Actors in Europe's Foreign Policy*, London: Routledge.

Hilsman, R. (1990), *The Politics of Policy Making in Defence and Foreign Policy*, Englewood Cliffs: Prentice-Hall.

Hix, Simon (1998), 'The Study of the European Union II: The "New Governance" Agenda and its Rival' , *Journal of European Public Policy*, 5:1

Hocking, B. (ed.) (1993), *Managing Foreign Relations in Federal States*, Leicester: Leicester University Press.

Hocking, B. (ed.) (1999), *Foreign Ministries: Change and Adaptation*, Houndsmills: Macmillan.

Hocking, B. and D. Spence, (eds) (2000), *EU Member State Foreign Ministries. Change and Adaptation*, Macmillan: London.

Hoffmann, S. (1964a), 'Europe's Identity Crisis: Between the Past and America', *Daedalus*, 93:4.

Hoffmann, S. (1964b), 'The European Process at Atlantic Cross Purposes', *Journal of Common Market Studies*, 3:2.

Hoffmann, S. (1966), 'Obstinate or Obsolete? The Fate of the Nation-State and the Case of Western Europe', *Daedalus*, 95:3.

Hoffmann, S. (1991), 'French Dilemmas and Strategies in the New Europe', in R. Keohane, J. Nye and S. Hoffmann, *After the Cold War: International Institutions and State Strategies in Europe, 1989–1991*, Cambridge, MA: Harvard University Press.

Hoffmann, S. (1994), 'Europe's Identity Crisis Revisited', *Daedalus*, 123:2

Hoffman, S. (1995), *The European Sisyphus: Essays on Europe, 1964–1994*, Oxford: Westview Press.

Hoffmann, S. (2000), 'Towards a Common Foreign and Security Policy?', *Journal of Common Market Studies*, 38:2.

Holland, M. (1987), 'Three Approaches for Understanding European Political Co-operation: A Case-Study of EC–South African Policy', *Journal of Common Market Studies*, 25:4.

Holland, M. (1988), *The European Community and South Africa. European Political Co-operation Under Strain*, London: Pinter Publishers.

Holland, M. (ed.) (1991), *The Future of European Political Cooperation. Essays on Theory and Practice*, London: Macmillan.

Holland, M. (1994), *European Integration: From community to Union*, London: Pinter.

Holland, M. (1995), *European Union Common Foreign Policy. From EPC to CFSP Joint Action and South Africa*, London: Macmillan.

Holland, M. (ed.) (1997), *Common Foreign and Security Policy. The Record and Reforms*, London and Washington, DC: Pinter.

Hollis, M. and S. Smith (1990), *Explaining and Understanding International Relations*, Oxford: Oxford University Press

Holm, U. (1993), *Det franske Europa*, Aarhus: Aarhus Universitetsforlag

Holsti, K. (1976b), 'Toward a Theory of Foreign Policy: Making the Case for Role Analysis', in Stephen Walker (ed.), *Role Theory and Foreign Policy Analysis*, Durham, NC: Duke University Press, 1st edn.

Holsti, K. (1987a), 'National Role Conceptions in the Study of Foreign Policy' (orig. 1970), in S. Walker (ed.), *Role Theory and Foreign Policy Analysis*, Durham, NC: Duke University Press.

House of Commons (2001), *The Six-Nation Framework Agreement*, Defence Committee, First Report, Session 2000–2001, London, 14 February (available via www.parliament.uk).

Howorth, J. (2001), *European Integration and Defence: The Ultimate Challenge?*, Paris: WEU Institute for Security Studies, Chaillot Paper No. 43.

Hudson, V. and C. Vore (1995), 'Foreign Policy Analysis Yesterday, Today, and Tomorrow', *Mershon International Studies Review*, 39:2.

Hughes, R. (1991), *The Shock of the New*, New York: McGraw Hill.

Hurd, D. (1981), 'Political Co-operation', *International Affairs*, 57:3.

Hyde-Price, A. (2000), *Germany and European Order: Enlarging NATO and the EU* Manchester: Manchester University Press.

Ifestos, P. (1987), *European Political Cooperation. Towards a Framework of Supranational Diplomacy?*, Aldershot: Avebury.

Ignatieff, M. (1998), 'Identity Parades', *Prospect*, April.

Jackson, J. (ed.) (1972), *Role*, Cambridge: Cambridge University Press.

Jackson Preece, J. (1997), 'National Minority Rights vs. State Sovereignty in Europe: Changing Norms in International Relations?', *Nations and Nationalism*, 3:3.

Jakobsen, P. (1995), 'Multilateralism Matters, But How? The Impact of Multilateralism on Great Power Policy towards the Break-up of Yugoslavia', *Cooperation and Conflict*, 30:4.

Jeppeson, Ronald L., Alexander Wendt and Peter J. Katzenstein (1996), 'Norms, Identity and Culture in National Security', in P. Katzenstein (ed.), *Culture of National Security*, New York: Columbia University Press.

Jervis, R. (1983), 'Deterrence and Perception', *International Security*, 7:3.

Jönsson, C. (1984), 'Perceptions in International Politics and National Security', in By Bo Huldt and Atis Lejins (eds), *Security in the North*, Stockholm: Swedish Institute of International Affairs, Conference Papers 5.

Jönsson, C. and U. Westerlund (1982), 'Role Theory in Foreign Policy Analysis', in C. Jönsson (ed.), *Cognitive Dynamics and International Politics*, London: Frances Pinter.

Jönsson, C., S. Tägil and G. Törnqvist (2000), *Organizing European Space*, London: Sage Publications.

Jopp, M. and R. Warjovaara (eds) (1998), *Approaching the Northern Dimension of CFSP*, Helsinki and Bonn: Ulkopoliittinen instituutti and Institut für Europäische Politik.

Jørgensen, K. E. (1993), 'EC External Relations as a Theoretical Challenge: Theories, Concepts and Trends', in Frank R. Pfetsch (ed.), *International Relations and Pan-Europe. Theoretical Approaches and Empirical Case Studies*, Münster: LIT Verlag.

Jørgensen, K. E. (1996), *Det udenrigspolitiske samarbejde i Den Europæiske Union*, Copenhagen: Systime.

Jørgensen, K. E. (1997a), 'PoCo: The Diplomatic Republic of Europe', in K. E. Jørgensen (ed.), *Reflective Approaches to European Governance*, Basingstoke: Macmillan.

Jørgensen, K. E. (ed.) (1997b), *Reflective Approaches to European Governance*, London: Macmillan.

Jørgensen, K. E. (1998), 'The European Union's Performance in World Politics – How to Measure Success?', in Jan Zielonka (ed.), *Paradoxes of European Foreign Policy*, The Hague: Kluwer Law International.

Jørgensen, K. E. (1999), 'Modern European Diplomacy: A Reearch Agenda', *Journal of International Relations and Development*, 2(1).

Jørgensen, K. E. (2001), 'Four Levels and a Discipline', in K. M. Fierke and K. E. Jørgensen (eds), *Constructing International Relations: The Next Generation*, New York: M. E. Sharpe.

Jørgensen, K. E., T. Christiansen and A. Wiener (1999), 'The Social Construction of Europe', *Journal of European Public Policy*, 6:4

Jørgensen, M. W. and Louise Phillips (2002), *Discourse Analysis as Theory and Method*, London: Sage Publications and New Delhi: Thousand Oaks.

Katzenstein, P. (ed.) (1996), *The Culture of National Security: Norms and Identity in World Politics*, New York: Columbia University Press.

Katzenstein, P. (ed.) (1997), *Tamed Power: Germany in Europe*, Ithaca and London: Cornell University Press.

Keatinge, Patrick (1997a), 'Security and Defence', in Ben Tonra (ed.), *Amsterdam: What the Treaty Means*, Dublin: Institute of European Affairs.

Keatinge, Patrick (1997b), 'Strengthening the Foreign Policy Process', in Ben Tonra (ed.), *Amsterdam: What the Treaty Means*, Dublin: Institute of European Affairs.

Keohane, R. (1984), *After Hegemony. Cooperation and Discord in the World Political Economy*, Princeton: Princeton University Press.

Keohane, R. (ed.) (1986a), Realism Neorealism and the Study of World Politics in Robert O. Keohane (eds.) *Neorealism and its Critics*, New York: Columbia University Press

Keohane, R. (1988), 'International Institutions: Two Approaches', *International Studies Quarterly*, 32:4.

Keohane, R. (1989), *International Institutions and State Power. Essays in International Relations Theory*, Boulder: Westview Press.

Keohane, R. (1989a), 'Neoliberalism Institutionalism: A Perspective on World Politics', in Robert O. Keohane, *International Institutions and State Power. Essays in International Relations Theory*, Boulder: Westview Press.

Keohane, R. (1989b), 'International Institutions: Two Approaches', in Robert O. Keohane, *International Institutions and State Power. Essays in International Relations Theory*, Boulder: Westview Press.

Keohane, R. (1989c) 'Reciprocity in International Relations', in Robert O. Keohane, *International Institutions and State Power. Essays in International Relations Theory*, Boulder: Westview Press.

Keohane, R. (1990), 'Multilateralism: An Agenda for Research', *International Journal*, 45:4.

Keohane, R. (1993a), 'Institutional Theory and the Realist Challenge After the Cold War', in David A. Baldwin (ed.), *Neorealism and Neoliberalism. The Contemporary Debate*, New York: Columbia University Press.

Keohane, R. (1993b), 'The Diplomacy of Structural change: Multilateral Institutions and State Strategies', in Helga Haftendom and Christian Tuschhoff (eds), *America and Europe in and Era of Change*, Boulder: Westview Press.

Keohane R. (1993c), 'Sovereignty, Interdependence, and International Institutions', in Linda B. Miller and Michael Joseph Smith (eds), *Ideas and Ideals. Essays on Politics in Honor of Stanley Hoffmann*, Boulder: Westview Press.

Keohane, R. and S. Hoffmann (1990), 'European Community Politics and Institutional Change', in William Wallace (ed.), *Dynamics of European Integration*, London: Pinter.

Keohane, R. and J. Nye (1974), 'Transgovernmental relations and International Organization', *World Politics*, 27:1.

Keohane, R. and J. Nye (1977), *Power and Interdependence*, Boston: Little, Brown

Keohane, R. and J. S. Nye (1989), *Power and Interdependence* (2nd en), Glenview: Scott, Foresman and Company.

Keohane, R. and Joseph S. Nye (1993), 'Introduction: The End of the Cold War in Europe', in Robert O. Keohane, Joseph S. Nye and Stanley Hoffman (eds), *After the Cold War. International Institutions and State Strategies in Europe, 1989–1991*, Cambridge, MA: Harvard University Press.

Keohane, R. and L. Martin (1995), 'The Promise of Institutionalist Theory', *International Security*, 20:1.

Keohane, R., J. Nye and S. Hoffmann (1993), *After the Cold War: International Institutions and State Strategies in Europe, 1989–1991*, Cambridge, MA: Harvard University Press

Keukeleire, S. (1998), *Het Buitenlands Beleid van de Europese Unie*, Deventer: Kluwer.

King, G., R. Keohane and S. Verba (1994), *Designing Social Inquiry: Scientific Influence in Qualitative Research*, Princeton: Princeton University Press.

Kirchner, E. J. (1989), 'Has the Single European Act Opened the Door for a European Security Policy?', *Journal of European Integration*, 13:1.

Kirste, K. and H. Maull (1996), 'Zivilmacht und Rolkentheorie', *Zeitschrift für Internationale Beziehungen*, 3:2 (December).

Kostecki, W. (1996), *Europe after the Cold War. The Security Complex Theory*, Warsaw: Institute of Political Studies, Polish Academy of Sciences.

Kowert, Paul and Jeffrey Legro (1996), 'Norms, Identity, and Their Limits: A Theoretical Reprise', in Peter J. Katzenstein (ed.), *The Culture of National Security: Norms and Identity in World Politics*, New York: University of Columbia Press.

Krasner, S. (ed.) (1981), 'International Regimes', Special Issue of *International Organization*, 36:2

Krasner, S. (1988), 'Sovereignty – An Institutional Perspective', *Comparative Political Studies*, 21:1

Krasner, S. (1995), 'Compromising Westphalia', *International Security*, 20:3

Krasner, S. (1999), 'Logic of Consequences and Appropriateness in the International System', in M. Egeberg and P. Laegreid (eds), *Organizing Political Institutions. Essay for Johan P. Olsen*, Oslo: Scandinavian University Press.

Kratochwil, F. (1993), 'Norms versus Numbers: Multilateralism and the Rationalist and Reflexivist Approaches to Institutions – A Unilateral Plea for communicative Rationality', in John Gerard Ruggie (ed.), *Multilateralism Matters. The Theory and Praxis of an Institutional Form*, New York: Columbia University Press.

Kratochwil, F. and J. G. Ruggie (1986), 'International Organization: A State of the Art on an Art of the State', *International Organization*, 40:4.

Krenzler, H.-G. and H. C. Schneider (1997), 'The Question of Consistency', in E. Regelsberger, P. de Schoutheete de Tervarent and W. Wessels (eds), *Foreign Policy of the European Union. From EPC to CFSP and Beyond*, Boulder and London: Lynne Rienner.

Laclau, E. and C. Mouffe (1985), *Hegemony and Socialist Strategy – Towards a Radical Democratic Politics*, London and New York: Verso.

Larsen, H. (1997a), *Foreign Policy and Discourse Analysis: France, Britain and Europe*, London: Routledge.

Larsen, H. (1997b), 'British Discourses on Europe: Sovereignty of Parliament, Instrumentality and the Non-mythical Europe', in Knud Erik Jørgensen (ed.), *Reflective Approaches to European Governance*, Basingstoke: Macmillan.

Larsen, H. (1999), 'British and Danish Policies towards Europe in the 1990s: A Discourse Approach', *European Journal of International Relations*, 5:4.

Larsen, Henrik (2000a), 'Europe's Role in the World: The Discourse', in Birthe Hansen and Bertel Heurlin (eds), *The New World Order: Contrasting Theories*, London: Macmillan.

Larsen, Henrik (2000b), 'The Concept of Security in the European Union After the Cold War', *Australian Journal of International Affairs*, 54:3.

Laurent, P. H. and M. Maresceau (eds) (1998), *The State of the European Union, Vol. 4. Deepening and Widening*, London: Boulder.

Le Prestre, P. (ed.) (1997), *Role Quests in the Post-Cold War Era: Foreign Policies in Transition*, Montreal: McGill Queen's.

Legro, J. W. (1997), 'Which Norms Matter? Revisiting the "Failure" of Internationalism', *International Organization*, 51:1.

Lenzi, G. (ed.) (1998), *L'UEO a cinquante ans*, Paris: Institut d'Etudes de Sécurité de l'Union de l'Europe occidentale.

Lichbach, M. and A. Zuckerman (1997), *Comparative Politics: Rationality, Culture and Structure*, Cambridge: Cambridge University Press.

Light, M. (1994), *Foreign Policy Analysis*, London: Pinter.

Lincoln, G. (ed.) (1987), *The Eroding Empire. Western Relations With Eastern Europe*, Washington, DC: Brookings Institution.

Lindberg, L. N. (1963), *Political Dynamics of European Economic Integration*, Oxford: Oxford University Press.

Lindberg, L. N. (1968), 'Integration as a Source of Stress on the European Community System', in Joseph S. Nye (ed.), *International Regionalism. Readings*, Boston: Little, Brown and Company.

Lindberg, L. N. and S. A. Scheingold (1970), *Europe's Would-Be Polity. Patterns of Change in the European Community*, Englewood Cliffs: Prentice-Hall.

Lindberg, L. N. and S. A. Scheingold (eds) (1971), *Regional Integration. Theory and Research*, Cambridge, MA: Harvard University Press.

Lister, M. (1997), *The European Union and the South*, London: Routledge.

Long, D. (1997), 'Multilateralism in the CFSP', in M. Holland (ed.), *Common Foreign and Security Policy: The record and Reforms*, London: Pinter.

Lorenz, Pierre-Louis (1996), 'Luxembourg: New commitments, New Assertiveness', in Christopher Hill (ed.), *The Actors in Europe's Foreign Policy*, London: Routledge.

Lose, Lars G. (2001), 'Communicative Action and Diplomacy', in K. Fierke and K. E. Jørgensen (eds.), *Constructing International Relations. A New Generation*, New York: Armonk.

Lucarelli, Sonia (1998), *Western Europe and the Breakup of Yugoslavia. A Political Failure in Search of a Scholarly Explanation*, PhD. dissertation Florence: European University Institute.

Lundgren, Å. (1998) *Europeisk identitetspolitik. EU's demokratibistånd till Poland och Turkiet* PhD dissertation, Uppsala.

Lundquist, L. (1987), *Implementation Steering: An Actor-Structure Approach*, Lund: Studentlitteratur

Manners, Ian and Richard Whitman (2000), *The Foreign Policies of the European Union Member States*, Manchester: Manchester University Press.

March, J. G. and J. P. Olsen (1998a), 'The Institutional Dynamics of International Political Orders', Oslo: Arena Working Paper No. 5.

March, J. G. and J. P. Olsen (1998b), 'The Institutional Dynamics of International Political Orders', *International Organization*, 52:4

Maull, H., G. Segal and J. Wanandi (eds) (1998), *Europe and the Asia Pacific*, London and
New York: Routledge.

Maury, J.-P. (1996), *La construction européenne, la sécurité et la défense*, Paris: Presses
universitaires de France.

McLaren, L. M. (2000), 'Turkey's Eventual Membership of the EU: Turkish Elite Perspectives on the Issue', *Journal of Common Market Studies*, 38:1.

Mearsheimer, J. (1990), 'Back to the Future: Instability in Europe after the Cold War',
International Security, 14:4.

Mearsheimer, J. (1994), 'The False Promise of International Institutions', *International
Security*, 19:3 (Winter).

Mearsheimer, J. (1995), 'The False Promise of International Institutions', *International
Security*, 19:3.

Michelmann, H. J. and P. Soldatos (eds) (1994), *European Integration. Theories and
Approaches*, Lanham, MD: University Press of America.

Miller, L. and M. J. Smith (eds) (1993), *Ideas and Ideals. Essays on Politics in Honor of
Stanley Hoffmann*, Boulder: Westview Press.

Milliken, J. (1999), 'The Study of Discourse in International Relations: A Critique of
Research and Research Methods', *European Journal of International Relations*, 5:2.

Milward, A. (1992), *The European Rescue of the Nation-State*, Berkeley: University of California Press.

Missiroli, A. (1998), 'Coopération renforcée et flexibilité dans le deuxiéme pilier: un par-
cours d'obstacles?', in G. Lenzi (ed.), *L'UEO a cinquante ans*, Paris: Institut d'Etudes
de Sécurité de l'Union de l'Europe occidentale.

Missiroli, A. (2000), *CFSP, Defence and Flexibility*, Paris: WEU Institute for Security
Studies, Chaillot Paper No. 38.

Mitrany, D. (1943 [1946]), *A Working Peace System: An Argument for the Functional Development of International Organization*, Chicago: Quadrangle Books (1st edition,
London 1943).

Moisi, D. (1998), 'The Trouble with France', *Foreign Affairs*, 77:3.

Monar, J. (1997a), "The European Union's Foreign Affairs System After the Treaty of
Amsterdam: A Strengthened Capacity for External Action?", *European Foreign
Affairs Review*, 2:3.

Monar, J. (1997b), 'The Financial Dimension of the CFSP', in Martin Holland (ed.),
Common Foreign and Security Policy. The Record and Reforms, London: Pinter.

Monar, J. (1997c), 'Political dialogue with Third Countries and Regional Political
Groupings: The Fifteen as an Attractive Interlocutor', in Elfriede Regelsberger,
Philippe de Schoutheete de Tervarent and Wolfgang Wessels (eds), *Foreign Policy
of the European Union. From EPC to CFSP and Beyond*, London: Lynne Rienner
Publishers.

Moravcsik, A. (1991), 'Negotiating the Single European Act: National Interests and Conventional Statecraft in the European Community', *International Organization*, 45:1.

Moravcsik, A. (1993), 'Preferences and Power in the European Community: A Liberal
Intergovernmentalist Approach', *Journal of Common Market Studies*, 31:4.

Moravcsik, A. (1998), *The Choice for Europe: Social Purpose and State Power from Messina
to Maastricht*, London: UCL Press.

Morgenthau, H. (1948), *Politics among Nations: The Struggle for Power and Peace*, New
York: Knopf.

Morse, E. (1970), 'The Transformation of Foreign Policies: Modernization, Interdependence and Externalization', World Politics, 22:3.

Mouritzen, Hans (1991), 'Tension between the Strong and the Strategies of the Weak', Journal of Peace Research, 28:2.

Mouritzen, Hans (1993), 'The Two Munsterknaben and the Naughty Boy: Sweden, Finland and Denmark in the process of European Integration', Cooperation and Conflict, 28:4.

Müller, Harald (2001), 'International Relations as Communicative Action: A Critique of Utilitarian Theories of Action', in K. Fierke and K. E. Jørgensen (eds.), Constructing International Relations: The Next Generation, New York: M. E. Sharpe.

Neak, L., J. Hey, and P. Haney (eds) (1995), Foreign Policy Analysis: Continuity and Change in its Second Generation, Englewood cliffs: Prentice-Hall.

Nelsen, B. F. and A. C. G. Stubb (eds) (1998), The European Union. Readings on the Theory and Practice of European Integration (2nd edition), Boulder-: Lynne Rienner.

Neumann, I. (1998), Uses of the Other: 'The East' in European Identity Formation, Manchester: Manchester University Press.

Neumann, I. and O. Wæver (1997), The Future of International Relations: Masters in the Making, London and New York: Routledge.

Niblett, R. and W. Wallace (2001), Rethinking European Order: West European Responses, 1989–1997, Basingstoke: Palgrave.

Nørgaard, O., T. Pedersen and N. Petersen (eds) (1993), The European Community in World Politics, London: Pinter.

Norris, C. (1982), Deconstruction: Theory and Practice, London: Methuen.

Nugent, N. (2000), 'EU Enlargement and the "Cyprus Problem"', Journal of Common Market Studies, 38:1.

Nuttall, S. (1992), European Political Cooperation, Oxford: Clarendon Press.

Nuttall, S. (1997), 'Two Decades of EPC Performance', in E. Regelsberger, P. de schoutheete de Tervarent and W. Wessels (eds), Foreign Policy of the European Union. From EPC to CFSP and Beyond, Boulder and London: Lynne Rienner.

Nye, J. (ed.) (1968), International Regionalism. Readings, Boston: Little, Brown and Company.

Nye, J. (1975), Transnational and Transgovernmental Relations, London: Croom Helm.

Nye, J. and R. Keohane (1977), Power and Interdependence, Boston: Little Brown and Company.

Øhrgaard, J. C. (1997), 'Less than Supranational, More than Intergovernmental: European Political Cooperation and the Dynamics of Intergovernmental Integration', Millennium: Journal of International Studies, 26:1.

O'Neill, Michael (1996), The Politics of European integration, London: Routledge.

Onuf, N. (1989), World of Our Making: Rules and Rule in Social Theory and International Relations, Columbia, SC: University of South Carolina Press.

Owen, D. (1995), Balkan Odyssey, London: Victor Galancz.

Pedersen, T. (1998), Germany, France and the Integration of Europe: A Realist Interpretation, London: Pinter.

Peterson, J. (1995), 'Decision-Making in the European Union', Journal of European Public Policy, 2:1.

Peterson, J. (1998), 'Introduction: The European Union as a Global Actor', in John Peterson and Helene Sjursen (eds), A Common Foreign Policy for Europe? Competing Visions of the CFSP, London: Routledge.

Peterson, J. and H. Sjursen (eds) (1998), A Common Foreign Policy for Europe? Competing Visions of the CFSP, London: Routledge.

Petersen, N. (1998), 'National Strategies in the Integration Dilemma: An Adaptation Approach', *Journal of Common Market Studies*, 36:1.

Petite, M. (1997), "Le traité d'Amsterdam: ambition et réalisme", *Revue du Marché unique européen*.

Pfetsch, F. R. (ed.) (1993), *International Relations and Pan-Europe. Theoretical Approaches and Empirical Case Studies*, Münster: LIT Verlag.

Pfetsch, F. R. (1994), 'Tensions in Sovereigny: Foreign Policies of EC Members Compared', in W. Carsnaes and S. Smith (eds), *European Foreign Policy. The EC and Changing Perspectives in Europe*, London: Sage.

Piening, Christopher (1997), *Global Europe: The European Union in World Affairs*, Boulder: Lynne Rienner Publishing.

Pijpers, A. (1983), 'the Netherlands: How to keep the spirit of Fouchet in the Bottle', in Christopher Hill (ed.), *National Foreign Policies and European Political Cooperation*, London: George Allen & Unwin.

Pijpers, A. (1990), *The Vicissitudes of European Political Cooperation. Towards a Realist Interpretation of the EC's Collective Diplomacy*, Gravenhage: Gegevenes Koninklijke Bibliothek.

Pijpers, A. (1991), 'European Political Cooperation and the Realist Paradigm', in Martin Holland (ed.), *The Future of European Political Cooperation. Essays on Theory and Practice*, London: Macmillan.

Pijpers, A. (ed.) (1992), *The European Community at the Crossroads. Major Issues and Priorities for the EC Presidency*, Dordrecht: Martinus Nijhoff.

Pijpers, A. (1996), 'The Netherlands: The Weakening Pull of Atlanticism', in Christopher Hill (ed.), *The Actors in Europe's Foreign Policy*, London: Routledge.

Pijpers, A., E. Regelsberger and W. Wessels (eds) (1988), *European Political Cooperation in the 1980s. A Common Foreign Policy for Western Europe?*, Dordrecht: Martinus Nijhoff.

Price, Richard and Christian Reus-Smit (1998), 'Dangerous Liaisons? Critical International Theory and Constrictivism', *European Journal of International Relations*, 4(3) (September).

Pridham, G. (1994), *The International Dimension of Democratisation: Theory, Practice and Inter-regional Comparisons*, Leicester: Leicester University Press.

Pritzel, I. (1998), *National Identity and Foreign Policy: Nationalism and Leadership in Poland, Russia and Ukraine*, Cambridge: Cambridge University Press.

Putnam, R. (1993), 'Diplomacy and Politics: The Logic of Two-Level Games', in P. Evans, H. Jacobson and R. Putnam (eds), *Double-Edged Diplomacy: International bargaining and Domestic Politics*, Berkeley and Los Angeles: University of California Press.

Quermonne, J. L. (1988), *Le système politique de l'Union européenne*, Paris: Montchrestien.

Ravenhill, J. (1985) *Collective Clientilism. The Lomé Conventions and North–South Relations*, New York: Columbia University Press

Reflection Group (1995), *Report from the Reflection Group* SN 520/95 (REFLEX21), Brussels: Sectetariat-General of the Council of Ministers.

Regelsberger, E. (1988), 'EPC in the 1980s: Reaching Another Plateau?', in Alfred Pijpers, Elfriede Regelsberger and Wolfgang Wessels (eds), *European Political Cooperation in the 1980s. A Common Foreign Policy for Western Europe?*, Dordrecht: Martinus Nijhoff.

Regelsberger, E. (1990), 'The Dialogue of the EC/Twelve with Other Regional Groups: A New European Identity in the International System?', in Geoffrey Edwards and

Elfrieck Regelsberger (eds), *Europe's Global Links. The European Community and the Inter-Regional cooperation*, London: Pinter Publishers.

Regelsberger, E. (1997), 'The Institutional Setup and Functioning of EPC/CFSP', in Elfriede Regelsberger, Philippe de Schoutheete de Tervarent and Wolfgang Wessels (eds), *Foreign Policy of the European Union. From EPC to CFSP and Beyond*, London: Lynne Rienner Publishers.

Regelsberger, E. and W. Wessels (1996), 'The CFSP Institutions and Procedures: A Third Way for the Second Pillar', *European Foreign Affairs Review*, 1:1.

Regelsberger, E., P. de Schoutheete de Tervarent and W. Wessels (eds) (1997), *Foreign Policy of the European Union. From EPC to CFSP and Beyond*, Boulder and London: Lynne Rienner.

Remacle, E. (1992), *La politique étrangère européenne de Maastricht à la Yougoslavie* Brusselles: GRIP.

Remacle, E. (1997), 'La politique étrangère de l'Union ay-delà de la PESC', in M. Telò and P. Magnette (eds), *De Maastricht à Amsterdam. L'Europe et son nouveau traitè*, Brussels: Complexe.

Remacle, E. and R. Seidelmann (eds.) (1998), *Pan-European Security Redefined* Baden-Baden: Nomos.

Rhodes, C. and S. Mazey (eds) (1995), *The State of the European Union, Vol. 3, Building a European Polity?*, Boulder and London: Lynne Rienner and Longman.

Richardson, J. (ed.) (1996), *European Union: Power and Policy-Making*, London and New York: Routledge.

Risse, T. (1998), 'Let's talk! Insights from the German Debate on Communicative Action and International Relations', Paper presented at the Third Pan-European International Relations Conference, Vienna.

Rittberger, V. (ed.) (1993), *Regime Theory and International Relations*, Oxford: Clarendon Press.

Rose, G. (1998), 'Neoclassical Realism and Theories of Foreign Policy', *World Politics*, 51:1 (October).

Rosenau, J. (1990), *Turbulence in World Politics*, Princeton: Princeton University Press.

Rosenau, J. (1992), *Governance, Order and Change in World Politics*, Cambridge: Cambridge University Press.

Rosenau, J. N. (1970), *The Adaptation of National Societies: A Theory of Political Systems Behaviour and Transformation*, New York: McCaleb-Seiler.

Rosenau, J. N. and M. Durfee (1995), *Thinking Theory Thoroughly*, Boulder: Westview Press.

Ross, Marc H. (1997), 'Culture and Identity in Comparative Political Analysis', in M. Lichbach and A. Zuckerman (eds), *Comparative Politics: Rationality, Culture, and Structure*, Cambridge: Cambridge University Press.

Ruggie, J. G. (1991), 'Embedded Liberalism Revisited', in Emanuel Adler and Beverly Crawford (eds.), *Progress in Postwar International Relations*, New York: Columbia University Press.

Ruggie, J. G. (ed.) (1993), *Multilateralism Matters. The Theory and Praxis of an Institutional Form*, New York: Columbia University Press

Ruggie, J. G. (1998a), *Constructing the World Polity. Essays on International Institutionalization*, London: Routledge.

Ruggie, J. G. (1998b), 'What makes the World Hang Together? Neo-utilitarianism and the Social Constructivist Challenge', *International Organization*, 52:4

Rummel, R. (ed.) (1990), *The Evolution of Europe as an International Actor: Western Europe's New Assertiveness*, Boulder, San Francisco and Oxford: Westview Press.

Rummel, R. (ed.) (1992), *Toward Political Union. Planning a Common Foreign and Security Policy in the European Community*, Boulder: Westview Press.

Rummel, R. (1996), 'Germany's Role in the CFSP: "Normalität" or "Sonderweg"?', in Christopher Hill (ed.), *The Actors in Europe's Foreign Policy*, London: Routledge.

Rummel, R. and W. Wessels (1983), 'Federal Republic of Germany: New Responsibilities, Old Constraints', in Christopher Hill (ed.), *National Foreign Policies and European Political Cooperation*, London: George Allen & Unwin.

Said, E. (1991), *Orientalism*, London: Penguin.

Said, E. W. (1995), 'East isn't East. The Impending End of the Age of Orientalism', *Times Literary Supplement*, 3 February 1995.

Salmon, T. C. (1992), 'Testing Times for European Political Cooperation: The Gulf and Yugoslavia, 1990–1992', *International Affairs*, 68:2

Sandholtz, W. and A. Stone Sweet (eds) (1998), *European Integration and Supranational Governance*, Oxford: Oxford University Press.

Schaber, T. and C. Ulbert (1994), 'Relexivität in den Internationalen Beziehungen: Literaturbericht zum Beitrag kognitiver, reflexiver und interpretativer Ansätze zur dritten Theoriedebatte', *Zeitschrift für Internationale Beziehunsen*, 1:1.

Schiffauer, P. and G. Jeffrey-Jones (1999), The Principle of Transparency: A Comparative Overview on the Legislation of the EU Member States and the Rules applied by Community Institutions *Working Papers, Political Series, POLI 106 EN, European Parliament, Directorate General for Research.*

Schmitt, Burkhard (2000), *From Co-operation to Integration: Defence and Aerospace Industries in Europe.* Chaillot Paper No. 40, Western European Union Institute for Secutiry Studies, Paris.

Schmitter, P. C. (1969), 'Three Neo-functional Hypotheses About International Integration', *International Organization*, 23:3.

Schmitter, P. C. (1992), Interests, Powers and Functions: Emergent Properties and Unintended Consequences in the European Polity *Stanford: Stanford University and Centre for Advances Studies in Behavioural Sciences, Working Paper.*

Schröder, G. (1999), 'Speech to the French National Assembly', Paris, 30 November.

Schweller, R. (1996), 'Neorealism's Status-Quo Bias: What Security Dilemma?', in B. Frankel (ed.), *Realism: Restatements and Renewal*, London: Frank Cass.

Schweller, R. and D. Priess (1997), 'A Tale of Two Realisms: Expanding the Institutions debate', *Marshon International Studies review*, 41 (May).

Searing, D. (1991), 'Roles, Rules, and Rationality in the New Institutionalism', *American Political Science Review*, 85:4.

Searle, J. R. (1995), *The Construction of Social Reality*, New York: The Free Press.

Sidjanski, D. (1992), *L'avenir fédéraliste de l'Europe: la Communauté européenne, des origines au traité de Maastricht*, Genèva: Publications de l'Institut universitaire d'études européennes, 2nd Paris: Presses universitaires de France.

Singer, M. and A. Wildavsky (1996), *The Real World Order: Zones of Peace, Zones of Turmoil*, revised edition, Chatham, NJ: Chatham house Publishers.

Sjursen, H. (1997), 'Enlarging the Union', in S. Stavridis et al. (eds), *New challenges to the European Union: Policies and Policy-Making*, Aldershot: Dartmouth.

Sjursen, H. (1999), *Enlargement and the Common Foreign and Security Policy: Transforming the EU's External Identity?*, Oslo: ARENA, special issue.

Smith, H. (1995), *European Union Foreign Policy and Central America*, London: Macmillan.

Smith, H. (1998), 'Actually Existing Foreign Policy – or Not? The EU in Latin and Central America', in J. Peterson and H. Sjursen (eds), *A common Foreign Policy for Europe? Competing Visions of the CFSP*, London: Routledge.

Smith, K. (1998a), 'The Instruments of European Union Foreign Policy', in Jan Zielonka (ed.), *Paradoxes of European Foreign Policy*, the Hague: Klumer Law International.

Smith, K. (1998b), 'The Use of Political Conditionality in the EU's Relations with Third Countries: How Effective?', *European Foreign Affairs Review*, 3:2.

Smith, K. (1999), *The Making of EU Foreign Policy. The Case of Eastern Europe*, London: Macmillan.

Smith, M. E. (1998a), 'Rules, Transgovernmentalism, and the Expansion of European Political Cooperation', in Wayne Sandholtz and Alec Stone Sweet (eds), *European Integration and Supranational Governance*, Oxford: Oxford University Press.

Smith, M. E. (1998b), 'What's Wrong with the CFSP? The Politics of Institutional Reform', in Pierre-Henri Laurent and Marc Maresceau (eds), *The State of the European Union, Vol. 4. Deepening and Widening*, Boulder: Lynne Rienner Publishers.

Smith, M. E. (1998c), 'Uncertainty, Problem-Solving, and Collective Preference Formation: The Expansion of European Foreign Policy Cooperation', Paper prepared for the IGCC/MacArthur Regional Relations Conference, Newport Beach, CA, May.

Smith, M. E. (1998d), 'Does the Flag Follow Trade?: Politicisation and the Emergence of European Foreign Policy', in J. Peterson and H. Sjursen (eds), *A Common Foreign Policy for Europe? Competing Visions of the CFSP*, London: Routledge.

Smith, M. H. (1994), 'Beyond the Stable State? Foreign Policy Challenges and Opportunities in the New Europe', in S. Smith and W. Carlsnaes (eds), *European Foreign Policy: The EC and Changing Perspectives in Europe*, London: Sage.

Smith, M. H. (1996a), 'The EU as an International Actor', in J. Richardson (ed.), *European Union; Power and Policy-making*, London: Routledge.

Smith, M. H. (1996b), 'The European Union and the Changing Europe: Establishing the Boundaries of Order', *Journal of Common Market Studies*, 34:1.

Smith, M. H. (1997), 'The Commission and External Relations', in G. Edwards and D. Spence (eds), *The European Commission*, London: Longman.

Smith, S. (2000a), 'Wendt's World', *Review of International Studies*, 26:1.

Smith, S. (2000b), 'International Theory and European Integration', in Mike Williams and Morten Kelstrup (eds), *International Relations Theory and the Politics of European Integration*, London: Routledge.

Smith, S. and W. Carlsnaes (eds) (1994), *European Foreign Policy: The EC and Changing Perspectives in Europe*, London: Sage.

Snyder, G. (1996), 'Process Variables in Realist Theory' in B. Frankel (ed.), *Realism: Restatements and Renewal*, London: Frank Cass.

Spence, David (1999), 'Foreign Ministries in National and the European Context', in B. Hocking (ed.), *Foreign Ministries – Change and Adaptation*, Houndrulls: Macmillan and New York: St. Martin's Press.

Spirtas, M. (1996), 'A House Divided: Tragedy and Evil in Realist Theory', in B. Frankel (ed.), *Realism: Restatements and Renewal*, London: Frank Cass.

Stark, H. (1992), 'Dissonances franco-allemandes sur fond de guerre serbo-croate', *Politique Étrangère*, No. 2

Stavridis, S. and C. Hill (eds) (1996), *Domestic Sources of Foreign Policy: West European Reactions to the Falklands Conflict*, Oxford: Berg.

Stevens, Christopher (1996), 'EU Policy for the Banana Market', in Helen Wallace and William Wallace (eds), *Policy-making in the European Union*, Oxford: Oxford University Press.

Stockholm International Peace Research Institute (SIPRI) (ed.), *SIPRI Yearbook, Armaments, Disarmament and International Security* (Oxford: Oxford University Press, annually).

Taylor, P. (1983a), *The Limits of European Integration*, London: Croom Helm.

Taylor, P. (1983b), *International Organization in the Modern World: The Regional and the Global Process*, London: Pinter.

Telò, M. and P. Magnette (eds) (1996), *Repenser l'Europe*, Brussels: Editions de l'Université de Bruxelles.

Telò, M. and P. Magnette (eds) (1997), *De Maastricht à Amsterdam. L'Europe et son nouveau traité*, Brussels: Complexe.

Telò, M. and E. Remacle (eds) (1998), *L'Union européenne après Amsterdam. Adaptations institutionnelles, enjeux de la différenciation et de l'élargissement* Brussels : Fondation Paul-Henri Spaak.

Tewes, H. (1998), 'Between deepening and Widening: Role Conflict in Germany's Enlargement Policy', *West European Politics*, 21:2 (April).

Tietje, C. (1997), "The Concept of Coherence in the Treaty on European Union and the Common Foreign and Security Policy", *European Foreign Affairs Review*, 2:2.

Tigner, B. (1998), *Europe Fights Back. New Strategies for Europe's Defence Industries*, Background Report, 1998 European Defence Procurement Conference, Brussels, 23 April.

Tonra, B. (1996), *Dutch, Danish and Irish Foreign Policy in EPC/CFSP 1970–1996*, PhD dissertation, Trinity College , University of Dublin.

Tonra, B. (1998), *Europeanisation of National Foreign Policies in the EU*, Paper prepared for the third Pan-European Relations Conference and Joint Meeting with the ISA, Vienna, May.

Tonra, Ben (2001), *The Europeanisation of National Foreign Policy: Dutch, Danish and Irish Foreign Policy in the European Union*, Aldershot: Ashgate.

Tonra, B. and T. Christiansen (eds) (1998), *CFSP and Beyond. Theorising European Foreign Policy*, Aberystwyth: Centre for European Studies, Department of International Politics, University of Wales.

Torreblanca Payá, J. I. (1997), *The European Community and Central Eastern Europe (1989–1993): Foreign Policy and Decision-Making* (PhD. dissertation, Madrid: Instituto Juan March de Estudios e Investigaciones).

Tréan, Claire (1991), 'La France dans le nouvel ordre européen', *Politique Étrangère*, No. 1.

Van Evera, S. (1997), *Guide to Methods for Students of Political Science*, Ithaca and London: Cornell University Press.

Van Ham, P. (2000), 'Europe's Common Defence Policy: Implications for the Transatlantic Relationship', *Security Dialogue*, 31:2 (June).

Vertzberger, Y. (1990), *The World in Their Minds: Information Processing, Cognition, and Perception in Foreign Policy Decisionmaking*, Stanford: Stanford University Press.

Vesterdorf, B., Judge-Rapporteur, Court of First Instance (1999), *Report for the Hearing of 4 March*, Case T-14/98, Luxembourg.

Von der Gablentz, O. (1979), 'Luxembourg Revisited or The Importance of European Political Cooperation', *Common Market Law Review*, 16.

Wæver, O. (1990), 'Three Competing Europes: German, French and Russian', *International Affairs*, 66:2

Wæver, O. (1994), 'Resting the Temptation of Post Foreign Policy Analysis', in W. Carl-
    snaes and S. Smith (eds), *European Foreign Policy: The EC and Changing Perspectives
    in Europe*, London: Sage.
Wæver, O. (1995), 'Identity, Integration and Security: Solving the Sovereignty Puzzle in
    EU Studies', *Journal of International Relations*, 48:2.
Wæver, O. (1996), 'European Security Identities', *Journal of Common Market Studies*, 34:1
Wæver, O. (1997), 'Figures of International Thought; Introducing Persons instead of
    Paradigms', in I Neumann and O. Wæver, *The Future of International Relations:
    Masters in the Making*, London and New York: Routledge.
Wæver, O. (1998), 'Explaining Europe by Decoding Discourses', in Anders Wivel (ed.),
    Explaining European Integration, Copenhagen: Copenhagen Political Studies Press.
Walker, R. J. B. (1990), 'Security, Sovereignty, and the Challenge of World Politics', *Alter-
    natives*, 15:1.
Walker, R. J. B. (1993), *Inside/Outside: International Relations as International Theory*,
    Cambridge: Cambridge University Press.
Walker, S. (1979), 'National Role Conceptions and Systemic Outcomes', in L. S. Folkowski
    (ed.), *Psychological Models in International Politics*, Boulder: Westview.
Walker, S. (ed.) (1987), *Role Theory and Foreign Policy Analysis*, Durham, NC: Duke Uni-
    versity Press
Wallace, H., W. Wallace and C. Webb (eds) (1983), *Policy-Making in the European Com-
    munity* (2nd edn) Chichester: John Wiley and Sons.
Wallace, W. (1978), 'A Common Foreign Policy: Mirage or Reality?', in Bernard Burrows,
    Geoffrey Denton and Geoffrey Edwards (eds), *Federal Solutions to European Issues*,
    London: Macmillan.
Wallace, W. (1983a), 'Political Cooperation: Integration Through Intergovernmental-
    ism', in Helen Wallace, W. Wallace and c. Webb (eds), *Policy Making in the European
    Community*, Chichester: John Wiley and Sons.
Wallace, W. (1983b), 'Introduction: Cooperation and convergence in European Foreign
    Policy', in Christopher Hill (ed.), *National foreign Policies and European Political
    Cooperation*, London: George Allen & Unwin.
Wallace, W. (ed.) (1990), *The Dynamic of European Integration*, London: Pinter Publish-
    ers for the Royal Institute of International Affairs.
Wallace, W. (1991), 'Foreign Policy and National Identity in the United Kingdom', *Inter-
    national Affairs*, 67:1
Wallace, W. (1994), *Regional Integration: The West European Experience*, Washington,
    DC: The Brookings Institution.
Wallace, W. (1996), *Government Without Statehood: The Unstable Equilibrium*, Oxford:
    Oxford University Press.
Walt, S. (1987), *The Origins of Alliances*, London: Cornell University Press.
Waltz, K. N. (1979), *Theory of International Politics*, New York: McGraw-Hill.
Weiler, Joseph and Wolfgang Wessels (1988), 'EPC and the Challenge of Theory', in
    Alfred Pjpers, Elfriede Regelsberger and Wolfgang Wessels (eds), *European Political
    Cooperation in the 1980. A Common Foreign Policy for Western Europe?*, Dordrecht:
    Martinus Nijhoff.
Weldes, J. (1996), 'Constructing National Interests', *European Journal of International
    Relations*, 2:3.
Wendt, A. (1987), 'The Agent-Structure Problem in International Relations Theory',
    International Organization, 41:3.

Wendt, A. (1991), 'Bridging the Theory/Meta-theory Gap in International Relations', *Review of International Studies*, 17:4.

Wendt, A. (1992), 'Anarchy is what States Make of It: The Social Construction of Power Politics', *International Organization*, 46:2.

Wendt, A. (1994), 'Collective Identity Formation and the International State', *American Political Science Review*, 88:2.

Wendt, A. (1995), 'Constructing International Politics', *International Security*, 20:1

Wendt, A. (1999), *Social Theory of International Politics*, Cambridge: Cambridge University Press.

Wessels, W. (1980), 'New forms of Foreign Policy Formulation in Western Europe', in Werner J. Feld (ed.), *Weston Europe's Global Reach. Regional Cooperation and World-wide Aspirations*, New York: Pergamon Press.

Wessels, W. (1982), 'European Political Cooperation: A New Approach to European Foreign Policy', in David Allen, Reinharde Rummel and Wolfgang Wessels (eds), *European Political Cooperation: Towards a Foreign Policy for Western Europe*, London: Butterworth Scientific.

Wessels, W. (1991), *The EC Council: The Community's Decision-Making Centre*, Boulder: Westview.

Wessels, W. (1997), 'An Ever Closer Fusion? A Dynamic Macropolitical View on Integration Processes', *Journal of Common Market Studies*, 35:2.

White, B. (1978), 'Decision-Making Analysis', in T. Taylor (ed.), *Approaches and Theory in International Relations*, London: Longman.

White, B. (1998), 'The European Challenge to Foreign Policy Analysis', *European Journal of International Relations*, 5:1.

White, B. (2001), *Understanding European Foreign Policy*, Basingstoke: Macmillan.

Whitman, R. (1997), *From Civilian Power to Superpower? The International Identity of the European Union*, Basingstoke: Macmillan.

Whitman, R. (2000a), '*The State of the Art in the Foreign Policies of the European Union Member States II*' Paper presented at the ISA Annual conference, Los Angeles, 15–18 March.

Whitman, R. (2000b), 'Conclusion', in I. Mannas and R. Whitman (eds), *The Foreign Policies of the European Union Member States*, Manchester: Manchester University Press.

Willaert, P. and C. Marques-Ruiz (1995), 'Vers une politique étrangère et de sécurité commune: état des lieux', *Revue du Marché unique européen*, 3:1.

Williams, M. (1997), 'The Institutions of Security: Elements of a Theory of Security Organisations', *Cooperation and Conflict*, 32:3 (September).

Williams, M. (1998), 'Identity and the Politics of Security', *European Journal of International Relations*, 4:2.

Wish, N. (1980), 'Foreign Policy Makers and Their National Role Conceptions', *International Studies Quarterly*, 24:4.

Wivel, A. (ed.) (1998), *Explaining European Integration*, Copenhagen: Copenhagen Political Studies Press.

Wright, V. (1996), *The National Co-ordination of European Policy-Making*, London, Routledge.

Yahuda, Michael (1998), 'Europe and China', in H. Maull, G. Segal and J. Wanandi (eds.), *Europe and the Asia Pacific*, London and New York: Routledge.

Young, O. (1972), *The Actors in World Politics*, New York: Free Press.

Zehfuss, M. (1998), *Never War Again? The Politics of Constructing a Military Role for the Federal Republic of Germany*, Sussex: paper presented at the Annual BISA Conference, University of Sussex, December.

Zielonka, J. (ed.) (1998), *Paradoxes of European Foreign Policy*, The Hague: Klüwer Law International.

INDEX

Note 'n' after a page reference indicates a note number on that page.